SEX
Magicians

SEX
Magicians

The Lives and
Spiritual Practices of
Paschal Beverly Randolph,
Aleister Crowley, Jack Parsons,
Marjorie Cameron, Anton LaVey,
and Others

MICHAEL WILLIAM WEST

Destiny Books
Rochester, Vermont

Destiny Books
One Park Street
Rochester, Vermont 05767
www.DestinyBooks.com

Text stock is SFI certified

Destiny Books is a division of Inner Traditions International

Cataloging-in-Publication Data for this title is available from the Library of Congress

ISBN 978-1-64411-163-5 (print)
ISBN 978-1-64411-164-2 (ebook)

Printed and bound in the United States by Lake Book Manufacturing, Inc. The text stock is SFI certified. The Sustainable Forestry Initiative® program promotes sustainable forest management.

10 9 8 7 6 5 4 3 2 1

Text design and layout by Debbie Glogover
This book was typeset in Garamond Premier Pro with Appareo, Nixrift, and Gill Sans MT Pro used as display fonts

To send correspondence to the author of this book, mail a first-class letter to the author c/o Inner Traditions • Bear & Company, One Park Street, Rochester, VT 05767, and we will forward the communication.

Contents

Foreword

Yes, hello. I'm writing to you from Thee Nest, the Lower East Side home and working studio of the infamous Genesis Breyer P-Orridge, my dear friend, mentor, and co-creator. I cannot claim to be an expert on Sex Magick, yet my introduction to the practice and education on certain techniques was quite fortunate and unique.

Thirteen y-eras ago in 2006, at the ripe young age of nineteen, I moved into Thee Gates Institute, Genesis and Lady Jaye's Brooklyn brownstone, with my new boyfriend, Markus Fabulous Persson, who played keyboards for Psychic TV at the time. Markus and I resided in the first-floor apartment while the Breyer P-Orridges occupied the uppermost realms.

Serendipity and the magical current of the universe that places us precisely where and when we need to be somewhere dropped me off at the doorstep shores of my loving tribe. I didn't know this at the time, of course. Growing up in small, conservative towns meant that I had never heard of Genesis, TOPY/TOPI, Crowley, Brion Gysin, the cut-up method, sex magic, or any related practices or personalities of that particular cultural underground.

It didn't take long for Gen and Jaye to take a smiling shine to my humble innocence and eagerness to learn. They took me under their experienced wings and were as happy to share their unusual and colorful world with me as I was delighted and dazzled by the myriad of raw creativity; enchanting histories; and libraries of the great minds, magicians, outsiders, cultural engineers, and taboo breakers.

Markus would playfully refer to our evenings spent at Gen and Jaye's apartment as the Psychic TV School of Magick. He was right, though. It was a thorough by-proxy cultural education. We were sent back downstairs each night with a different occult book to read, art book to thumb through, or Pee-Wee's Playhouse VHS to watch. It worked on a one-out-at-a-time basis, so if we wanted new material we had to devour and return what was loaned to us previously.

At one fortuitous point during my time living at Thee Gates Institute, Genesis offered to give us personal mentorship and training in the sex magic techniques practiced by the Temple Ov Psychic Youth (TOPY, but since changed to the Temple Ov Pandrogenous Individuals [TOPI]). Every month on the 23rd, starting at precisely 11:23 p.m. (23:23), we would enter our individual private ritual spaces and create and charge a Three Liquid Sigil.

In short, the Three Liquid Sigil is a magical creation (drawing, collage, Polaroid series, painting, sculpture, poem, writing, etc.) produced with manifestational intent in a ritual space (alongside any desired ritual talismans) and then christened with three specific bodily fluids: spit, blood, and cum (referred to as "Ov" by TOPY). Before applying the sexual fluids, it was integral that the practitioner brought themself to orgasm while looking at the freshly created sigil and envisioning their intent as consensus reality. Once the semen or post-orgasm vaginal fluids were applied to the sigil, the ritual was completed and the sigils were handed over to Genesis. The results/intents were not to be dwelled upon but rather forgotten so that the symbiotic universe and subconscious mind would freely dance together and allow those specific desires to unfold.

During my distinctive sex magic process with Genesis, each month we would revisit the sigil from the prior 23rd and retrospectively discuss the effectiveness of the month's working. This discourse allowed me to piece together my own unique universe of symbols, connotations, archetypes, and language. To speak directly to my personal muse, or Holy Guardian Angel as Crowley called it, required that I understand how to be precise, concise, and effectual in my sigil communications with the outer and inner realms of being. Rewiring the subconscious mind to implement a change in behavior, thought process, awareness, and relation to the outside world can be a trickster dance indeed.

Not only did the manifestational power of pleasure and orgasm become wildly apparent through the workings, but I realized the fundamental and universally potent mechanism behind these monthly ritual actions. The true work and challenge of the Three Liquid Sigil was not doing something at a specific date and time each month, creating a piece of art, spitting, bloodletting, having an orgasm. The real work, I soon learned, was what happened in the weeks, days, or hours before the ritual while concretely deciding: What DO I actually WANT to be, experience, or otherwise manifest? I was training myself to take my world into my own hands instead of passively allowing life and time to sweep me down the river toward death as they pleased.

The magicians explored in this compendium of sex magic history each have a unique way of approaching the rewiring of the subconscious mind and utilization of the orgasm. Each has a specific magical tool or technique that sets them apart from the others. This goes to show that there's no one correct path. In fact, I've found the opposite to be true. Utilizing magic to know thyself and change your reality is a personal journey that requires imagination, creativity, and doing things your own way.

The tools that were passed down to me from Genesis and TOPY were a strong foundation for me from which to springboard and find my own way on the great path of no path. Just as humans have to actively work to keep their relationships from becoming stagnant, dull, or distant, I am continually putting effort into making my relationship with the chaosmos as exciting, intimate, and evolved as possible. I'm a cackling coyote on the edge of the abyss, dancing beyond the veils, and flirting with the archetypes.

JAI KALI MA!
HANNAH HADDIX
JUNE OV 2019

Free Thinkers, Visionaries, and the Origins of Western Sex Magic

Sex magic is a term that invariably elicits a reaction in anyone who hears it, often something between curiosity and trepidation. It remains a field of study and practice that is truly occult, in that the combination of sex and spirituality remain obscure, mysterious, and absurd to most people. To propose that sexual energy can be harnessed to perform magic is where the majority lose familiar points of reference to our contemporary culture and become skeptical, even wary.

Defining the term *sex magic* at the earliest opportunity seems important in terms of contextualizing the behaviors and beliefs of the subjects of this book, although, as these short biographies will reveal, there is much subjectivity and ambiguity to its meaning. Sex magic is a form of magical practice that is charged by sexual energy. In sex magic, sex is the means to the magical end; at the moment sex in itself becomes the end, then the wary will have been justified that it is nothing more than a way to broaden or improve one's own sex appeal by cloaking it as spiritual or occultish.

The power of sex has driven human culture from the very dawn of our essence as a species. It is the means by which the majority of humans have found their strongest capacity to develop powerful emotional bonds, of love and lust, with others. It has been proved to give great benefits to both physical and psychological health, as well as being a source of pleasure. The over-pursuit or repression of sexual desire is—according to a swath of twentieth century psychiatrists, at least—the primary source of our anxieties and psychological imbalances. It is what separates adult from child, and sexual desire is an insuperable prerogative for human love. For all the power sex has in generating love, health, and well-being, it has an equally well-documented dark side and has been weaponized by both governments and individuals to devastating effect in innumerable and horrific ways since the dawn of civilization, and the degree to which sexual freedoms are suppressed has been a defining factor of most major religious and political ideologies.

The effects of sex on our psychological and physical well-being are not the remit of this book but rather its effect on a specific part of human spiritual mind, that element of the subconscious that is loosely defined as "magical." Magic, in this sense, has nothing to do with stage performers who use sleight of hand and illusionary tricks to entertain an audience into believing the impossible has occurred before their very eyes. To make this point clear, Aleister Crowley, perhaps the most famous and notorious figure in the history of magic and the occult, decided to alter the spelling to "magick" in his own works to distinguish entertainment from the occult art of magic. (I will note here that I will keep with the traditional spelling, since much of the magic I'll be writing about occurred long before Crowley was born, and plenty who succeeded him do not necessarily conform to Crowley's particular conception of it.) Furthermore, he gave a succinct and pragmatic definition of what he understood magic to be: "the science and art of causing change to occur in conformity with the Will."[1] In Crowley's era, the human will was at the center of much interest concerning its role in psychology. Friedrich Nietzsche understood "will" as the fundamental quality of the universe that pervades all things. In their respective fields, Nietzsche and Crowley were among the vanguard who created the post-Christian world that still dominates Western culture today; a world in which submission to God is no longer taken as a philosophical and spiritual certainty, and suddenly faced with a crushing responsibility for him or herself, the post-Christian must try to engage with that which drives them, that which brings the essential sense of meaning to existence. Influenced by Nietzsche, Crowley came to believe that certain individuals, with training, could exert the force of their own will upon the subconscious mind, through magical and meditative practice, and then subsequently generate a form of power that could be expended to cause mysterious yet tangible changes to the universe surrounding them. Crowley made sure to point out that fundamental laws of physics could not be broken—at least not by any magicians of whom he was aware. Telekinesis and such are not in the realm of magical possibility according to Crowley. But engaging with what Carl Jung defined as the collective unconscious, within which resides a set of universal atavistic archetypal representations of common and basic fears, pleasures, and instincts, was, according to Crowley, very much possible and part of the essence of magic. The vast enlightenment that can come from these meditative-magical experiences and, more ominously (to some), the power they can bestow upon an individual are, and have always been, the main draw of the practice of the dark arts of magic.

Needless to say, the methods required to generate such powers require considerable effort. Crowley was not alone in pushing himself to incredible and sometimes absurd extremes in the pursuit of increasing access to the powers of his own magical subconscious. It is the introduction of a psychological reasoning and the implication of scientific ideas and theories into magic that make Crowley such an important figure. For many, the mysteries of magic are better as just that—mysterious. But Crowley was a student of chemistry at the University of Cambridge, as well as a contemporary of Planck, Einstein, and Bohr; Crowley saw magic in quantum theory, relativity, and the atom bomb, and he saw physics in his adventures into the magical subconscious. One of the other great contributions Crowley made was to open a path to a more subjective and personal interpretation of magic. While he propounded his own system and his Thelemic religion as being a path to truth—gaining many followers in doing so—he also removed what he considered as blinds to magical development. The ancient grimoires that reveal the magic of, for example, King Solomon, of both dubious and obscure origin, tell of a powerful king who ruled his kingdom with the help of seventy-two demons. These demons have been recognized as a bundle of ancient pagan deities, branded demonic by the followers of Abrahamic religions. But each deity/demon was vital to its native culture and, like all polytheistic gods, had certain special powers, frailties, and caprices that it may exert if called upon by a devoted magician. Solomon's methods for evoking his demons involve preparations so elaborate as to render them impossible for anyone much lower in status than a king (obtaining a lion-skin belt, for example, would raise some serious ethical and practical issues, and that's just the start of things). Crowley dismissed the paraphernalia as being placed there to try to stop just anyone from unlocking the secrets of this particular form of powerful magic (which became known as the Goetia, from the *Ars Goetia,* Ancient Greek for "Arts of Sorcery"). Crowley postulated that, theoretically, anyone could strip away the labors of ancient magic and train the mind to do the work, relying on symbolic representations of the various tools to encourage the mind to enter into the necessary meditative state. Furthermore, he believed that while the reclusive Eastern gurus, meditating for decades to reach enlightenment, were certainly capable of great spiritual advances, similar results could be attained by harnessing the far more accessible power of human sexuality. For Crowley at least, the moment of orgasm is the only common moment—for most people—when our conscious mind subsides long enough for us to notice it. Thus, through sex, we have a direct passage to our unconscious minds and can therefore begin to manipulate it, send symbolic messages to it, and engage in the arts of magic through the willful command of our own sexual powers. In essence, sex magic is a form of shortcut to enlightened and powerful states—both benevolent and maleficent— that would otherwise likely require many years of solitary meditation; highly impractical in the modern world.

In a practical sense, the performance of sex magic in the Western tradition is now an occult branch of psychology, in that it allows the magician to access and meddle with the subconscious mind. Modern psychology is almost universal in acknowledging the benefits of mindfulness and meditation, exercises that at one time were considered occult practices but have now entered the realm of normal. Both, in essence, are means of shutting down the conscious mind—which so defines the human species—and activating the more ancient subconscious. The sex magician can move at least one step further than this. Once accessed, the magician can manipulate the subconscious, interact with it, even project it before themselves and see its form. These forms tend to have a degree of commonality shared among all those who perceive them; consistent with the aforementioned Jungian ideal of the collective unconscious. An analogue would be the hallucinations produced by psychedelic drug use, although as the early experiments of Albert Hofmann and others attest, the introduction of chemical components in the body can lead to an uncontrolled and terrifying state of being, albeit one that can bring similar enlightenment. There are many magical traditions of both East and West that incorporate drugs and alcohol into their rituals, but they are not always necessary to achieve the end of opening up the subconscious mind.

That sex magic is an art is an acceptable designation for most twenty-first century Westerners. To think of it as a science is more controversial. Once, magic and science were inseparable. The scientific method and the intellectual produce of the Age of Reason, for all their great value, remain somewhat inflexible when it comes to the mysterious. There are, as our advances in the sciences proceed at a pace that is truly unprecedented, occasional discoveries allowing a thin thread to be spun across the distance that separates the scientific and the esoteric. One example was the 2016 discovery of biophotons in mammalian brains.[2] Neurons in the human brain are capable of producing light photons, with a range of light from infrared to ultraviolet. Their purpose and function are not yet established, but it is suggested that they serve as information transmitters; it is not a huge speculation to suggest that such information could be transmitted beyond the confines of the flesh and bone of the human head. In another sense, the discovery that the human brain is capable of producing its own light gives a sense of pre-science to one of Crowley's well-known proclamations: "every man and every woman is a star."

In occult theory, meditative and magical practice should allow the magician to access and manipulate these strange functions of the human brain. How such a thing might actually work is obscure, unresearched (in any scientific sense), and largely condemned as pseudoscience. Yet, humans are drawn to practice magic today as much as any time before, and the numbers who report its efficacy are significant. Perhaps the more credible, rational explanation is that the implantation of a desire upon the subconscious is an active means of assisting a person to go through life in a more mindful way. An example is the modern chaos magic technique called "sigil magic," developed from the practices of Austin Osman Spare. In this, the magician creates a sigil, or a simple symbol, representing a desire. The sigil is meditated upon, and then the image is held in the mind at the moment of orgasm, as the subconscious mind surfaces momentarily. This then imprints a symbolic statement of intent upon the subconscious. The magician may then discover that their stated desire does indeed become reality, as long as it conforms to the basic rules of probability and physics. The rational explanation is that the subconscious sets to work guiding the magician toward oppor-tunities to fulfill this particular desire that might otherwise have been missed. For example, the magician has a mundane desire for a new job. After sigil magic, the subconscious leads the magician to a seemingly chance encounter with someone who is looking for a new employee in a field in which the magician is skilled. Furthermore, the subconscious relays confidence and charm to the conscious, allowing the magician to make a good impression and advance in life accordingly. More radically, there are magicians who believe the magical power extends far beyond relaying messages to one's own subconscious, and some energetic, quantum, or atomic interaction is possible; essentially an interaction with God, if we understand God as some vague binding force in the universe; the "God particle," otherwise known to physics as the Higgs boson, for example. Speculations are endless, and there are no truths to be uncovered here beyond that which an individual may uncover about themselves and their own powers through the practice of magic, sexual or otherwise.

Sex magic, at least in the Western tradition, is a far more recent development than many people realize. It was not until the nineteenth century that tentative exploration of the relationship between sex and magic began in earnest in the West. This is partly due to the widening of the aperture in the wall that has long divided the sacred cultures of West and East, as technological improvements in transport and the expansion of great empires, whether British, French, or Ottoman, began to overlap in the two hemispheres. Prior to the eighteenth century, if some audacious soul had voyaged to the remnants of Babylon or the heart of the Indian subcontinent and discovered the "devil-worshipping" Yazidi or the practitioners of Tantra, any attempt to enlighten his compatriots to such exotic forms of the mystical and sacred would have likely endangered his freedom and even his life. Such was the strength of the chokehold that the Christian dominion held upon Europe for ten centuries. Practitioners of magic (or, often, merely those suspected of it) were subject to sustained and violent persecution. Any deviance from the proscribed norms of sexual behavior also induced similar responses. Elaborate forms of torture, genius conceptions of the deviant human mind, worked the bodies of those who had sinned against God into states of unimaginable pain and suffering. The price for ecstasies and mysteries was often carnage. It is not surprising that very few people dared consider investigating the radical union of sex and magic until the dawn of the Victorian era; hardly a time of easygoing sexuality, but still, following the Enlightenment and the imposition of the rule of law, an epoch of relative safety for those exploring unorthodox religious, sexual, and intellectual avenues.

The modern Western tradition of sex magic has been influenced by an Eastern tradition that has fermented and flowered across thousands of years. The most advanced practitioners of the West still cannot lay claim to a system as advanced and delicate as Kundalini, a means of sexual enlightenment in the Indian tradition of what is known to the West as "Tantra." But this book is not concerned with attempting to unveil the complexities of the Eastern traditions. Western sex magic is still in its infancy and remains an obscure and controversial activity, liable to draw howls of derision from devotees of rationalism and the scientific method. Despite the resistance of society, the pioneering practitioners examined here have opened a path that is leading to a discrete and independent form of sex magic.

Sex alone tends to be the most feared form of human behavior to any authoritarian entity, from the Christians to the Communists, knowing as they do that sexual liberation, most especially female sexual liberation, will likely lead to the complete dissolution of their repressive systems. Even the Roman Republic turned against the magical-sexual powers of the ancient cult of Dionysus, at one time burning to death five thousand of its members in a general panic (an act that would later influence the preferred Christian method of executing witches), an act strongly criticized by Livy,[3] the great historian. The empire saw the rise and fall of the anarchic Emperor Caligula, who reveled in sex, violence, and his own outrageous divinity, and whose beloved wife, Milona Caesonia, was accused of being a witch.[4] Other strange unveilings of this world occurred from time to time, but almost always—like Caligula—history found a way to utilize them as propaganda for the established order. In the seventeenth century a defrocked Parisian priest, Abbé Etienne Guibourg, was engaged by Madame de Montespan, the mistress of King Louis XIV, to perform black masses with the intention of securing the continued sexual interest of the Sun King. Guibourg laid a black velvet pall across the altar upon which the king's mistress then lay naked. The mass was notorious not only for the sexual nature of the ritual and the invocation of the demons Astaroth and Asmodeus, but also because at the moment of orgasm the Abbé cut the throat of an abducted baby as a dramatic, demonic sacrifice.[5] Such excesses are, of course, completely unnecessary and contrary to the teachings of any sane practitioner of the occult.

Following the Enlightenment, cautious steps were made by pioneers such as the Swedish mystic Emmanuel Swedenborg, who alluded in his writings to divine unions within the bounds of marriage. Another precursor was the English poet William Blake, who posited that evil energy comes from the body and good energy from the soul but that the two are inseparable in man. Body energy is sexual, and much of Blake's poetry is concerned with early forms of sexual liberation as well as a profound mysticism that captivated the Romantic era, with its vigorous appetite for the paranormal, spiritual, and esoteric.

From the relative mystical freedoms afforded by the Romantic era came the first figures who could be considered practitioners of modern, Western sex magic. The Romantic movement also threw away some of the dryness of the eighteenth century and allowed dreams and fantasy to infiltrate Western culture once more: sexual fantasy motivated the imaginations of the esoterically inclined. The Catholic Church's longstanding attempts to discredit any theological rivals by (somewhat ironically) denouncing them as sexually perverse began to backfire as these tales of orgiastic rites performed according to savage, pagan traditions began to seem glamorous and exciting, even if they were entirely fabricated.

Early pioneers also began to tentatively suggest the possible health benefits of a spiritual-sexual union between husband and wife, inspired by the surge in interest in Kabbalah, an ancient esoteric discipline within Judaism, which is still denounced to this day among some conservative Jews as a devil-worshipping sex cult. In western Europe, Kabbalism was mixed with Christian beliefs, as the hardline Christian view that sex was sinful began to run out of steam. At the same time, the secular materialist worldview was proposing that sex was merely a biological end with no greater significance, another challenge to the centuries of negative significance attached to sex by Christianity. So, Kabbalah, as well as Eastern traditions that viewed sex as capable of revealing a sense of the spiritual constant in a world that might otherwise seem transient and meaningless, began to attract those departing the crumbling Christian moral order.

The United States during the late nineteenth century became a kind of laboratory of religious cults and orders. Some were heavily oriented around sex, albeit more often believing that increased restrictions on sexual acts were the path to a life closer to God. One notable example was the Shakers, an egalitarian millenarian Christian sect founded in the late eighteenth century. They were famed for their convulsive, ecstatic body movements they displayed when in deep religious communion with God. However, they preached total celibacy and abstention from all sexual acts, a policy that led to the communities being somewhat short-lived, for reasons that are self-evident. On the other hand, a group known as the Oneida Community believed quite the opposite. Established by John Humphrey Noyes, a Vermont native who set up in Oneida, New York, in the 1830s, the Oneida Community saw sex as the most powerful means of drawing *closer* to God; this was certainly a time and place where sexual spirituality was happening, and women were afforded freedoms and roles in the community that were unthinkable anywhere else in the United States at that time. But, in spite of this, there was a strong suspicion that Noyes founded the community with his own polyamorous desires in mind more than any true spiritual aims; the commune did not survive Noyes's death in 1886. From this unique cultural backdrop, Western sex magic emerged as a loose set of practices, philosophies, and mystical principles that over time were developed into codified systems.

The first figure this book will explore is the founding father of modern sex magic, Paschal Beverly Randolph, a mixed-race New Yorker born into abject poverty who became an adventurer who attended the court of Napoleon III, as well as establishing the first Rosicrucian order in the United States (Rosicrucians being a community of mystics), which exists to this day. From his spectacular contribution a tradition emerged of radical thinkers and occultists who have gathered many followers, to the extent that "occultists" (a somewhat broad appellation under which we can safely place the majority of sex magicians) are now the fastest growing religious grouping in several Western countries,[6] including the United Kingdom and the United States. Some, like Ida Craddock, faced exceptional adversity due to their beliefs, and her life ended in tragedy directly attributable to her views and writings on sexual magic. Others, such as Crowley, became iconic figures familiar to the public and the press, who dubbed him "the wickedest man in the world," much to his delight. Crowley's influence can seem overbearing, and my own induction into the magical world was as an admirer of Crowley many years ago; but it was when I discovered his contemporary and rival Austin Osman Spare that I found the magical figure with whom I felt the strongest personal connection. Spare did not care much for the theatrics of Crowley and his followers, seeing magic and especially sex magic rather as a source of artistic power—and while there is something to be said for Crowley's poetry, Spare's paintings and drawings are among the most important British artworks of the twentieth century.

The internet age has seen an upsurge in interest in chaos magic, of which Spare is considered the great prophet. Its anarchic, post-modern focus on symbiotic and individual magical experiences appeal far more to the spiritually adventurous millennial than do the solemn, ceremonial airs of Crowley's religion, Thelema. Others have deployed magic to drive themselves to the highest echelons of artistic achievement: in literature, Burroughs, and in music, P-Orridge—although both have wide multidisciplinary output that blend magic and art as one. In science, Jack Parsons openly used magic while making spectacular and unconventional breakthroughs in rocketry. In terms of magic for magic's sake, Crowley's only rival is the equally theatrical and charismatic founder of the Church of Satan, Anton Szandor LaVey. If Crowley thrust magic—and sex magic—into the public eye, LaVey sealed it into popular culture. Tales of the supposed depravity at his infamous Black House in San Francisco reported by an enthralled media fascinated and shocked

America, while the Satanic Bible was available to buy at supermarkets, gas stations, and local bookstores across the nation in the late 1960s, selling in huge numbers and attracting major Hollywood stars, artists, and a variety of people from every walk of life to Satanism and LaVey. Whichever figure appeals and speaks to the reader most, any legitimate passage into the occult, magic, and the practice of sex magic will likely be as confusing and meandering as each of the lives presented here were, at least at times. There is no set path.

1

Paschal Beverly Randolph (1825–1875)

From the most improbable beginnings, Pascal Beverly Randolph can now be credited as the man who unchained the beast of Western sex magic from its centuries of secrecy. Yet, in spite of the quantum leap in Western sex magic understanding that he personally inspired, his legacy has been reduced almost to the kind of obscurity that would have seemed inevitable at his birth. He was born into abject poverty in the United States and began his adult life early, as most impoverished children do. Before he reached his midteens he was sailing to distant ports as a cabin boy, voyages that allowed him to amass a unique anthology of occult knowledge, gathered from Europe, Persia, and India. Once he left the sea, he embarked on a land life almost as itinerant, never settling for long in a city. His radical and singular writings have since been passed among social historians, African American scholars, and Rosicrucians (a seventeenth-century European spiritual and cultural movement of which Randolph is considered to be the founder of the first American order), though none of these groups seem entirely keen to include Randolph as one of their own. He developed the first known sex-magic system in the West, coining the term *magia sexualis* (meaning sex magic), and his writings have influenced every significant practitioner in the field since, whether or not they are aware of it.

Randolph was born on October 8, 1825, at 70 Canal Street in the

Five Points slum, Lower Manhattan, New York City (the neighborhood, long demolished, was where the Civic Center and western parts of Chinatown stand today), to barmaid Flora Clark. At that time the neighborhood was gaining international notoriety for the extreme levels of destitution and the dilapidation of the tenements there; only parts of London's East End could compare to the brutality of Five Points. It is claimed that Five Points had the highest murder rate of any place in human history, and it was ravaged by pollution, disease, and violent racial conflict between Irish immigrants escaping the potato famine and black Americans who were legally emancipated in 1799 but had seen minimal advancements in terms of civic rights and freedoms by 1825. In fact, due to a variety of Byzantine enrollment, race, and residency laws, the black electorate in New York in 1825 amounted to 16 men from a total city population of about 150,000. This social context was of special importance to Randolph: Vermont-born Flora's ancestry was English, German, Native American, and Malagasy, making Randolph one-eighth African by descent, or in the parlance of the day, an octoroon.

Randolph's father, entirely absent from his upbringing, remains a mysterious figure. Randolph later claimed that his father was a descendant of the famous Randolph family of Virginia, established in the 1670s by William Randolph I, an English colonist, tobacco merchant, and slave owner; he and his wife, Mary Isham, were described as the Adam and Eve of the state of Virginia by their contemporaries. However, there is no genealogical or historical record that sheds any further light on Randolph's claims, and his father may have merely carried the famous name by chance.

Randolph claimed that his mother had married William Beverly Randolph after her first husband had disappeared, only for him to show up again some time later, leaving her with two husbands. In all likelihood it seems that the young Randolph was simply another illegitimate child to an impoverished New York mother who had briefly attracted the interest of a—possibly—wealthy man. Whomever his father really was, he paid no attention to either his "wife" or son, and Clark was left to raise the child alone among the brothels and groggeries of Five Points.

When Randolph was six years old, his mother was placed in the almshouse of the notorious Bellevue Hospital. She had contracted smallpox, and the hospital was overflowing due to the cholera epidemic that ravaged much of the world from 1831 to 1832. Randolph had to stay there, too, since she was his only parent. Here he amused himself by communicating with the ghosts who haunted the attic room where the children slept; Randolph claimed the spirits would make the sound of cannonballs rolling across the floorboards and sometimes whip the bedsheets from children's sleeping bodies during the night. His mother, facing death, became a seeress and threw herself into mysticism as she was wracked by the pox. His mother succumbed to the disease, dying when Randolph was aged somewhere between six and seven years old. He was partially raised from this point on by his half sister Harriet Jennings, who began to instruct him in the Roman Catholic faith. Impoverished, he also began working as a beggar for a "ci-devant English actress"[1] who used his begging to supplement her earnings as a prostitute. Randolph described himself at this age as having a "massive brain . . . but a thin, weak and puny body—therefore an unbalanced character,"[2] and he notes that until his fifteenth year he was "cuffed and kicked" about, and little more: "At less than ten years of age I had become proficient in knowledge of the shady side of human nature."[3] His time on the streets brought him one advantage (albeit one he impressed upon himself through considerable willpower): he learned to read and write. His sources were billboards and signs, and Randolph read and wrote whatever he could. This gave him the idea that he was capable of far more than life had offered to him up to now.

In America in the 1830s his African lineage made him a black man, for whom career opportunities were few. Sailors, perhaps less attached to notions of soil, have long been more accepting of men willing to do hard and dangerous work, regardless of race or religion. So, in 1837, aged only twelve, he found himself employed as a cabin boy sailing from

New Bedford, Massachusetts, on a voyage to Cuba and then England.

Over the next few years, his experiences at sea introduced him to new languages (he spoke French, as well as reasonable Turkish and Arabic), and more importantly to new customs of spirituality he found alive in the port towns of the East. Aside from the acquisition of new knowledge, life as a cabin boy was miserable for Randolph, and he contemplated suicide. He found the rites of passage inflicted upon the boys by the older sailors humiliating and brutalizing and was relieved to leave the sea following an injury sustained while chopping wood when he was twenty.

He then found himself in Portland, Maine, and began a semblance of schooling as well as learning the dyer's and barber's trades in the hope of finding less infernal work, but he was also harboring far grander ideas than dyeing, and his enflamed passion for Spiritualism gave him the confidence to make his first important declaration. Spiritualism was a belief system influenced by theologist Emanuel Swedenborg, who in the late eighteenth century had claimed to have the ability to communicate with the spirits of the dead. By the mid-nineteenth century it had grown into a major system of belief in the English-speaking world, with millions of Spiritualists in search of wisdom and solace using mediums and other methods to attempt to contact spirits residing in an ever-evolving afterlife. According to his own account, on his twenty-first birthday in 1846, Randolph appointed himself Supreme Hierarch of the Brotherhood of Eulis, creating his own magical order. He would have to wait another eight years until he would be able to found the physical Lodge of Eulis, but his path was being laid out before him. While he would engage with a variety of occult and esoteric movements of his times, the Brotherhood of Eulis, necessarily secret, was the platform from which Randolph would teach his methods of magia sexualis.

The next decade or so was a time of explosive learning for Randolph as he pursued his schooling in Maine, and he was able to write in the ornate, exclusive, and highbrow style, filled with classical and literary allusions, that was expected of the mid-nineteenth-century man of letters. Rather than taking up the more established practice of translating ancient texts for a contemporary audience, he presented himself as a "seer," one who recounts his own experiences with spirits—a personal approach that ensured a broader appeal for his prolific self-published writing. He experimented with seances, scrying with magic mirrors, hashish visions, and channeling, all of which he would compile in the book *Seership,* published in 1864. Furthermore, by the early 1850s Randolph had established himself as a "physician," treating patients with forms of clairvoyant medical diagnosis. In 1853, the year before he permanently established himself there, he began working for two French doctors in New York, who referred their patients to him for his Spiritualist cures. One patient in particular came to see him, along with his wife, complaining of what can easily be inferred as ten years of impotency, which had driven him to misery. Randolph was so touched by the couple's fundamental kindness toward him that he resolved to find the cure for his new friend's condition no matter how long it took. The technique he applied was to act as a subject, and then by using a trance state, he was able to make a diagnosis and prescribe treatment through clairvoyance. The method was common and fairly typical of the times, but Randolph's discoveries were far less so. After 118 sessions and much experimentation, he was able to offer successful treatment to his patient.

The nineteenth century was an era obsessed with so-called vital forces, which were imperative to the will, and the epoch was a laboratory of new chemical, philosophical, and spiritual techniques designed to increase male vitality, which was most obviously all at least somewhat euphemistically referring to sexual potency. From the mid-century on, the age of Vril was in full swing. The enemy of the potent, morally superior, and strong-willed male, however, was masturbation. While the rabidity of anti-onanism of the eighteenth century had subsided somewhat, there was a severe and general paranoia about the ill effects of masturbation on both men and women. Some of the best-known European physicians and thinkers of the eighteenth century had described masturbation as "the heinous sin of self-pollution" (British surgeon John Marten), "productive of . . . generally incurable disorders . . . there is perhaps no sin productive of so many hideous consequences" (British physician Robert James), and "a violation of one's duty to himself" (Prussian philosopher Immanuel Kant). In 1838, French psychiatrist Jean Esquirol wrote that masturbation caused insanity, and the American doctor John Harvey Kellogg—on a lifelong mission against masturbation—advised veganism and circumcision as ways to warn young men away from this sin (the latter still routinely administered to American children to this day as a matter of course). Other medical journals advised electric shock therapy, suturing the vulva, cauterization, castration, chastity belts, and full surgical removal of the genitals. It is perhaps unsurprising, then, that there was some neurosis attached to the subject in Randolph's day.[4]

Randolph shared the view that the vital forces could be depleted through masturbation, since nervous fluid came from the genitals and was transformed by the body into its joy and will-giving mysterious energy, reinforcing spiritual and physical well-being. Expending it through masturbation, then, logically led to depletion of nervous energy and to states of depression and impotence. Randolph administered elixirs to recharge the body, calling them *"Phymelle"* and *"Amylle,"* but most importantly, he deduced that orgasm achieved through sexual intercourse had the exact opposite effect of masturbation. In spite of the literal loss of fluids, the combination of them in sex would, through love, create an "aeroform" that would fully replenish both partners, on the condition that both were fulfilled. In simple terms, Randolph administered aphrodisiac elixirs, which may have been more effective as placebos than as actual medicine, and then instructed his male patients to make sure their wives also had orgasms (the existence of the female orgasm being something of a medical controversy in the nineteenth century) and to refrain from other, unfulfilling, forms of sexual release. The path to spiritual health, happiness, and joy was to be found in sex.[5]

By 1855, Randolph was seeing fifty patients a day, and his reputation as a doctor specializing in spiritual-sexual health matters grew rapidly around New York City. One of the French doctors for whom

Randolph performed these clairvoyant diagnoses, Monsieur Bergevin, was a member of the Société Magnétique in France, an important association of Mesmerists, practicioners of a hugely popular form of hypnosis. It was he who wrote letters of introduction for Randolph before his departure for Europe that year.

His first stop, and his primary motive for the trip, was London in May. Randolph came bearing a variety of messages and texts as the representative of several of the principal advocates of American Spiritualism, who saw an opportunity to present their work to a fresh audience in Great Britain. This opportunity came in the form of the 1855 World Convention that had been announced by the influential Welsh social reformer Robert Owen. Owen was now eighty-four years old and a well-known advocate of utopian socialism and had brought great advances in schooling and the treatment of workers at his cotton mills in Scotland, promoting welfare, temperance, and education, while renouncing corporal punishment in his workers' schools and encouraging education and dance as well as religious freedom of belief. At the age of eighty-three, one year before the convention, Owen had converted to Spiritualism, which was still largely unheard of in Britain. Owen had organized the convention to "inaugurate the commencement of the millennium," and Randolph arrived looking to spread the word of Spiritualism to social reformers and millennialist utopians with Owen's support. In spite of his recent conversion, however, Owen remained firmly on-message during the convention, eschewing spiritualism for topics on social reform. Although Owen published one of Randolph's articles in his journal, he declined to accept Randolph's offer to speak. Randolph took offense and left London for Paris rather than remain at the convention.

Randolph was able to preach spiritualism to the French on his several visits to Paris in the mid- to late-1850s, but the French Mesmerist scene, far more exciting and mysterious than the Anglo-American pragmatic approach, was where Randolph had much to learn. Eccentric and dramatic figures like Baron du Potet and Louis-Alphonse Cahagnet haunted the salons of Paris, playing out their psychic roles in a theater of flapping capes, magnet tricks, and hypnotism. Mesmerism, named for the German physician Franz Anton Mesmer, had swept France in a frenzy of mysterious healers and miracle workers through the early- to mid-nineteenth century. Mesmer had proposed a system for manipulating what he called animal magnetism, the invisible life force surrounding everything. He also developed a healing technique whereby a liquid containing iron was poured into the body before magnets were applied to the skin. Patients reported, upon the placement of the magnets, feeling a magnetic fluid flowing through their bodies that healed various ailments. Mesmer would also employ the passing of hands over the body and other techniques, including playing the glass harmonica, as methods of energetic rehabilitation to the various ridicule and fascination of wealthy Parisians. Mesmer first introduced hypnotism to the popular consciousness, so to speak, as a means of contacting the spirit world. As Enlightenment rationalism declined and was replaced by Romanticism, Mesmer's esoteric ideas took hold and were in full swing by the time Randolph arrived in Paris.

While there, Randolph was introduced to occult luminaries such as Éliphas Lévi, Edward Bulwer-Lytton, Kenneth R. H. MacKenzie, and, most astonishingly, to the emperor of France, Napoleon III, an avowed Rosicrucian. Both Lévi and the mighty emperor were impressed by Randolph's knowledge and ability as a seer. Randolph said that he "played and conquered at both chess and écarte, no word being spoken, the games simultaneous and the players in three separate rooms,"[6] while in the emperor's presence at the Tuileries. He reportedly made predictions about Lévi's life with peculiar accuracy, although there is no record of what the divinations actually were, and he had (somewhat flattering) visions of Lévi as Apollonius of Tyana, the miracle-working Pythagorean philosopher whose history was once blended into that of his apparent contemporary, Jesus Christ.

On these tours Randolph also befriended two men who proved to be particularly influential on his life: the English Rosicrucian Hargrave Jennings and the mystic and US Army General Ethan Allen Hitchcock.

Hitchcock was responsible for introducing Randolph to Abraham Lincoln, in whom he would find a good friend, while Jennings brought Randolph to the Paris Rosicrucian Supreme Grand Lodge, where—although accounts are somewhat vague—it seems he made a good impression as a seer and guest speaker. Whatever went on with Randolph and the Paris Rosicrucians, he felt not only compelled but also qualified to begin work on the establishment of the first Rosicrucian lodge in the United States upon his return there, and it seems that Emperor Napoleon III gave his blessing to Randolph to do so, perhaps seeing an opportunity to strengthen his hand in the United States as he braced himself through a period of extraordinary political turbulence in Europe. In any case, Randolph patronized and founded the Temple of Rosicrucia in Boston in 1858, and before long Rosicrucian Rooms, spaces where Rosicrucians would gather together and hold semipublic salons, had proliferated across America under Randolph's guidance.

Randolph's great strength as an occultist was his willingness and ability to recount, in relatively straightforward terms, his own practical experiences and visions with a clarity that was completely unknown to the reader of the obfuscating, high-romantic works of Lévi. Between 1858 and 1860 he published a series of pamphlets on hashish (which he was now selling as a magical aid under the name of "protozone"), clairvoyance, and instructions on how to make a mirror of the dead for the purposes of contacting spirits. In spite of all this, his frankness also reveals itself in the desperate letters he wrote to benefactors describing his miserable financial state. These financial woes, along with his lifelong search for love and acceptance that was rarely achieved in his multiple passing affairs with beautiful women, led him to a period of darkness. He attempted suicide, and the experience, along with his induction into the Rosicrucians, led Randolph to renounce Spiritualism for Christianity. He felt that Spiritualism had possessed him, and that he had allowed spirits to drain his physical and mental health to the point where he had become suicidal. Cynics pointed out that Randolph was merely ahead of the curve as Spiritualism reached its natural saturation point, but his own words on the subject seem to paint a man genuinely haunted by the imbalances caused by trance states: "I frequently resolved to break my fetters, but some good-natured miracle-seeker would persuade me to sit in a circle, just once more, in order that some great defunct Napoleon, Caesar, Franklin, or Mohammed, might, through my lips, give his opinion on the subject, and edify some dozen or so with metaphysical moonshine and transcendental twaddle. I would consent, 'just to oblige,' and then, good-bye reason, sanity adieu, common sense farewell! Like the reformed inebriate, who, so long as he tastes not, is safe from the destroyer, but who is plunged into a deeper misery the instant he yields to the tempting 'one glass more,' so the medium. Nothing can rescue him or her but the hand of God, who is 'mighty to save.'"[7]

His benefactors responded to his pleas and gave him the opportunity to lecture to groups of prominent spiritualists, and perhaps rescue himself from financial ruin. Randolph, however, chose this moment to publicly launch his attack on Spiritualism and denounce it as evil. Now having alienated his primary support base, Randolph was reaching out alone into untested fields of mysticism, risking all he had in the pursuit.

This testing period, which also saw the outbreak of the American Civil War, resulted in Randolph cautiously beginning to reveal himself as a sex magician. Inspired by his earlier trips to Persia, Palestine, and Egypt, he reinvented himself as "The Rosicrucian" and gave lectures and privately distributed pamphlets that explained the Rosicrucian order as merely a reintroduction of Eastern mysteries to European Christianity. He, as always, provided details of his own personal experience with the sex magic of the East.

One night—it was in far-off Jerusalem or Bethlehem, I really forget which—I made love to, and was loved by, a dusky maiden of Arabic blood. I of her, and the experience, learned—not directly, but by suggestion—the fundamental principle of the White Magick of Love; subsequently I became affiliated with some dervishes and fakirs of who, by suggestion still, I found the road to other knowledges; and of these devout practicers of a sublime and holy magic, I obtained additional clues—little threads of suggestion, which, being persistently followed, led my soul into labyrinths of knowledge themselves did not even suspect the existence of. I became practically what I was naturally—a mystic, and in time chief of the lofty brethren; taking the clues left by the masters, and pursuing them farther than they had ever been before; actually discovering the *elixir of life;* the universal Solvent, or the celestial Alkahest; the water of beauty and perpetual youth, and the philosopher's *stone. . . .*[8]

At the same time, he began teaching emancipated slaves to read and write, published two novels (making him a pioneer of African American literature), and befriended President Lincoln—dedicating one of his books to him[9]—after making recruitment drives for young black men to join the Union army. Later, he was aboard the funeral cortege train for his friend Lincoln in 1865, but at the first stop he was dismissed from the train of the Great Emancipator on the grounds that he was the only black man aboard.[10] In 1861, Randolph made a successful public lecture tour of California, and while his lectures were largely concerned with the fulfillment of the will and forms of concentrated magical experience, he began to drop hints that sex was a part of his system of belief. Privately, he was more explicit. He distributed pamphlets titled *The Anasairetic Mystery—A New Revelation Concerning Sex* and *The Mysteries of Eleusis,* which dealt overtly with sex as a means of magical progression. His followers became numerous and international, and this singular figure of the Victorian age—a black man, a sex magician, friend of Lincoln, defender of women, abolitionist, and Rosicrucian— seemed to be finally achieving the preeminent position he had so desired and long worked toward. He established the first Grand Lodge of Eulis in California, and at the conclusion of the Civil War he had his own publishing house in Ohio, which was printing his texts on scrying, mysticism, and sex magic. The Hermetic Brotherhood of Luxor—a sex magic movement that endured into the twentieth century—was secretly founded in 1870 and was largely based upon Randolph's teachings at the Lodge of Eulis. The Hermetic Brotherhood of Luxor was the only organization offering practical instruction in the Western occult prior to the 1888 foundation of the Hermetic Order of the Golden Dawn, a cult that traced its descent to Renaissance magicians like John Dee and beyond. The brotherhood's founder, Max Theon, was inducted by Randolph on a visit to London, and the influential views on sex magic, which later instructed the founders of the fraternal magical order Ordo Templi Orientis (O.T.O.), were given to the brotherhood by Randolph.

The ideals of Eulis were nonetheless bound by the traditions of Christian attitudes toward sexuality. Randolph opposed free-love movements, believing them to be vehicles of vice, divorce, and spiritual pain. Rather, he instructed his followers to treat sex between husband and wife as a divine experience that may "launch Genius, Power, Beauty, Deformity, Crime, Idiocy, Shame or Glory on the world's great sea of Life, in the person of the children we may then produce."[11] There was a eugenic element to Randolph's sex magic, in that he believed children conceived in the presence of a divine force were more likely to be "good." It was, then, necessary to evoke this divine force during sex, with special emphasis on its presence at the moment of ejaculation.

While details of what occurred in meetings of the Brotherhood of Eulis are obscure, it was enough to attract the attention of the authorities as rumors of initiations, "officiating girls," and "strange oaths"[12] veered from the tolerated teaching of theoretical magic, to the intolerable demonstration of practical magic. Furthermore, he had incited the wrath of his former friend and head of the Theosophical Society, Madame Blavatsky, one of the most famous and influential occultists in the world. She began referring to him simply as "The Nigger,"[13] and Randolph's racial background became, again, a weapon to be used against him. Blavatsky and Randolph met many times as she toured America, but the nature of their enmity remained secret as the entire relationship was, according to them both, conducted telepathically.

It seems probable that Blavatsky was threatened by her charismatic rival, as well as being a staunch opponent of sex as a means to spiritual enlightenment.

A net was closing around Randolph, just as it seemed his revolutionary ideas were finding a broad enough audience to survive. The Rosicrucian Rooms were shut down, and amid heightening moral sensitivities, he was briefly jailed for the distribution of obscene literature. About 1873, he married Kate Corson, a young woman whose company published one of Randolph's texts, but his marriage seems not to have brought him happiness. Now in his forties, he was growing bitter and frustrated at his difficulty with finding acceptance for his esoteric ideas, while those things carrying the safer Rosicrucian label were given credit. In March 1874 his wife gave birth to a son, Osiris Budh. In early 1875, Randolph published an account of a meeting of the Brotherhood of Eulis over which he personally presided, and it reveals an organization in good health—financially, structurally, and with a growing membership and well-defined objectives for future expansion. It seemed that, in spite of difficulties, things were not altogether bad for Randolph, and in July of that year he wrote to a friend that the birth of his son had given him strength to "win new victories" and had led him to feel no longer afraid of "a lack of greenbacks, friends and faith in God."[14] Nine days after the letter was written, Randolph was found dead, by suicide. He was fifty years old.

His death, while on the face of it caused by Randolph's own hand, was nevertheless claimed by an embittered Blavatsky, who pronounced cryptically to Gustav Meyrink, a friend of both Blavatsky and Randolph: "He's shooting at me, The Nigger. Ah, now he's dead, the Devil's got him."[15] Meyrink asked Blavatsky what she meant, and she claimed that the magical war between them had reached a head as Randolph had picked up a gun and then psychically tried to materialize the bullet in her heart. At the last moment the effort of this extraordinary attempt at magic had overwhelmed him, driven him insane, and he had turned the gun on himself. Meyrink recorded being bemused by the pronunciation, until sometime later when he discovered that Randolph had indeed shot himself on the day in question.

Randolph's legacy remains unfulfilled; perhaps a life of turns and contradictions, as well as a knack for driving away friends and supporters, made him too difficult to categorize. Or perhaps the racism and sexual conservatism of the times have yet to be corrected so that his enormous influence and courageous pioneering of sex magic into Western society, among other occult ideals, can be recognized. He is without doubt the source of the marriage of sex and will that proved to be the foundation of the more famous systems of sex magic of the O.T.O. and Crowley, and therefore the most important figure of the genesis of Western sex magic.

Selected Works by Paschal Beverly Randolph Concerning Sex Magic

Paschal Beverly Randolph's writing is available from many publishers.

1868 ✦ *After Death, or, Disembodied Man. The World of Spirits; Its Location, Extent, Appearance; the Route Thither; Inhabitants; Customs, Societies: Also Sex and Its Uses There, Etc., Etc.; with Much Matter Pertinent to the Question of Human Immortality. Being the Sequel to "Dealings with the Dead."*

1896 ✦ *Eulis! The History of Love, Its Wondrous Magic, Chemistry, Rules, Laws, Moods and Rationale: Being the Third Revelation of Soul and Sex: Also, Reply to "Why is Man Immortal?", the Solution of the Darwin Problem, an Entirely New Theory.*

1931 ✦ *Magia Sexualis,* published in French posthumously by Maria de Naglowska. Published in English as *Magia Sexualis: Sexual Practices for Magical Power,* 2012.

2

Ida Craddock
(1857–1902)

Among the early liberators of both sex and magic into the general culture, the tragic and mystical Ida Craddock might be considered the martyr for the cause. The opening line of her public suicide note is unequivocal about her motives: "I am taking my life, because a judge, at the instigation of Anthony Comstock, has decreed me guilty of a crime which I did not commit—the circulation of obscene literature—and has announced his intention of consigning me to prison for a long term."[1]

The obscene literature in question was her spiritual and sexual essays, particularly "Heavenly Bridegrooms" and "Psychic Wedlock"; the latter proposed a form of sexual initiation into mysticism by three levels, or degrees, preceding the comparable system of the O.T.O. by several years. Her second suicide letter, addressed to her mother, states, "the world is not yet ready for all the beautiful teachings which I have to give it."[2]

Craddock was born, like Crowley, into a Quaker family. Unlike Crowley, however, Craddock's father, Joseph T., a native of Maryland but making his living in "corrupt and contented"[3] Philadelphia, had turned against his faith and become irreligious in adulthood after his first marriage ended with the death of his first wife, Mary, leaving the inventor in charge of four young children. It appears this misfortune was the catalyst for his renunciation of the benevolent Christian God.

Ida was a product of his second marriage, to Lizzie Selvage, the daughter of French immigrants. After remarrying, the elder Craddock succumbed to tuberculosis when Ida was only four months old, his dying words to his wife a demand that she keep Ida away from religion. Not only did Lizzie not fulfill her husband's deathbed request, but she became an evangelical Quaker, terrifying the precocious and sensitive Ida with the recriminations that awaited her both on Earth and in the afterlife should she allow a man to so much as kiss her or hold her hand. Lizzie enforced her fanatical beliefs on her daughter with violence and discipline.

The Quakers (also known as the Society of Friends) were founded in the seventeenth century by the English dissenting preacher George Fox. Fox lived through a time of extraordinary variety of religious thought in England, which was under the control of Lord Protector Oliver Cromwell. Cromwell led the republic known as the English Commonwealth following the English Civil War, and the country was ablaze with religious fervor. Cromwell was, like any military dictator of a new and unstable theocratic republic, highly paranoid about any perceived threat to his regime and himself and generally persecuted those who began preaching religious views that diverged from Puritanism. So many dissenting voices arose, however, that silencing them all proved near impossible, and Fox turned out to be a particular case. Arrested and imprisoned, he was granted an audience with Cromwell, and the sincerity and profundity of Fox's spiritual views left Cromwell in tears, and he almost granted Fox the right to continue preaching what would become known as Quakerism. However, "Old Ironsides," as Cromwell was known, was not swayed by his emotions for long, and Fox was forced to continue his preaching in the shadows.

By the nineteenth century the Quakers had grown in popularity and remain one of the most recognizable protestant groups in both England and the United States. This is partly due to the various eccentricities of Quakers, such as always using the archaic singular pronoun "thee" and their simple dress code, but also due to their forthright political stances as abolitionists, pacifists, and teetotalers. Furthermore, they seemed to have a knack for business, establishing some of the most famous names in British commerce and banking such as Cadbury's, Carr's, J.S. Fry & Sons, Clarks shoes, Barclays and Lloyds banks, various power plants both coal and nuclear, as well as the charitable organizations Oxfam and Greenpeace, sportswear company Nike, and the Japanese electronics giant Sony, among others (although the eponymous breakfast oats company owned by PepsiCo has nothing to do with them). Divisions among the Quakers in the nineteenth century led to many members leaving to join rival groups due to theological differences. One of the fundamental beliefs of the Quakers was that of Inner Light, which represented the God within (an idea that was descended from the Ancient Greek concept of *entheos*, from which our word "enthusiasm" is derived—a quality displayed in abundance by the Quakers). This was at odds with more standard Christian beliefs that posited Christ's death was the salvation of mankind, and it was through his death that the sins of humanity would be atoned, and thus humanity saved from death and separation from God, allowing man access to the Kingdom of Heaven. Were God already within man, then Christ would have died for nothing.

Testing out her Quaker entrepreneurial skills, Lizzie went into the medicine business, selling Indian hemp (cannabis oil) as a cure for various ailments—such as colds, bronchitis, nausea, night sweats, and, tellingly, tuberculosis—in an early appearance of Western medicinal marijuana. It was a success, and Ida, along with her half sister, a maid, her mother, and a female lodger, enjoyed a New Jersey summer house complete with a horse named Daisy, suggesting that in spite of her mother's uncompromising religiosity, there was comfort and recreation in Ida's childhood.

Able to read fluently from the Bible at two-and-a-half years old, Ida was destined for literary work. Her first publication, at age twenty—a review of Johann Wolfgang von Goethe's *Faust* for the *Saturday Evening Post*—was well received, and she was invited to make further contributions. Alongside her writing, Craddock became proficient in stenography and became a women's shorthand tutor. A curious concurrence of the nineteenth century was that many prominent stenographers also happened to be (for reasons that are obscure beyond both appealing to progressive natures) vanguards of the sexual reform movement.[4] It was through this channel that Ida became interested in both women's rights and Swedenborgian mysticism, which included direct communication with angels, demons, and spirits. She applied to be the first female undergraduate student at the University of Pennsylvania and was accepted, only to be blocked by the board of trustees. It would not be the last time her gender proved an obstruction in the pursuit of her will.

By thirty years old, Craddock was in San Francisco teaching stenography at a women's college and working as a bank clerk, having finally shaken off her Quaker upbringing. She became drawn to the occult, and involved herself with Blavatsky's Theosophical Society, attending a Unitarian church where Theosophical classes were held. In 1889 she spent a month in Alaska and was fascinated with the native Alaskan culture, in particular their customary phallic worship. She produced an article on the subject and a heavily censored version was published. Thus began Craddock's life's work, a voyage into the long-abandoned—in Christian society, at least—milieu of sex and religion.

Her first notoriety came as she published an article in defense of *The Danse du Ventre,* a popular belly-dancing spectacle at the Chicago World's Fair of 1893. Among the other attractions, including an ostrich farm, Thomas Edison's embryonic moving pictures, and George Ferris's first ever Ferris Wheel, was Cairo Street and its *Egyptian Theatre.* Dreamy dances of veiled women took place to the accompaniment of Arabic instruments, flutes, tambourines, drums, incense, and howling cries. The titillating show, impossibly tame by the standards of today, was a hit, and its popularity did not suffer from the press accusations of it being a "horrible orgie" from the "waste of Oriental slums" and a "heathen show."[5]

In response to the outcry among journalists of the yellow press and the easily scandalized, Anthony Comstock, a thick-set man with a mustache like a gala curtain, rose to prominence as a self-appointed warrior for American decency. Having seen the show, he used his great belly to imitate the movements of the dancers to a group of reporters, excusing the fact that he couldn't perform it quite as they had, saying, "I am not as little as they are."[6]

In 1873, the year after Randolph was jailed in Boston, Comstock had set up the New York Society for the Suppression of Vice, a private force of religious fundamentalists affiliated with the Young Men's Christian Association funded by conservative luminaries such as J. P. Morgan and Samuel Colgate. A determined lobbyist, Comstock soon saw the passing of an eponymous law that suppressed wholesale any literature he deemed "obscene, lewd or lascivious,"[7] and he extended this suppression to the US mail, outlawing the sending of contraceptives and any written material pertaining to contraception, sex, or abortion. Comstock oversaw the enforcement of his law personally, employing gangs of private investigators, using all manner of underhanded tactics to expose the purveyors of the obscene, as well as ferociously lobbying Congress to appoint him in the role of Volunteer Postal Inspector In Chief. He was soon boasting of the numbers of arrests made under his command and, more despicably, the number of suicides he had induced with his raids on the carnal, the improper, and the immoral. Unsurprisingly, women's suffragists and advocates of sexual freedom were among his prime targets.

His efforts to halt *The Danse du Ventre* failed, however. Although the fair's director general, George R. Davis, complied with Comstock's demands for a full investigation, the wily Davis managed to keep his popular show going. He was no doubt motivated by the fair's mounting debt and the more horrifying events surrounding the self-proclaimed Satanist and serial killer H. H. Holmes's slayings at the next-door World's Fair Hotel, which was hardly enticing visitors to come and spend. Craddock took the fight with Comstock to the press, and in the furor and scandal managed to attract the attention of some important allies in the cause. She printed and sold her essay, also titled "The

Danse du Ventre," herself after Comstock criminalized its publication and delivery by post, and it was read eagerly by her supporters in New York. She noted the details of the dance and defended it as a "religious memorial of purity and self-control," as well as noting the presence of six tassels on each dancer's outfit representing the five days of a woman's period, plus the sixth day for the resumption of sexual intercourse. This showed a ritual respect for the rhythmic nature of the female body that Craddock believed was lacking in the Christian world when compared with the customs of the Muslim and Jewish worlds. Furthermore, she saw in the belly dance an equivalent of the male technique of *karezza,* or ejaculation control. She saw that a woman could gain a degree of sexual self-control through certain physical techniques, and as in karezza, this heightening of the sexual self was a potent method for bringing a third party into sex: God.[8]

Enjoying her victory, she then began to produce a prolific output of lectures and essays as interest in her work grew. In her essay "The Wedding Night," she details techniques of penetration for the bridegroom, recommending that he avoid bringing his wife to orgasm through clitoral stimulation "for the reason that it is a rudimentary male organ, and an orgasm aroused there evokes a rudimentary male magnetism in the woman, which appears to pervert the act of intercourse, with the result of sensualizing and coarsening the woman." The more patient approach required to bring his wife to a vulva orgasm would have a more profound spiritual and health-giving effect on both bride and bridegroom. She recommended the philosophy of yoga as a sexual solution to most of the marital problems of the West, discussed lubrication, the hymen, how both partners should primarily aim to pleasure the other rather than themselves—deeply contrary to society's prevailing attitude about the "marital rights" of men—and how to invoke the Divine Central Force into sex. She also set out attacking Comstockian morals, blaming him for the suffocating repression that was strangling the well-being of nineteenth-century America.

Comstock's response was to imply that Craddock, who was blond, blue-eyed, and pretty, was a woman of loose morality and had learned so very much about the practical nature of sex by behaving in decidedly un-Christian ways with her fancy men. She was prepared for this, though: in the final paragraph of "The Danse du Ventre," she made her first allusion to her "marriage." Further questioning how a spinster virgin could be so familiar with the "final quivering of passion"[9] led her to explain more precisely that her husband "is in the world beyond the grave, and had been for many years previous to our union."[10] She never revealed his earthly name in public, but only gave his spirit name as Soph, an angel with whom she shared a conjugal bed every night. She detailed in the essay "Heavenly Bridegrooms" her experiences with her husband and how Soph had brought her sexual enlightenment through the three degrees of initiation. In "Psychic Wedlock," the most influential of her sex magic essays, she elaborated upon these three stages. The first, which she termed *Alphaism,* is essentially using masturbation to teach self-control over the orgasm. In the second stage, *Dianism,* both partners delay and withhold orgasm during sex using various techniques, until the sensation of orgasm can be achieved without ejaculation in the male or exhaustion in the female, so that sex can theoretically continue indefinitely. Finally, the third stage explained the evocation of the deity into sex as a third party, first as what she termed "The Great Thinker," that the ultimate state may be achieved through a divine joy arising from the sexual ecstasy being given to—as opposed to received from—the other partners, both divine and fleshly. All this came from her marriage to the angelic Soph, and their sex life was so active and wild, it was said,[11] that the neighbors frequently complained about the noise. She wrote of her experiences with Soph: "When the orgasm approached, Soph begged me not to give way just yet. Twice this occurred and I felt he would enjoy as prolonged a union just before the culminating point quite as much as I . . . as it was, however, I had a partial orgasm at the moment, in spite of myself. At first Soph thought I could not continue; but I did manage to, to his delight . . . at each one of these successful attempts at suppression I felt myself growing stronger and stronger."[12]

That she really was a virgin at this point, as she claimed (although she had much to say on the notion of virginity), seems doubtful. Members of the O.T.O., years after her death, curious to uncover more about this figure who was so influential on their movement, discovered in her diaries that Craddock had probably had two lovers[13]—one younger man who was unsatisfying in his approach to normal sex, and later an older former clergyman who had become a heretical mystic (whom she likely met through her Theosophy classes) and was able to bring her to states of divine sexual ecstasy through his knowledge of both male and female karezza techniques. But neither of these affairs seems to have endured, while Soph would share her bed every night.

It would not be long before such radical thinking would attract counterattacking forces seeking to defend the moral, Puritan status quo of the age. While it seemed that, with "The Danse du Ventre" saved, Comstock was defeated for now, it was Craddock's mother Lizzie, who would begin to become her most powerful adversary. In 1894 she attempted to have her daughter placed in an asylum for the insane. The public declaration of marriage to an angel, and the recounting of her sex life with her ethereal spouse, was too much for the Quaker to bear. It was unsuccessful, and Craddock had the foresight to send her papers to an editor in England who promised to secure them, should her mother try to burn them as she had threatened to do. In 1898, Lizzie succeeded in her asylum plan, and Ida was forcibly admitted to the Pennsylvania Hospital for the Insane. After three months of incarceration, she was released by doctors who judged her again to be sound of mind. Surviving this, she then had to contend with an enraged Comstock, who was determined to pursue his personal vendetta against her until the bitter end. She was arrested and charged with obscenity in 1899 at the behest of Comstock and released only when Clarence Darrow, advocate of free speech and famous defense attorney, posted her $500 bond. Craddock was not deterred, and in fact decided to rise to the challenge, writing upon moving to Comstock's New York turf: "I have an inward feeling that I am really divinely led here to New York to face this wicked and depraved man Comstock in open court."[14] Comstock was to prove, however, a formidable opponent. In 1902 Craddock fell afoul of the obscenity law in New York for distributing copies of "The Wedding Night" by post, and endured three months of hard labor in grueling and terrible workhouse conditions, following a trial in which the judge refused to even allow the jury to read the offending article. Released, Craddock was immediately re-arrested under the Comstock Law and convicted once more. Support flooded in from advocates of free speech and her other political allies, but to little effect. Facing the choice of either pleading insanity and thereby admitting that her life's work and her angelic marriage were but a figment, or serving a much longer prison sentence, Craddock slashed her wrists and inhaled the gas from her cooker. There she died, aged forty-five.

Her public suicide note continued: "Perhaps it may be that in my death, more than in my life, the American people may be shocked into investigating the dreadful state of affairs which permits that unctuous sexual hypocrite Anthony Comstock to wax fat and arrogant and to trample upon the liberties of the people, invading, in my own case, both my right to freedom of religion and to freedom of the press."[15] Having paid the ultimate price, Craddock had her revenge: the public backlash against Comstock hounding her to suicide led to the disbandment of the New York Society for the Suppression of Vice. Comstock's power and influence declined as a wave of social change washed him away. He became a mentor to a young J. Edgar Hoover and attracted the ire of George Bernard Shaw, who frequently ridiculed him in the press.[16] He died in New Jersey in 1915, his legacy the destruction of 15 tons of books, 284,000 pounds of printing plates, and 4 million pictures, and the responsibility for 4,000 arrests and 15 suicides, including that of Craddock.

While her influence on the general understanding of social change in the early twentieth century may be overshadowed by more prominent figures, her status in the esoteric world of magic is well established. Crowley incorporated Craddock's concepts of divine sexual ecstasy into his hugely influential *The Book of the Law*. He also wrote of her in the *Blue Equinox,* under the reverent guise of "Baphomet X° O.T.O.," saying of "Heavenly Bridegrooms" that it is "one of the most remarkable human documents ever produced, and it should certainly find a regular publisher in book form. . . . She seems to have had access to certain most concealed sanctuaries. . . . She has put down statements in plain English which are positively staggering. This book is of incalculable value to every student of occult matters. No Magic library is complete without it."[17] Furthermore, in recent years, the O.T.O. posthumously inducted her into the Order of the Eagle in recognition of her contributions to esoteric sexuality,[18] and among sex magicians worldwide Craddock is acknowledged as one of the principal figures in the foundation of modern sex magic.

Selected Works of Ida Craddock Concerning Sex Magic

Ida Craddock's collected essays are available within *Sexual Outlaw, Erotic Mystic: The Essential Ida Craddock* by Vere Chappell.

1894 ✦ "Heavenly Bridegrooms"

1899 ✦ "Right Marital Living"

1990 ✦ "Spiritual Joys"

1900 ✦ "The Wedding Night"

3

Aleister Crowley (1875–1947)

It is now impossible to consider, discuss, or write about the modern occult without making some reference to Crowley. His influence is so great that every magical path, order, school, and philosophy—even those that seek to revive the occult world that existed centuries before his birth—are largely defined by their adherence to or defiance of Crowley. In this regard he might be considered an occult analog to the position held by the Beatles in popular music. It seems appropriate, then, that on the far left of the back row of the sleeve art of the Beatles' most celebrated LP, *Sgt. Pepper's Lonely Hearts Club Band,* Crowley can be seen staring menacingly out among the curious cardboard celebrity troupe. Sandwiched between Sri Yukteswar Giri and Mae West, Crowley's place in popular cultural eternity has been sealed.

His status as an icon began long before any of the Beatles were born, however, and it was all his own work. Crowley is perhaps the only figure in the history of magic who has managed to fully transcend the occult and become an international celebrity, no matter how distorted his image became in that process. In 2002 a public vote at the BBC, bastion of the modern British establishment, placed Crowley as the seventy-third greatest Briton of all time, this time sandwiched between King Henry V, the Lancastrian English king immortalized by William Shakespeare, and the equally noble and notable medieval king of Scotland, Robert the Bruce. Crowley's spirit had survived into the new millennium, the zeitgeist of which he had both predicted and helped to form. He was an idol to counterculture figures of the 1960s, including Jimmy Page of Led Zeppelin, who used some of his vast wealth to buy Crowley's former home, known as Boleskine, on the shores of Loch Ness in Scotland. To the 1960s counterculturalists, Crowley was not only a magician but also one of the most ferocious individual forces of social change ever known, opening the way for a revolution in thought about the spiritual self, drugs, and sex.

Crowley was born Edward Alexander Crowley on October 12, 1875, in Royal Leamington Spa, Warwickshire, England. Like Craddock, Crowley was raised in a strict religious family. His father, Edward Crowley, was a fanatical preacher and member of the Exclusive Brethren. The Exclusive Brethren was a radically conservative sect that formed in 1848 after a schism within the Plymouth Brethren, itself an already radical sect of Quakers. The Exclusive Brethren preached a fundamentalist reading of the biblical word of God as the literal truth, as well as forcefully condemning all non-members as sinners.

Crowley Sr. would read a Bible verse to his young son and wife, Emily Bertha (née Bishop), every morning after breakfast, and celebrating Christmas was forbidden as it was a pagan festival. The family was wealthy, and Edward Sr. was the scion of a Quaker brewing dynasty (curiously the Friends decided that while consuming alcohol was forbidden, earning money from brewing it for others was perfectly acceptable). After some business ventures in his youth he had retired at age twenty-six to concentrate on his spiritual life. He traveled the country preaching the teachings of the Exclusive Brethren.

In 1877, Crowley Sr. sold his shares in the Crowley brewery and reinvested his money in a Dutch waterworks company. Following this change of career, and after many years of abstinence, he began—rather ironically—drinking alcohol again. His waterworks investments seem to have motivated him to choose the spa town of Leamington as his new home, investing in a large property and maintaining several servants, and these were the surroundings into which his diabolical son would be born.

The younger Crowley, or Alec as he was known during his childhood, recalled a happy, comfortable existence until about the age of ten years old. There were difficulties in the family: his father's insistence that they socialize only with other members of the brethren meant that his young wife was forcibly cut off from the rest of her family. But the small family of three (a younger sister died within hours of being born when Crowley was four years old) and their four servants enjoyed a life of luxury and travel, while young Crowley attended exclusive Evangelical Christian boarding schools.

While he was away at school at the age of eleven, Crowley noted a disturbing dream he'd had one night about his father dying. When he woke the following morning, he received the news that his father had passed away during the night from tongue cancer. Here began a highly turbulent period of Crowley's life. The strong paternal figure had been pulled from him, and he began a pattern of destructive behavior that would lead his mother to label him "the Beast"—a nickname he gleefully adopted for the rest of his life. The death of his father also affected Crowley financially. Upon his majority, he stood to inherit £50 thousand, which equates to about £2 million ($2.6 million) in today's money. He was rich and thus freed from the need to work to make his living. Crowley could now consider himself an aristocrat, and it was a distinction he would embrace with considerable enthusiasm while being typically unconcerned with any actual legitimacy as a nobleman, albeit with some justifiable social reasoning, as the nineteenth-century aristocrat was more than ever defined by his bourgeois accumulation of wealth rather than ancient peerages.

Before he came of age, Crowley had to navigate the rest of his teenage years without a father. He referred to his teenage years as his "boyhood from Hell," specifically referring to this period after the death of his father. Until then pious to the point of competitiveness, he had his first feelings of religious doubt when his mother embarked on a radical interpretation of the teachings of the brethren, cutting ties with friends of the family and denouncing them as heretics who were condemned to Hell. The fallacious logic that allowed his mother to suddenly declare once exemplary Christians on the path to Paradise to be incorrigible sinners was not lost on Crowley. He saw hypocrisy and bigotry in his mother, and began to see it through the entire opaque pall of his faith.

His school life also became a ritual terror as he found himself the target for Reverend Henry D'Arcy Champney, the headmaster at the school for sons of the Plymouth Brethren, which Crowley attended. Champney was so intensely pious he claimed never to have had sex with his wife and spent much of his time and energy attempting to make sure the boys did not indulge in masturbation—unsuccessfully in Crowley's case, at least. The young headmaster also exposed the boys to disease by forcing them to welcome impoverished measles, mumps, and ringworm patients into the school, believing that those who fell sick among his schoolboys did so as a result of divine punishment for some hidden misdeed. Crowley, a curious child, found himself often subjected to routine corporal punishment, but other forms of discipline were crueler and more unusual, including long terms of solitary confinement and exposure to the elements. This led to Crowley contracting albuminuria, a life-threatening kidney condition, and his uncle Jonathan Crowley removed him from the school. Following complaints from the elder Crowley to the authorities, the school soon closed down. The younger Crowley had refused to denounce his headmaster, later explaining that he was as loyal to his enemies as to his friends, but it seems likely confusion and fear would have played a role in his reticence.

Surviving the illness, to the surprise of his doctors, Crowley gathered strength and began to grow into a strong and handsome young man. He seduced one of the family maids on his mother's bed (leading to the maid's dismissal upon discovery of the deed), and then, continuing a fascination for explosives that he had developed at school, the sixteen-year-old Crowley blew up a jar of gunpowder in the garden, knocking himself unconscious and blinding him for six weeks. He later remarked that his "famous Guy Fawkes day"[1] and the subsequent loss of vision was the beginning of his development of his other senses.

In 1895 he was enrolled at Trinity College, Cambridge, and furthermore he was now entitled to his inheritance. Rich and far from his oppressive relatives, Crowley was given his first taste of true freedom. He wanted to distance himself as much as possible from his former self and decided a name change would be a useful symbolic entry into manhood. Alec, his childhood pet name, was not suitable for a Cambridge scholar, and Edward Alexander, his birth names, seemed dull. He decided, since the family was distantly descended from Irish blood at a time when a great sentiment of nativist Celtic romance was spreading through Britain, to settle on the Gaelic variant of his birth name, Alexander: Aleister.

Crowley was an excellent student, and he veered toward a career in the diplomatic service in his studies. He then studied chemistry, finally leaving Cambridge without bothering to complete his degree. But he developed other passions as he went; for mountaineering, chess, and poetry in particular. He spent large amounts of his fortune on book-collecting and was soon drawn to the Decadents, who were lighting up the painting and literature of the era with thrilling and daring works of art: Felicien Rops, J-K Huysmans, Algernon Charles Swinburne, James Abbott McNeill Whistler, and Aubrey Beardsley were among those he admired. This interest led him to what made the Decadents so feared by the established world—an open delight in perversity and divergent sexuality. His first homosexual experience came at Cambridge and, having conquered the ultimate sin—as preached by his father—he finally had the cataclysmic crisis of faith that saw him turn his back on the Christian God for good. This experience also served to presage some of Crowley's most important sex magic developments years later. Looking for some form of spiritual guidance, it seemed logical to turn to the great enemy of God: he picked up a copy of Arthur Edward Waite's *The Book of Black Magic and of Pacts,* published in 1898, and was enthralled.

In London, Crowley—after a persistent search—was finally introduced to a man who could begin to slake his thirst for magical knowledge. Samuel Liddell Mathers was known at the time as MacGregor Mathers (like Crowley he was indulging in a fantastical Celtic personal history), and he was head of the Golden Dawn. Although as Crowley entered the neophyte grade of the order he was underwhelmed by the bourgeois dullness of the Golden Dawn, he nevertheless skipped through the initiations, quickly becoming one of its most powerful and prominent figures. In doing so, he made both allies and enemies—the latter including William Butler Yeats, a high-ranking member of the Golden Dawn and perhaps the most famous poet in the English-speaking world at the time. Crowley did not make a distinction between good and bad magic—or white and black—believing that any magic that led to development of the True Will to be worthy of performance, especially magic related to the Great Work: knowledge of and conversation with one's Holy Guardian Angel, or in other words, the ultimate form of mystical self-development. Yeats believed that Crowley's fundamentally amoral approach to magic would bring the order into disrepute and unleash great forces of evil upon humanity. From the outset, Yeats and Crowley were at one another's throats. They were love rivals for one of the female members of the order, Florence Farr, and Yeats felt usurped by the vivacious young magician who had become close to Mathers in place of him. Crowley was also an ambitious poet, but his poetic talents paled next to the Nobel Prize winner, and he became jealous—albeit while claiming it was in fact Yeats who was jealous of his talents. Yeats accused Crowley of performing low black magic upon his fellow magicians, including sticking pins in effigies of them.

This animosity would lead the pair into an all-out magical war, with its critical moment coming during the dramatically titled "Battle of Blythe Road."[2] Threats of blackmail and legal troubles began to erupt, and Crowley—now styling himself as the Laird of Boleskine following his purchase of the enormous property in Scotland—kept a low profile and divided his time between Boleskine and Paris, where Mathers was fighting in his corner. His advancement by Mathers to the Second Order had been overruled in London by a rebel contingent led by Yeats. This insubordination angered Mathers, and the pair devised a plot whereby Crowley would return to London and, disguised, demand that every member swear allegiance to the Second Order of the Golden Dawn or be expelled. Crowley was going to ride into the middle of the warzone and put the onus on the rebels to prove themselves. Mathers gave him a talisman and warned him of psychic attacks and magic that would be cast upon him, saying that burning fires or fires that refused to be lit would be sure signs he was being assaulted. In London, Crowley reported that his cab had to be stopped after the paraffin lamps set fire to the hood, while the second cab's horse bolted. When he arrived, his raincoat spontaneously combusted, and he found it impossible to light the fire in the hearth. His colorful talisman, a Rosy Cross, had bleached white. All of this Crowley considered to be deeply foreboding.

Crowley headed to Blythe Road, where the rebels had congregated in the flat of one of their members. He was dressed as a Highland warrior with the black cross of a Crusader on his chest, and he began stomping up the stairs, making the sign of the pentagram while screaming curses upon the rebels. Yeats and a white magician bouncer appeared and kicked Crowley down the stairs before a police constable appeared and told Crowley to move along. Suffering a tactical defeat, Crowley withdrew. Wanting to press his advantage, Yeats then performed a ritual that intended to send a vampire to sit at Crowley's bedside table and drain him of his vital energy as he slept. In a more mundane but strategic counterattack, Crowley took the rebels to court on charges of withholding documents, while the rebels expelled Mathers, Crowley, and their supporters, making Yeats the new head of the order. The judge, highly amused by the eccentric and ludicrous nature of the case, ruled in favor of Yeats, and Crowley left the arena defeated in the war.[3]

Crowley spent the next few years, as he advanced through his twenties, on vanity-publishing poetry, magic, and traveling the world to climb mountains. He built a reputation as a daring and skillful mountaineer, conquering several of the world's most challenging peaks, including in 1905 leading the first ever expedition up Kanchenjunga (otherwise known as K2) , which although ultimately aborted, was a major advance toward conquering the 28,000-foot mountain—a feat not achieved until an Italian expedition finally made it to the summit in 1954.

After the failed attempt at K2, Crowley returned to Boleskine and to magic. He began the notorious Abramelin operation, a six-month-long magical ritual that, through immense self-discipline and difficulty, allows the magician to contact their Holy Guardian Angel. Contact with the Holy Guardian Angel was, to Crowley, the ultimate and sole objective of the practice of magic, and this was his first major attempt to accomplish it. He abandoned the attempt part-way through after deciding to make a gesture of chivalric generosity. Rose Kelly was a young widower now in love with a married man and who was also the sister of Crowley's good friend, the painter Gerald Kelly. Rose's parents had forced her to choose between two suitors, both of whom were keen to marry her for love and neither of whom she had any feeling for. Crowley saw the solution and asked Rose to marry him. That way, he could carry on with mountain climbing and magic while she would be free to conduct her affair without the impropriety of being unmarried. Furthermore, as she was not particularly cultured or educated, Crowley was sure they would feel little more than friendly affection for one another. Rose accepted, and one morning they slipped away to have the ceremony performed by a lawyer, unbeknown to Gerald Kelly. Crowley and Rose sat in the cab in silence, not sure what to say to one another. "I only have to emancipate her," he told himself. "I don't have to live with her."[4]

The elopement created a scandal when it was uncovered, with both of Rose's suitors and Gerald Kelly furious. To maintain a veneer of respectability, Crowley took Rose on a honeymoon to the west of Scotland. Once they'd drunk enough champagne, the silent awkwardness between them suddenly turned into Crowley composing and reading her Romantic poetry, and his halfhearted desire to consummate the marriage out of boredom turned into a passionate sexual affair. Now fired up by love, he wrote Rose poems and decided to take her on a much grander honeymoon to Naples, Cairo, Ceylon, and China. It was in Egypt that Rose would prove to be one of the most valuable figures in Crowley's magical life. They stayed in Cairo, and Crowley constructed a temple in their luxurious flat; he was keen to show off his magic skills to his new wife. In possibly one of the greatest romantic gestures of all time, Crowley arranged for himself and Kelly to spend a night in the King's Chamber, deep inside the Great Pyramid at Giza, with Crowley attempting to use conjuring to fill the chamber with light before they spent a night of sex and magic together there. In the flat, she watched with curiosity as he performed his conjuring, hoping to show her sylphs he had commanded into the room. Instead, Rose went into a trance each time and repeated the words: "They are waiting for you."[5]

On the third day she fell into her trance during his ritual and said, "He who waits is Horus." Crowley was intrigued by this more specific pronunciation: Rose's knowledge of mythology was zero, and he wondered how she'd come to know the name of the falcon-headed Egyptian sky god. He grilled her about Horus, and she was able to answer questions on the god's appearance as well as his planet and numbers—answers that would be very hard to guess correctly, but Rose's answers were indeed correct. Still skeptical, Crowley took her to the Boulak Museum in Cairo and told her to identify what she had seen. Rose made her way through the rooms, walking past many images of Horus, leaving Crowley satisfied that it had all been a coincidence, until she stopped before one particular piece and confidently pronounced, "There he is." Crowley took a look at the piece and saw an eighth-century-BCE wooden stele depicting the sun god Ra-Hoor-Khuit with his son, Horus. She had indeed picked out the correct god, but what truly astonished Crowley was the museum catalogue number of the piece that was noted on a card—666.

Amazed at this synchronicity, he now believed that Kelly was in contact with the god Horus. He taught her how to invoke the god, and she began to recount instructions on how Crowley might receive word from Horus. First, he discovered that it was an envoy of Horus named Aiwass that was trying to speak to him. Then, after several days studying the stele and its hieroglyphs, Rose fell into a trance in their home temple, and Crowley prepared himself for something major. He sat down, and from behind him he heard a voice, that of Aiwass. The voice was deep and spoke perfect, unaccented English. Crowley frantically began to transcribe what the voice was telling him, while the entranced Rose sat in as the conductor. Through Aiwass, the sky goddess Nuit, mother of Osiris, Isis, Set, Nepthys, and Horus, began to speak; her first proclamation being: "Every man and every woman is a star." The transcription would go on to include three narratives in the first person, one from Nuit, one from Hadit (a form of Horus representing the inner self), and one from Ra-Hoor-Khuit (an active form of Horus, who is the god of war and vengeance). These narratives would form *The Book of the Law,* Crowley's best-known and most influential work. He claimed he was merely a conduit for the words of his Holy Guardian Angel Aiwass, who was, in turn, speaking on behalf of these three deities. "There is no law beyond do what thou wilt" and "the word of sin is restriction" are the most potent phrases, which Crowley recognized as the end of one age and the beginning of another; specifically, he saw the world in 1904 entering the age of Horus, promising a time of great increases in both pleasure and violence.

The age of Horus was the age of the son, who followed on from the age of Osiris, the slain male god. Osiris's epoch coincided with the long patriarchal period that came about following the agricultural revolution. Religions proliferated and narrowed down to male figures in the sky, the sun was worshipped as the bringer of good harvests, and the phallus became the predominant preoccupation of human worship. Prior to this had been the age of Isis, the mother, when lunar mysteries of fertility were the most important aspects of human survival and therefore a strong focus for religion and society—women were worshipped. Now the age of the child Horus would come to the fore; more innocent, more driven by simple desires for pleasure, but also more capable of remorseless violence. The catalyst for all this was Crowley and *The Book of the Law,* which would, while relatively little-read, nevertheless bleed so deeply into society that there's hardly a counter- or subcultural movement that doesn't owe it a debt. Christianity, already beginning to look bloated and fragile as a worthy intellectual and spiritual preoccupation in the West, took another devastating blow from Crowley, who had inverted its basic principles and formed a coherent philosophy of unrestricted will, sexual liberation, and personal freedom.

Naturally, many people have questioned the veracity of Crowley's claim to have been a mere conduit for a higher power gifting a kind of supreme knowledge to the world, particularly as certain themes had foreshadowing in his earlier learning and beliefs. But Crowley himself seems to have been dubious about the nature of the manuscript and what to do with it. He chose not to follow Aiwass's instructions to build an island fortress and distribute the book in many languages. Instead, he put the book away after making a few copies of it, seeming—for once—to have been afraid of what he had done. He returned to Boleskine, delighted that his wife had proved to be such a powerful seeress, and they engaged in sex magic rituals to keep up momentum and protect themselves. He made the "cakes of light," as described by Aiwass, that contained honey, wine, olive oil, Abramelin oil, and Rose's menstrual blood and left them out as they would, according to the prophecy, attract beetles that he could either eat to gain great power or crush to destroy an enemy. He sent the beetles to the Natural History Museum in London, who returned the samples, saying—according to Crowley—that they were new to entomology. Finally, using anal sex with Rose as a means of gathering magical power, he sent the demon Beelzebub to attack Mathers (with whom he was also in conflict by this time) in retaliation for what Crowley believed was a magical attack upon him, causing his hunting dogs to all die and Rose to be assaulted by a stranger. In 1905, Rose gave birth to their first child, a girl, who was named Nuit Ma Ahathoor Hecate Sappho Jezebel Lilith Crowley, although for practicality's sake, they simply called her Lilith.

This high point in his magical career was followed by a more literal high point in his mountaineering career—although this would turn rapidly into a very low point indeed. The second attempt to climb K2 ended in tragedy as, following a rebellion against his leadership, Crowley stubbornly refused to leave an ice shelf where they had been stuck for several days. He told his mutinous party that descending at the time they had decided to was dangerous, but he let them go. Sure enough, four of the seven were killed in an avalanche as they went down, three local porters and one of his European party. When Crowley made a safe descent of the same pass, he refused to stop and assist the survivors with their rescue efforts and headed back to Darjeeling alone. Frustrated at what he saw as weakness and folly that had cost him the possibility of breaking the world altitude record, he collected the expedition funds that belonged primarily to one of the surviving climbers, the Swiss Jules Jacot-Guillarmod. It was not until Jacot-Guillarmod later blackmailed Crowley with the threat of exposing his pornographic poems that Crowley agreed to return the money. Crowley was unrepentant, but the callous act blackened his name among mountaineers, and his climbing days were as good as done.

He sent for his wife and child to meet him in India. While he waited for their ship to come in, he busied himself by learning Persian, hunting big game, and sacrificing goats to Kali. One night, during a public festival, Crowley realized he was being followed. He tried to give his pursuers the slip but found himself pinned to a wall by six shadowy figures. He managed to get a hand in his pocket and draw his Webley revolver and fire, sending them scattering. Panicked at having possibly killed a man and the thought of a long stint in an Indian jail, he performed the ritual of the Rose Cross in his mind, something he had trained many years to do as a member of the Golden Dawn. This specific ritual is designed to work like a veil for the aura (as opposed to, for example, the Lesser Banishing Ritual of the Pentagram, which lights up the aura). It is protective and can render the magician psychically invisible. In any case, Crowley was invisible enough to escape back to his lodgings without further incident. The following day's newspapers confirmed that police were looking for the killer of two men.

As soon as Rose and Lilith arrived, the Crowleys headed to Rangoon and on to China. He was in a state of deep depression by now, physically, emotionally, artistically, and psychically exhausted. He embarked on a grueling daily repetition of the Preliminary Invocation of the *Goetia* (a Renaissance system of summoning seventy-two demons that once allegedly belonged to the biblical King Solomon) for months on end. He told Rose, who was three months pregnant, to go back to Calcutta with Lilith and collect their belongings; he intended to head to the United States to raise funds for a third attempt at K2. Distraught, she eventually gave in and went back to India alone. Crowley diverted to meet an old friend from the Golden Dawn, Elaine Simpson, whom he tried to convince to perform sex magic with him to invoke more Egyptian deities, but she refused. He headed on to the United States and then finally arrived back in Liverpool to pick up a telegram informing him that Lilith had died of typhoid in Rangoon. The Crowleys fell apart: Aleister's health declined, and he spent much of the next year in a depressive sleep or in hospital, while Rose became a severe alcoholic. Their second child, Lola Zaza, seemed certain to die but managed to pull through in one of the few bright spots for Crowley in this period. Eventually, he became exhausted of his suicidal wife and couldn't bear to watch her die, and so he filed for divorce in 1909.

Crowley was gently parodied by the author W. Somerset Maugham—later to become a literary giant with the novels *Of Human Bondage* and *On the Razor's Edge*—in his 1908 novel, *The Magician,* which Crowley found flattering. He then set up a biannual journal called *The Equinox,* the first edition of which announced the formation of his own magical order, mysteriously known as the A∴A∴ but nicknamed the *Argentium Astrum* (or Silver Star). The order had an initiatory structure aimed at enlightening and improving the individual through pursuit of one's true will. It attracted notable figures from its outset, including the father of chaos magic, Austin Osman Spare, discussed later in this book, and one of Crowley's most important companions, friends, lovers, and magical counterparts, Victor Neuburg.

Crowley was suffering from heartbreak, and to avoid the temptation of allowing Rose another chance to save their marriage, he decided to head to Algeria with Neuburg. Neuburg was a graduate of Trinity College, Cambridge, and from a wealthy family. Crowley described him as "a vegetarian, a mystic, a Tolstoyan, and several other things all at once. He endeavored to express his spiritual state by wearing the green star of Esperanto, though he could not speak the language; by refusing to wear a hat, even in London, to wash, and to wear trousers. Whenever addressed, he wriggled convulsively, and his lips, which were three times too large for him, and had been put on hastily as an afterthought, emitted the most extraordinary laugh that had ever come my way; to these advantages he united those of being extraordinarily well-read, overflowing with exquisitely subtle humour, and being one of the best natured people that ever trod this planet."[6] The relationship between the two men was one of great feeling and would prove to be one of the longest-lasting of Crowley's life.

The two men had no real aim in heading out to the Algerian desert other than experiencing its peace and wildness, camping, and staying in ancient hostels as they walked. Crowley had brought with him his papers on Enochian magic, and it occurred to him that this might be the place to successfully perform this most notorious form of magic. He had made a failed attempt in Mexico in 1900 to use the Enochian calls, but he felt more confident now as a magician. The system was devised by the English Elizabethan court magicians Dr. John Dee and Edward Kelley. Over seven years Dee and Kelley received communications from angels who revealed an angelic language that could be used to evoke and command spirits and demons. Enochian magic, so called because Dee asserted that the last man to have known the language of the angels was the Old Testament figure of Enoch, is considered by some magicians to be the most difficult, complex, and dangerous form of magic there is, capable of unleashing a whole range of psychological maladies, if not actual angels and demons.

Out in the desert, Crowley took out a large piece of topaz jewelery and began meditating upon it while making the Enochian calls. Neuburg transcribed what appeared in the topaz: "An angel with opalescent shining garments . . . his face is black, and his eyes white without any pupil or iris. The face is very terrible indeed."[7] The vision lasted an hour, and the first of the thirty calls was complete. Neuburg shaved his head but for two horns that he spiked up diabolically, and Crowley led him by a chain deep into the desert, reading aloud from the Qur'an, a sight surely quite spectacular to the region's native nomadic and village-dwelling people. Each day, as the calls progressed, Crowley was besieged by powerful visions of angels, fire, monsters, and other subtler synesthetic experiences. Great mysteries were being revealed to him, and creatures came to test and provoke him. He built an altar to Pan out of rocks and, for the first time, engaged in true sex magic. He had indulged in sexual acts as a part of his magical workings before (rituals that use magic are referred to as "workings"), but this was an overt attempt to use the emotional, physical, and psychic power of sex to enhance the magical experience. To properly worship Pan required sacrifice; in this case the spilling of semen was substituted for the spilling of blood. As the sensual powers of the magicians are aroused, this was a much more powerful form of sacrifice than killing an animal. Neuburg penetrated Crowley anally, and Crowley focused on the evocation and the calls. Afterward, he claimed that his visions were so powerful it left him in a state of prolonged spiritual ecstasy.

Each of the thirty stages, or aethyrs, of the calls is progressively initiatory. The Enochian magician progresses from the thirtieth aether, which is closest to the physical plane, through to the highest; those numbering nine to one, are reserved only for the greatest master magicians. Guarding them, according to Dee and Kelley, is the tenth aethyr, the home of Choronzon the gatekeeper, the deadliest and most powerful demonic entity of all.

Crowley was robed in black. Neuburg stayed in the magician's circle with a consecrated dagger, given the responsibility of physically controlling Choronzon should it try to exit the triangle of art, a literal triangle in the sand with the Hebrew god-names scratched in it, within which the demon would be evoked. They swore oaths to do their duties, and Crowley performed the banishing rituals to increase his magical state of mind and clean the area of negative energy. Then, unusually for Crowley, he performed an animal sacrifice, slitting the throat of a pigeon and letting its blood spill on the triangle as a purification. Crowley assumed the thunderbolt pose from his yogic system and began the tenth Enochian call.

Choronzon appeared soon enough, screaming terrible words that would unlock the gates of Hell. Choronzon began mimicking Crowley's voice and tempting Neuburg to leave the safety of the magic circle, but Neuburg was not fooled. The demon then appeared in the form of women, trying to seduce him out. Neuburg scribbled furiously the exchange between him and Choronzon, including its refusal to comply with the sounding of the god-names—among magicians considered to be a failsafe method of controlling a demonic entity and letting it know you are competent. Choronzon finally tricked Neuburg into throwing sand, and it was able to enter the circle where, in the form of a naked and feral man, it tried to rip Neuburg's throat out with his teeth. Neuburg reached for his dagger and shouted the god-name YHWH at it, causing it to retreat. Eventually, among more threats and attempts at violence, Choronzon continued the vision and gave Crowley a prophecy of how more mysteries would be revealed to him. Then he dispersed, and they took apart the holy place, wondering what had just happened. The remaining nine calls were completed, and Crowley was inducted among the highest adepts of all magicians; his profound experience with sex magic in the Algerian desert, and not to mention his witnessing of live demon-wrestling by Neuburg, would count as some of the most dramatic magical experiences ever described.

Now divorced, Crowley continued his relationship with Neuburg as well as numerous women, one of whom would capture his heart. Leila Waddell was a beautiful violinist and magician from Australia, and in her Crowley found a new artistic muse. He called her Laylah and referred to her as his Scarlet Woman, Divine Whore, and Mother of Heaven, all in reference to the Thelemic expression of the divine feminine, the goddess Babalon. He wrote one of his most notable works, *The Book of Lies,* with her as one of the central figures in this collection of ninety-three poems, word games, rituals, and Kabbalistic texts. Following its publication, Crowley received a surprise visit from Theodore Reuss, the founder and head of the O.T.O. Reuss calmly accused Crowley of having divulged the secrets of the O.T.O.'s closely guarded higher orders to the world and demanded he take the O.T.O.'s oath of secrecy, as was compulsory for all those initiated into them. Crowley protested his innocence, saying he had no idea what Reuss could be talking about as he'd never gained access to the higher degrees of the O.T.O. Reuss then produced a copy of the recently published *Book of Lies* and explained it was all there, in plain text. Exactly which chapter Reuss opened the book to was never disclosed by Crowley, Reuss, or Waddell, but Crowley did say, "He went to the bookshelves and, taking out a copy of *The Book of Lies,* pointed to a passage in the despised chapter. It instantly flashed upon me. The entire symbolism, not only of freemasonry but of many other traditions, blazed upon my spiritual vision. From that moment the O.T.O. assumed its proper importance in my mind. I understood that I held in my hands the key to the future progress of humanity,"[8] all of which suggests that it was chapter 36 with which Reuss was concerned, the chapter containing a ritual he had devised and called the Star Sapphire. In the ritual he uses the Rosicrucian imagery of the rood, the cross, and the rose as devices; Reuss said that in doing so Crowley must have understood the sexual symbolism of these things. Amazed that it had never occurred to him that they were phallic and yonic symbols joined together in ritual—and that this had been the case for centuries—he jumped at the chance for initiation of both he and Waddell into the O.T.O's ninth degree. It was here that he would learn about the real power of sex magic.

The O.T.O. was extremely unusual—unique, in fact, among secret societies at the end of the nineteenth century—in that it allowed women to be full members. This was, of course, crucial to an order that pursued a strongly sexual passage to spiritual enlightenment. The order was co-founded in Germany about 1903 by Reuss and Carl Kellner, who had traveled the East together in search of the secrets of enlightenment and studied the philosophy of yoga in India. On returning, Reuss became a student of the works of Randolph, through which he was able to devise his great secret, the power of sex. The O.T.O. openly traced its origins to the original Bavarian Illuminati, making it a direct descendant of both the Hermetic Brotherhood of Light and the Illuminati, two secular, humanist, anti-Papist, anti-Royalist orders of Freemasonry born at the height of the Enlightenment. While the former survived, the latter was suppressed, giving rise to a thousand conspiracies about the continued existence of the Illuminati in a staggeringly wide variety of guises, from Nazis to contemporary pop stars to Marxists. Reuss and Kellner made steps for the O.T.O. to evolve the structure of its parent organizations, most notably allowing women to enter and giving them equal footing with men. Furthermore, the O.T.O. was founded upon tantric principles, and sex magic was its core.

The techniques used in the higher degrees of the O.T.O.—what Crowley later described as the Supreme Secret—follow a similar pattern to those devised by influential pioneers such as Ida Craddock. The preparation for initiation into these degrees is a fairly exhaustive process of Masonic iterations of oneself as a free and fearless man or woman: gestures, such as placing daggers to one's throat and gripping the thumb of the Emir, the officer leading the ceremony; oaths; songs to Pan; devotions; renditions of *Tristan and Isolde* by Richard Wagner; consecrations; blessings of Death; exaltations; and the conferment of various titles, not least that of Master Magician. Instructions on historical uses of sex as a means of marrying with God (or any god) were given. Passages from the Bible are quoted that reveal that the Christian God of the Old Testament (referred to explicitly by the O.T.O. as the enemy) in the books of Isaiah and Hosea makes direct reference to sex with harlots and wives of whoredom as means to approach more closely the Kingdom of God, while noting that the more influential texts of the New Testament, specifically the famous Epistle of Paul to the Romans, were nothing more than forgeries designed to eliminate the power of sex magic from the faith. Blood sacrifices among the Jews, Catholic black masses, Russian orgies in which a priestess is inseminated by many men in the dark with the goal of conceiving a holy child, the sexual nature of the classical fables, the Kama Sutra, succubi and incubi, are all evidence of the longstanding desire to access the power that is borne from the mix of religious and sexual ecstasy.

Crowley, as ever, thrust himself into the O.T.O. with full vigor. He visited Russia and in 1913 wrote the Gnostic Mass that is still used by the O.T.O. today, and the next year he set about compiling his philosophy of Thelema (biblical Greek for "Will"), aiming to make it the official tenet of the O.T.O. He returned to Britain and began practicing sex magic rituals with Neuburg on a regular basis, having great success in evoking and conversing with the gods Mercury and Hermes. The sex magic of the O.T.O. is essentially a form of ego destruction through the breaking of sexual taboos; the highest taboo being that of the passive partner in homosexual anal sex. To Crowley, this was an ecstatic destruction of a major blockage in his ego, a final blow to the mores of his Plymouth Brethren father, who believed homosexuality to be such a horrendous sin and crime that its name could not even be spoken. As the orders go higher, so the taboos to be broken become more perverse, going as far as coprophagy.

Neuburg and Crowley had extraordinary visions brought on by their sex magic, including becoming the goddess Astarte and being placed inside a bull's carcass and drowned in blood while orgasming from being violated by a high priest. Crowley drew blood from Neuburg, cutting numbers in his chest in sacrifice to Jupiter. In another vision, Neuburg was an initiate and Crowley a beautiful dancer; Neuburg was to watch the erotic dance and try not to become aroused—if he did, he faced a choice of either raping the dancer or being castrated by a god. He was aroused, but he declined to rape the dancer, and the god had pity on Neuburg for the tenderness he had shown and merely expelled them from his temple without castration. It was not all tenderness though; Neuburg was the victim of Crowley's sometimes violent jealousy, and he became paranoid that the great magician was cursing people close to him, causing them to die. Through his love affair with Crowley, Neuburg had written poetry that enabled him to establish himself as a poet of note. But when the relationship ended, Neuburg never recovered his powers. On leaving Crowley, the Great Beast emphatically cursed him to his face.

In 1914, Crowley began again looking for ways to tackle K2, but this time his efforts were disrupted by the outbreak of the Great War. He offered his services but was rejected; he was almost forty and not considered good soldierly material. He went once more to the United States, where he was caught up in one of the most curious episodes of his life. New York City at that time had a large German population, and many of them were mobilized in trying to discourage the United States from joining the war against Germany. The United States was the upstart superpower in the world, rising to challenge the incumbent superpower, Great Britain, and a neutral status for the United States seemed like the best policy for pressing their rising advantage over the old imperial power. In spite of his whims, Crowley had always been patriotic and harbored romantic and idealistic feelings toward his homeland. It was a surprise, then, that the now notorious Crowley could be found producing pro-German propaganda in New York. Prior to this, he had been content to practice sex magic with the local prostitutes and otherwise spend time with Waddell, but one day on a tram he encountered an Irishman who led him to an underground circle of pro-German propagandists and agitators. Soon enough, posing as an Irishman, he was producing pro-German, anti-British articles for their two main English-language papers. He also supported Irish home rule and, with an eye for spectacle, made a declaration of Irish independence in front of the Statue of Liberty. All of this was considered extremely treasonous during a war that was by now eating its way through millions of young male lives. The British press assumed that the devil worshipper and black magician had such debased morals it was of no concern to him that his compatriots were dying by the thousands in Flanders. As it turns out, diary entries by Crowley suggest another set of circumstances: that he was in fact in the employ of the newly formed British Secret Intelligence Service, sent to infiltrate the German propagandists and produce articles of such ridiculousness that the American public would begin to take the German cause less seriously and start to support the idea of intervening on the side of the British.

When the United States did enter the war in 1917, Crowley wrote words in his diary to the effect that his work was done there.[9] Even more curiously, Crowley's role may have been far more direct than merely making the Germans appear ridiculous. He arrived in New York with Waddell aboard the RMS *Lusitania,* now infamous as the boat that was sunk by a German U-Boat, with a loss of almost 1,200 lives, including 128 Americans. This incident is commonly regarded as the turning point of American public opinion toward favoring the war. Crowley had actively encouraged the sinking of the ship he came in on, convincing his German circle that it would somehow get the Americans to stay out of the war once and for all (while being fully aware that it would have the opposite effect). Perhaps he specifically chose the ship he came in on so he would know to avoid it should he have to return to Britain during the war, or perhaps simply its high status as a famous passenger liner was his motive.

By 1917, Crowley was facing the fact that he had spent literally all of his inheritance: he was broke. He and Waddell had been arguing, and he left her in New York to travel around the United States looking for ways to earn some money. He returned even worse off than before, but that summer his luck turned. He was made an editor of pro-German magazine *The Fatherland,* providing him with a regular salary, and some of his poetry publications even began to make money for the first time. He took a break from sex magic to concentrate on more traditional disciplines of yoga and meditation, although he fueled both with a copious drug intake. He befriended the writer William Seabrook and gathered a variety of lovers in the search for his next

Scarlet Woman—finally finding her in the form of a schoolteacher named Leah Hirsig.

After the war Crowley returned to England, broke once again. He was also struggling to maintain his heroin habit since the drug had been outlawed—in a curious international effort that occurred in the middle of the Great War and involved the legal complicity of apparent enemy nations. Once freely and readily available, heroin had gone from the drug of choice to send to soldiers at the front, to take for toothache or, as in Crowley's case, bronchitis, to an outlawed substance carrying hefty penalties for possession. He was also under constant and often menacing assault by the press, who found great mileage in producing more and more fearful stories about the Great Beast 666, and Crowley was threatened by a confused and scared general public. In January 1920, Hirsig gave birth to his child, Anne Leah (nicknamed Poupée), in Fontainebleu, and Crowley and his Scarlet Woman decided to head to Italy and establish an Abbey of Thelema on the island of Sicily.

With Hirsig he headed to a tiny port town in northern Sicily called Cefalù, and there they found an ancient villa that was ideal for their purposes. Although it lacked basic amenities, it was isolated, had a stream running nearby, and offered plenty of natural beauty. Furthermore, Crowley might have felt that he was following a predestined path for a Romantic English poet, albeit a hundred years after Keats, Byron, and Shelley made their ways to Italy. He designated the large central room as the temple, installing a copy of the Stele of Revealing he had made in Cairo, a throne for himself and his Scarlet Woman in the east and west, respectively, and he drew a circle in the middle containing the altar. He also nicknamed the Abbey of Thelema the Whore's Cell, and Crowley consecrated it by performing sex magic with his lover Ninette Shumway. Shumway had two sons who came along, and soon others began to arrive to study and live in the Abbey. Hirsig, arriving after Shumway, was Crowley's real object of love, and this immediately caused a jealous rift between the two women, worsened by the endless supply of drugs and alcohol the Beast made sure was available at the Abbey. His reasoning was to provide enough so that desire for heroin and booze could not distract either his students or himself from the pursuit of their True Will, but the results tended to debauchery. It wouldn't be long before the Abbey descended into filth and tragedy. Italy at this time, before Mussolini set about modernizing the country, was still a largely rustic society and had all the diseases that went with that. So, it was not long before all of the Thelemites were struck down with dysentery. Hirsig in particular gave up on hygiene, causing visitors to be disgusted at her dirtiness. Crowley wanted Hirsig to put him through sexual experiences that caused revulsion in him as a continued attempt to fully break himself from his ingrained Christian morality, and so they engaged in a sado-masochistic relationship in which Crowley was the passive party, while Hirsig was free to be as creatively depraved as she desired, including forcing Crowley to eat her feces off the altar.

Their daughter Anne Leah, sickly from birth, died in October 1920, sending Hirsig, again pregnant, into a state of intense grief that resulted in a miscarriage. Shumway was also pregnant by Crowley, with no complications. This caused Hirsig to suspect Shumway of having cursed her, intensifying their enmity. The actress Jane Wolfe, among others, came to stay, and Crowley set her to work painting the *Chamber of Nightmares,* a room filled with intoxicating and terrifying murals. More visitors came, and Crowley gave them intermittent instruction in meditation, rituals, and astral projection, but much of the time he spent indulging in heroin with Hirsig.

Crowley was in a state of extreme grief over the loss of his child, and some of the major magical operations he attempted at the Abbey were failures, largely, he believed, because of his emotional distress. After reading in Shumway's diary that she had indeed cursed Hirsig's children, Crowley intervened, sending Shumway back to Cefalù. Sex became free and rampant, and the participants cared little about whether or not the children were present, something that worried several of the Abbey's students. Crowley did successfully perform a ritual to turn Hirsig into the Thelemic goddess Babalon, which raised her spirits, but he was still sunk in depression. Rereading classic texts of antiquity, Crowley felt inspired to try to emulate some of the ancient rituals. He encouraged Hirsig—who had taken a vow in which she swore, "I dedicate myself wholly to The Great Work. I will work for wickedness, I will kill my heart, I will be shameless before all men, I will freely prostitute my body to all creatures"—to offer herself to a goat as a ritual. She stripped naked and bent down on all fours for the goat as Crowley tried to encourage it to mount her, but the goat remained apathetic. Eventually Crowley took the goat's place: "I atoned for the young he-goat at considerable length."[10] This nonevent would become one of the most notorious scandals surrounding Crowley in the media, but they got their real chance to lash out at the "Wickedest Man in the World," as he was now known to the British press, when one of his young followers, Raoul Loveday, died from enteritis after drinking water from the mountain spring. The further tragedy, combined with Crowley's ever deepening battle to get off heroin, and the general state of intestinal sickness of the largely British contingent trying to cope with the unsanitary Mediterranean waters, pushed Crowley toward a breaking point.

The *Daily Express,* long one of the most shameless fabricators of yellow journalism and scandal, wrote hysterically about Crowley's supposed devil worship, animal sacrifice, and depravity. The campaign lasted months and was sustained on a daily basis, accusing Crowley of having caused Loveday's death by forcing him to drink cat's blood. Furthermore, they accused Crowley of having gained a taste for cannibalism after eating a couple of his porters during the disaster on K2. Crowley threatened legal action, but the *Express* issued the standard tabloid response of a sneering "catch us if you can"; they knew full well that in the unlikely event he pursued them in the courts and won, the losses sustained would be far outweighed by the gains that had come from booming sales of the newspaper that gave daily updates on the filth and fury happening in Sicily. He was again in financial difficulty, and it was perhaps some kind of relief when Mussolini, having come to power in 1923 courting the support of the conservative Catholics of Italy, decided to shut down the wild Abbey and expel its occupants.

Over the next ten years Crowley moved from Tunis to Paris and then Berlin, partly to escape the growing tabloid frenzy that now followed him. In Paris he met and befriended the occultist Israel Regardie, taking him under his wing and making him his secretary. In 1925, two years after the death of Reuss, he was elected head of the O.T.O., a position of great magical esteem, and a platform that allowed him to spread the word of Thelema far and wide. The O.T.O. under Crowley became a major Thelemic organization. He flirted with supporting National Socialism in the era of the Ahnenerbe and an apparent Nazi interest in the occult, but when, in 1933, Hitler turned against the occult and began to persecute its practitioners—having decided on a path of Christian conservatism—Crowley declared Hitler an enemy. He had a variety of Scarlet Women, although one was to commit suicide and another was certified as insane after Crowley left them.

As with Randolph and Craddock, popular attention to Crowley's ideas soon led to legal accusations of obscenity. His notoriety in the press peaked in 1934 as what became known as the "Black Magic Libel Trial" got under way. Reporters and onlookers crammed outside the courtroom to try to get a word or two from the Great Beast 666, who had decided to sue a woman named Nina Hamnett for a scandalous book she had published on the Abbey of Thelema. Crowley lost the case, but it was nevertheless one of the most unusual of the century, with Crowley being goaded to perform black magic in the courtroom, as well as told by the judge to try to turn himself invisible. Crowley's wit and intelligence were strong assets, but the case was lost when a copy of his early book of obscene poetry, *White Stains,* was produced, turning the jury against him.[11]

In 1937 a young woman named Pat MacAlpine gave birth to Crowley's first son, whom he named Ataturk Crowley. It inspired him to return to publishing books, which he had more or less given up on through the 1930s, returning him to the public eye for reasons other than the endless lurid and sensational tabloid stories about his life. He also returned to heroin to cure his asthma once more. Having kicked the habit in 1929, the sixty-four-year-old found himself again at its mercy as the Second World War broke out. He spent the early part of the war in London, approaching the Blitz with amusement at the relentless destruction of the capital, remarking after a German bomb missed him by twenty yards that if it'd been much closer to him then London would have immediately become a "more wholesome place."[12]

He was beginning to ail, however, and a life of alcohol and drug abuse was taking its toll. His doctor gave him a straightforward choice: leave London or die of heart failure. He departed for Torquay, but his role in the war, like in the Great War, had not been as a passive observer. He was closely linked to MI5 at this time, and it seems likely (although it cannot be proved as MI5's World War II activity remains classified information to this day) that he was operating once again as an unusual agent for British intelligence. Admiral John Godfrey was interested in deploying astrology as a means of trying to read the likely behavior of Hitler, and he employed the Jewish-Hungarian astrologer Louis de Wohl, who was an acquaintance of both Crowley and spy-turned-author Ian Fleming of 007 fame. Crowley, encouraged by Fleming it seems, offered his services as an interrogator of Rudolf Hess following his famous and dramatic landing in Scotland, an interesting proposal given Hess's serious interest in astrology and the occult.[13] One thing he did seem to contribute was the "V for victory" sign, made famous by Winston Churchill—it was a gesture whereby the index and middle fingers are raised to form a V shape. This hand gesture has a long history in England, supposedly dating back to the Battle of Agincourt during the Hundred Years' War, when English archers used it to mock aristocratic French knights who had threatened to cut off their fingers before the devastating English victory. Since then it has been the primary means of insulting someone with a hand gesture in England, and Crowley thought that this potent symbol, recognizable to every Englishman and -woman, transformed into a gesture of victory would serve as a powerful magical counter to Hitler's hooked cross, or swastika. According to Crowley,[14] he proposed it to MI5, and Churchill agreed and adopted it, creating his most iconic image; raising the defiant dorsal V sign, with its double meaning of victory and piss off, cigar in mouth; Churchill's later claims that he did not understand the offensive nature of the sign, due to his aristocratic heritage, rank among his most ludicrous pronouncements.

During the war Crowley also tried to build a second Abbey of Thelema, but the attempt proved fruitless. More interesting things were occurring in California, however, where the O.T.O. began its Agape (Greek for "Love") Lodge in the 1930s. In 1942 the lodge was booming and counted among its members the rocket scientist Jack Parsons, discussed later in this book, and future O.T.O. head Grady McMurty. Despite drawing notable and powerful members, Crowley was concerned about rumors that Agape Lodge's head, Wilfred Smith, was encouraging an atmosphere of debauchery instead of spiritual enlightenment. That year, Crowley removed Smith from his role, replacing him with Parsons, and decided to keep a closer eye on this American outpost of Thelema. The plan was for the lodge members to pitch together and bring their commander in chief out to California so he could enjoy a sunny and magical retirement. This was scuppered, however, by the FBI who decided that Crowley was Hitler's personal black magician and documented him as a "notorious moral pervert,"[15] therefore killing any visa application before it began. This depressed Crowley, not least because he was concerned about losing control of the rapidly expanding Agape Lodge, which did not settle down under Parsons's leadership. Over the next few years, he became futher distressed by reports of Parsons's rogue magical acts and the lodge's failure to maintain regular gnostic masses and other O.T.O. traditions that were supposed to be joined with all the sex magic and drugs.

Unable to go to the O.T.O., the O.T.O. came to him in the form of McMurty, who, as an American soldier, decided to use some of his leave to meet the master. Crowley took a shine to McMurty and, over the course of several visits, initiated him into the IXth order of the O.T.O. and made him his heir to the throne. Other visitors came and went as the war drew to a close, and reporters gathered outside his home: they were waiting for the ailing Beast to die. They would not have to wait too long to get their lurid headlines.

On December 1, 1947, Aleister Crowley died of heart failure and complications of bronchitis. He had been depressed, somewhat lonely, addicted to heroin, and impoverished for much of the 1940s. He had not seen the great spiritual revolution in his name take place, although he had always given the year 2005 as its probable commencement. He was ridiculed in the press, and his extensive and brilliant works had been thoroughly overshadowed by his reputation as a sexual pervert, drug addict, and black magician. However, it would take only twenty years from his death for the reappraisal to begin, and his influence, not least "do what thou wilt shall be the whole of the law," became the great catalyst for the most profound period of rapid social change humanity had seen for centuries. Now there can be no doubt that, as long as someone, somewhere is talking about sex and magic, then Crowley's name will live on.

SELECTED WORKS BY ALEISTER CROWLEY CONCERNING SEX MAGIC

Aleister Crowley's writing on sex magic is often heavily veiled in Thelemic symbolism. All of the essays below are collected on websites dedicated to resources on Thelema or Western Esoterism.

1904 ✦ *Liber CCXX: Liber AL vel Legis—The Book of the Law*

1912 ✦ *Liber LXVI: Liber Stellae Rubeae. A secret ritual of Apep, the Heart of IAO-OAI, delivered unto V.V.V.V.V. for his use in a certain matter of Liber Legis, and written down under the figure LXV*

1913 ✦ *Liber CCCXXXIII: The Book of Lies*

1914 ✦ *Liber CDXV: Opus Lutetianum or The Paris Working*

1914 ✦ *Liber XXIV: De Nuptiis Secretis Deorum cum Hominibus. On the Secret Marriages of Gods with Men*

1943 ✦ *Magick without Tears*

4

Maria de Naglowska
(1883–1936)

Maria de Naglowska's remaining dim light of renown in the twenty-first century is largely due to her credit as the translator of Randolph's *Magia Sexualis,* her love affair with Julius Evola (who is described later in this book), and a vague conception of her as a Satanist. Her influence and radical insights into the world of sexual mysticism are, however, far more valuable than this summation suggests. To begin with, her translation of *Magia Sexualis* is not only a compendium of Randolph's most important writings on sex magic, but it also includes a large amount of text that has no direct source link to Randolph but that Naglowska claimed were transmitted to her orally by Randolph from beyond the grave.

Naglowska was born in Saint Petersburg in 1883 to a noble family with strong Tsarist leanings. Her father was General Dimitri de Naglowski, the provincial governor of Kazan, and her mother, Catherine Kamaroff, of aristocratic descent (permitting the nobiliary particle "de" in the family name). Her father's prominence in the state system of the Russian empire was such that he began to attract the attention of the radical underground that had begun to proliferate in Kazan as it went through rapid industrialization. The area had known centuries of conflict between Russian and Tatar, Christian and Muslim, but it was a new element of insurgency that would devastate the lives of the Naglowskis. In 1895 a member of the radical intellectual Nihilist movement—famous for their assassination of Tsar Alexander II in 1881—infiltrated the de Naglowski estate, posing as a servant. The general, famous for his heroics driving the Turks from the Balkans in the Russo-Turkish War of 1877–1878, was precisely the kind of worthy sacrifice the Nihilists sought as a means of enacting revolutionary political change. General de Naglowski was poisoned by the posing servant and died, and Maria's mother died shortly afterward of an illness; though the nature of her sickness is lost to the historical record, it does not require a great leap of imagination to conclude that she suffered the same fate as her husband.

Now orphaned, Naglowska was entrusted to an aunt who sent her to the Smolna Institute of Saint Petersburg, a school reserved exclusively for members of the aristocracy. She had already received a classical education from her mother, and with the kind of resolve that would become characteristic in her adult life, she adapted quickly to the school and excelled as a student. She took an interest in the politics of her country, unsurprising given how much special interest the political radicals of Russia were giving to her own class and indeed her family. At twenty-two years old she witnessed the unfolding of the 1905 Russian Revolution, as various agrarian, nationalist, student, and trade union groups shook the empire, which was already reeling from the humiliating and devastating defeat in the Russo-Japanese war of 1904–1905. The height of the revolt saw the mutiny aboard the battleship *Potemkin,* later immortalized in Sergei Eisenstein's 1925 cinematic masterpiece, *Battleship Potemkin*. Naglowska, undoubtedly aware of the great danger she was in, kept to close-knit aristocratic circles as events unfolded. About this time, she fell in love at a concert with a violin soloist named Moise Hopenko, an event that would be the catalyst for the dramatic course of her life. The couple were forced to elope first to Berlin, then Geneva, where they married. The de Naglowski family had no intention of accepting their daughter's marriage, due to her new husband being Jewish.

In Geneva, Naglowska was partially cut off from her family wealth, so she began teaching Russian at a small language school she founded and continued her studies at the University of Geneva. She was able to earn enough to fund her husband's musical training as he became a virtuoso violinist. She gave birth to three children in Switzerland: Alexandre, Esther, and Andrei. Alexandre was circumcised, even though only Jewish through his father, a fact that displeased the Genevan Russian community who had until then been willing to assist the couple. While in Geneva, Hopenko became an active Zionist, influenced by the ideas of Theodor Herzl, whom he had befriended before Herzl's death in 1905. Hopenko sent his wife back to Russia, where she pleaded with her family to recognize the marriage; but they were unrelenting. As far as the Naglowskis were concerned, she was an unmarried mother with Jewish children, and therefore a pariah. They refused to give their daughter her full share of money and possessions, but she nevertheless returned to Geneva with the funds to send her husband to Palestine, where he had been invited by the Zionists to attend the Academy of Music. Hopenko left a month before the birth of his third child and never returned to his wife. Naglowska changed her daughter's name from Esther to Marie and gave her newborn—who would remain uncircumcised—the name of her motherland's patron saint, Andrei. These gestures led to her being tentatively reinstated to the Russian community in Geneva, but she was forced to teach and work as a journalist full-time to support her young family.

Naglowska's political views were formulated in Geneva, and at a peace conference held at the Athenaeum she distributed her own literature expressing her libertarian convictions—an act that saw her arrested on charges of espionage and political radicalism. Her two youngest children were taken into care by Geneva's Social Services (Alexandre had already left Switzerland to join his father in Palestine), and Naglowska was banished from the city. She moved to Bern, and the children were pensioned to a German school, but her political activity saw her suffer the same fate as in Geneva. She tried to settle in Basel, but by now she was known to the authorities nationwide, and she had no choice but to leave Switzerland for good. She possessed a Polish passport, which allowed her to settle in Rome, and she took a room in the apartment of a wealthy friend.[1]

Despite this good fortune, Rome was not an easy place for a foreign single mother to get by in 1920. The years 1919 and 1920 are known as the *Biennio Rosso* (The Two Red Years) in Italy, as the country became paralyzed by left-wing industrial action. Benito Mussolini and his Fascist Blackshirts capitalized on the situation by allying with businesses and employing strikebreaking methods, which sometimes turned to violence, in an attempt to restore order to the war-fatigued state. Humiliation, as well as bloodshed, was a factor in Italy's post-war mentality, as the Allies largely ignored Italy's claims for reparations and *irredenta* (unredeemed property, such as the return of Italian lands that were not under Italian political control). In response to this crisis, the Romantic soldier-poet Gabriele D'Annunzio took a band of legionnaires to Fiume in Dalmatia, declaring the extraordinary Regency of Carnaro in 1919, with himself installed as the original *Duce,* or leader. The regency was a unique legal and political structure combining anarchist, democratic republican, corporatist, and syndicalist ideals. Infamously, he designated music as the fundamental principle of the state. The regency was recognized by the Soviet Union alone and incited strong and conflicting views in Italy: the Italians of Fiume welcomed D'Annunzio as a liberator, but he was denounced by Tomasso Marinetti, the famous Futurist, as a deserter. Mussolini watched with fascination, but the Italian government was less amused, and a naval bombardment in December 1920 forced the surrender of D'Annunzio and the decline of the short-lived state in what is modern Rijeka, Croatia. Another figure who watched this great adventure with interest was Evola, the radical traditionalist, Roman pagan occultist, mystic, sex magician, Dadaist, medium, ferocious opponent of democracy, and self-described "superfascist." About 1920, Naglowska took a job at the newspaper *Italia,* and through this it seems she met Evola, and they became close friends and lovers.

Through Evola, Naglowska was introduced to Rome's vigorous occult world, including the infamous UR Group, which Evola helped to found. The group's purpose, while somewhat mysterious, was to use Tantric and Buddhist practices mixed with Western Hermetic rituals and study to create a group of magical supermen who could change the world through their combined occult force. It included associates of the famous Italian shaman and alchemist, Giuliano Kremmerz, and other prominent occultists of the time. Naglowska's natural abilities as a mystic impressed the group, and she was a member for several years.

The relationship between Evola and Naglowska seems curiously ill-matched on the surface. How was it that Naglowska, the single mother with a fierce streak of libertarian independence, who actively proclaimed in her writing the need for a return to the Age of Isis and the values of matriarchy, and Evola, who by the same measure openly called for a new Age of Osiris, the sun god and delegate of all things masculine, could fall in love? It seems possible that Naglowska may simply have had the intellectual vigor—not to mention aristocratic pedigree—to shut Evola up and evoke his admiration, and vice versa.

Her occult education was not entirely under Evola's direction, however. She met Russian occultists in Rome, including remnants of the famous Sect of Khylsti, one of the few (perhaps only) sex-based religious groups to survive the blanket destruction of mystical sexuality imposed by Islam and Christianity over the past 1,500 years. As late as 1856 the sect was recorded as openly active, and the rituals would end with group sex, described by Baron von Haxthaused, who witnessed one ceremony: "The jumping grows wilder and wilder till the lights were extinguished and horrible orgies commenced."[2] Finally, it turned out that Communism posed an even greater threat to both mystics and the sexually adventurous in Russia than followers of Christ, and the Khylsti decamped to Rome. Rasputin was once a member: Naglowska claims to have encountered the great mystic in her youth, and she translated his biography into French.

Naglowska, however, attributed her rapid spiritual development to neither Rasputin nor Evola but to an unknown Catholic monk whom she befriended in Rome. The monk, evidently a heretic, taught Naglowska his conception of the holy trinity in the form of a triangle. According to Naglowska, one apex represented Judaism, the head, the Old Testament, and an age that was already dead; another the dying age of Christ and the heart; while the third—the Holy Spirit—represented the new age of sex and the feminine. Her conception of the feminine in the divine sense was a balance of both light and dark forces—the dark side being absent from the divine nature of the other two ages. This dark force was Satan, and her defense of the necessity of the metaphysical presence of the Lord of Hell (as he was known to Christians) stoked controversy and soon led to her being branded a Satanist—a label she did not necessarily reject in her writings and lectures on the subject. She explained, "We forbid our disciples to imagine Satan (= the spirit of evil or the spirit of destruction) as living outside of us, for such imagining is proper to idolaters; but we recognize that this name is true."[3] Evola much later wrote in his book *The Metaphysics of Sex* that Naglowska had "a deliberate intention to scandalize the reader," although he may have had an ulterior motive for this criticism—by the 1958 publication of this text Evola was being forced to defend himself and his worldview from accusations of pretence, obfuscating mysticism, and courting controversy and was trying to deflect these accusations onto his former sparring partner instead.

Her two sons now having left Italy for Palestine to live with their father, and her daughter, Marie, employed as a nurse (after a bout of typhus earlier in the decade that almost killed her), Naglowska decided, after a tour of Egypt, to leave Rome for Paris. The French authorities declined to give her a work permit, but she managed to survive by giving conferences at the cafés of Montparnasse, where she had taken a small room at l'Hôtel de la Paix on the Boulevard Raspail. By the end of the 1920s, Montparnasse's cafés were internationally famous as dense hives of intellectual activity. Several of the cafés and brasseries, such as Le Dome and

La Coupole (which are still going concerns today, albeit with a distinctly different clientele) had an occult corner where speakers had the freedom to lecture on whatever they wished, as long as it was intellectually worthy of the exacting assembly. Well before Naglowska arrived, a couple of other Russians—Vladimir Lenin and Leon Trotsky—had made Le Dome home, among the dozens of other luminaries who gravitated to the favorite café of Guillaume Apollinaire hoping to encounter the great poet of the age. However, the heyday of Montparnasse ended abruptly in 1914. The war left Apollinaire (who would succumb to the Spanish flu in 1918), Moise Kisling, and Georges Braque seriously wounded; Blaise Cendrars lost an arm; and others such as Fernand Leger and Ossip Zadkine suffered severe shell shock. Nevertheless, it remained a place where speech was free, a plate of meat and vegetables could be had for a few *sous,* and works by Leger, Amadeo Modigliani, Pablo Picasso, and Marc Chagall were nailed to the walls. By the 1930s, and Naglowska's arrival, some of the misty-eyed were proclaiming that the Montparnasse scene was dead—but it was quite a corpse that could still attract André Breton, Henry Miller, Jean Cocteau, Simone de Beauvoir, and Man Ray on a regular basis.

She called her series of conferences "A Doctrine of the Third Term of the Trinity," and in it she put forward her successor religion, that of the Mother, which was to overthrow that of the phallic Father religion of Judaism and the Son of Christianity. The Mother religion would reintroduce the flesh as mind renovator, and during a Mass of Gold the flesh would be glorified ritually through sex. Her conferences proved popular, as did her journal *La Fleche* (The Arrow) that ran from October 1930 to December 1933 in eighteen issues. She was able to begin renting a space on the Rue Bréa, which held audiences of around fifty people. The room looked onto a small winter garden that was known, appropriately enough, as the Square of the Occultists. Her following became devoted to Naglowska, the spiritual mother, and they began calling her La Grande Sophiale, in honor of her wisdom and femininity. Among those attending were the surrealists Breton and

Man Ray; the American occultist, adventurer, and occasional cannibal William Seabrook; French intellectual and philosopher of eroticism Georges Bataille; and Jean Paulhan, the muse for Pauline Réage's erotic masterpiece *L'Histoire d'O* (which was later adapted to film by Kenneth Anger).

La Sophiale gathered her followers into her small room on Halloween 1930 for the first Mass of Gold. The high priestess of the Brotherhood of the Golden Arrow removed her gold gown and laid on the altar, wearing only her diadem. The scene was lit with electric lamps that made her crown sparkle, and the surroundings were ornate and draped in gold tissue. The male initiates (the women were chosen by Naglowska herself—apparently, she preferred blondes) placed a chalice containing wine on her genitals ready for the mixing of the fluids of the male sex (godly, positive) and female sex (Satanic, negative). Naglowska reposed in a deep trance, her role was to be an object of desire and the conduit for the entry of God into the mass through the sexual arousal of the participants. The men then recited an oath: "I will strive by any means to illuminate myself, with the aid of a woman who knows how to love me with virgin love . . . I will research with companions the initiatory erotic act, which, by transforming the heat into light arouses Lucifer from the satanic shades of masculinity."[4] Here, "virgin love" refers to a woman who is able to use her sexuality purely for enlightenment, rather than desire, as opposed to being sexually inexperienced. Through ritual, the wine would be magnetized, then the initiates—usually seven—were to have sex with three priestesses, although there's no record of this occurring on the occasion of the inaugural mass, at least. The lights were raised, and Naglowska exited her trance and declared that the Mother religion of the Third Term of the Trinity was now constituted and the Mass of Gold over. She dressed, washed the feet of her disciples, and brought the Brotherhood of the Golden Arrow back to La Coupole for a night of partying. The consecrations took place twice a month from then on and were open to the public.[5]

At the same time as holding her masses and conferences, and regularly publishing texts, she worked on her magnum opus, the translation of Randolph's *Magia Sexualis,* published in 1931. Naglowska had always been interested in the magical potential of mirrors, and Randolph's mirror scrying was a major influence. The work is really a compilation of Randolph's writings, at least for about two-thirds of the book, while the rest is made up of Naglowska's own writings, apparently sourced from necromantic conversations with Randolph and other unidentified sources. In the work Randolph—and Naglowska—explain that sex is the fundamental universal force and "the most characteristic evidence of God." Details are given of the inner workings of Randolph's sex magic organizations, the Brotherhood of Eulis and the Hermetic Brotherhood of Light, guiding the reader through an introduction to basic sex magic that can allow the practitioner to build their physical strength, refine their senses, and experience visions. It goes on to show how to charge an effigy of a person you wish to affect magically in some way, create talismans filled with the force of a specific planet, and how to mix "fluid condenser"—a technique in which a person's blood or semen (usually, although sometimes tinctures of gold are used) are mixed with other materials to add extra power to magical workings.

Naglowska was beginning to attract both support and criticism beyond the boundaries of Montparnasse (she was banned from La Rotonde once word of her Mass of Gold reached the proprietor), and she was attacked by the intellectual and traditionalist René Guénon in his journal *The Veil of Isis* in 1932. Naglowska responded with a particularly caustic polemic, invoking Nietzsche and mocking Guénon's dour approach to mysticism, and indeed anyone who "does not sing or dance in this era where all is collapsing."[6]

She then published in runs of fifty copies each two works that were required reading for all initiates into the Brotherhood of the Golden Arrow—*La Lumière de Sexe* (The Light of Sex), published in 1932, and *Le Mystère de la Pendaison* (The Mystery of the Hanging) in 1934. The former details the process required for an initiate to graduate from the first degree of the brotherhood (which she called "Jackals of the

Courtyard") to the second (called "Venerable Warriors"). The former was a ritual re-creation of the story of Salome and John the Baptist, in which Salome, daughter of King Herod II, demands the head of John the Baptist and receives it on a silver platter. *The Mystery of the Hanging* took adepts from the second to the third degree (which she called "Magnificent Invisible Knights.") This ritual proved more shocking to some. It was another re-creation; this time a celebration of the Passion of Judas Iscariot as he hanged himself from a tree. It was a process of autoerotic asphyxiation, ritual hanging, and sensory deprivation as methods of heightening sensuality and mystical power. In Naglowska's words, "Only the one who has gone beyond this rite [initiatory hanging] can usefully unite with a properly educated woman because, knowing the indescribable happiness of Satanic pleasure, he cannot drown in the flesh of a woman, and if he performs with his wife the rite of the earth, he will do it to enrich himself and not to diminish himself."[7]

In 1935 she was traumatized by two powerful visions: one foretold that the coming war would be immense and catastrophic, and the other showed Naglowska her own imminent death. She packed up and left Montparnasse immediately and went to Zurich to live with her daughter. There she died aged fifty-two on April 17, 1936.[8]

Her fame as a religious and sexual revolutionary has barely managed to seep beyond the boundaries of Montparnasse, although an English translation of *The Light of Sex* was published in 2012, giving her work to a new audience. She is mentioned in passing by others—Evola for one, and she appears in Zeena and Nikolas Schreck's book, *Demons of the Flesh*. Her sexual and magical legacy is understated, but slowly gathering. She was first and foremost a Satanist, in a sense of the word, saying, "My Brothers, the Venerable Warriors of the Golden Arrow, will say: 'The Free Man in you was Satan, and He wanted eternal joy, but you, Freed Brother, you decided otherwise, because you were not only Satan but also He who lives, being Life.'"[9]

Selected Works by Maria de Naglowska Concerning Sex Magic

Maria de Naglowska's collected essays from her newspaper, *La Flèche,* are available in English within *Initiatic Eroticism,* edited by Donald Traxler.

1930 ✦ "The Mother, the Virgin, the Lover"

1931 ✦ "The Polarization of the Sexes and the Hell of Modern Morals"

1932 ✦ *Le Rite Sacré de l'amour Magique,* published in English as *The Sacred Rite of Magical Love*

1932 ✦ *La Lumière du Sexe,* published in English as *The Light of Sex: Initiation, Magic, and Sacrament*

1933 ✦ "The Key of Saint Peter"

1935 ✦ "Initiatic Eroticism"

5

Austin Osman Spare
(1886–1956)

The recovery of the legacy of Austin Osman Spare has been dramatic; pulled from near obscurity to his rightful place alongside Crowley as one of the most influential and revolutionary occultists of the twentieth century. Spare's flame was kept alive by Thelemite, magician, writer, and apprentice to Crowley, Kenneth Grant, and was finally able to ignite when his works became the foundation of the chaos magic movement in the 1970s.

A one-time friend of Crowley, and a founding member of his A∴A∴ organization, Spare left his mentor to create his own path in magic. In many ways he was the antithesis of Crowley: Crowley lived his life on a stage, liberated as a young man by the death of his father and a substantial middle-class inheritance; he was exuberant, provocative, and dramatic; and has become a byword for wild libertinage and wickedness. Spare, on the other hand, lived much of his life in poverty and tended to reclusiveness and humbleness, an introvert to Crowley's arch-extrovert.

Spare was born within the sound of Bow Bells, Cheapside, in East London, an incidence that bestowed the charismatic sub-ethnicity of Cockney upon the newborn. His father, Philip Spare, was a Yorkshireman who had come to London in 1878 at the age of twenty-one to join the City of London police. Philip met a local girl, Eliza

Osman, the daughter of a Royal Marine, and they were married in 1879. Austin, born in 1886, was the couple's fifth child (the eldest had died in infancy), and the family lived in a tenement reserved for policemen and civil servants on what is now Smithfield Street. They were simple flats, with shared toilets and bathroom facilities, but otherwise modern and comfortable by the standards of the day, with running water and gas. The Smithfield of Spare's childhood was still the place that had horrified and fascinated readers of Charles Dickens—the dirt, danger, and poverty of the East End were still apparent at the end of the nineteenth century. Furthermore, the area was dominated by two monolithic structures that defined its boundaries: the Smithfield meat market and the infamous Newgate prison, which was not demolished until 1902.

Spare recalled his early childhood with affection for his parents—his father was stern, but nevertheless invoked respect and warmth in his children. Spare's love for his father remained, while his feelings for his mother would turn to hatred in adulthood. He also recalled terror at his urban surroundings. An animal lover, the meat market haunted him throughout his life, and Newgate, suffused with seven hundred years of imprisonment, torture, and execution, was a potent symbol of suffering and horror for all East Londoners. Furthermore, in 1888, the Jack the Ripper killings began, and while Spare's father was not directly involved in the case, there can be little doubt—as it became the talk of the world—that a police housing tenement at the very epicenter of the slayings must have felt the Ripper's presence more powerfully than most.

When Spare was seven years old, the family left Smithfield and moved to a brand-new housing estate in Kennington, South London, a kind of entry-level estate for those arriving at the British lower-middle-class. Spare's father had astutely invested his wages in small rental properties, and the family was able to ascend to the modest reality of the English Dream: suburban respectability on a leafy avenue. The new money of Kennington attracted a menagerie of hawkers, beggars, and peddlers. Spare remembered men with top hats covered in fly-paper and, soon enough, scores of flies, as they attempted to prove the quality of their pest control product to local butchers. One-man bands, acrobats, goldfish salesmen, organ grinders, ashen-faced beggars, and drunks enlivened the new streets.[1] Among these was a figure known to Spare as Witch Paterson, who he came to refer to as his second mother.[2] It was through her that he would be introduced to two important elements in his development: witchcraft and sexuality.

Witch Paterson claimed (this all according to Spare; there are no other verifiable accounts of her existence) that she was descended from the Salem Witches of Massachusetts who had managed to escape Cotton Mather's violent purges. She seduced Spare, and he was fascinated at her capacity to transform herself from an unattractive older woman into a being of immense sexual interest to the young Spare— suddenly she appeared nubile and beautiful to him. She spoke in a kind of gypsy patois, and she began to instruct Spare in sorcery and divination. He was thrilled and terrified at her ability to materialize thoughts into forms that were visible to anyone present. Her usual technique was to perform a skillful and profound reading of a person's character before revealing details about their future. If the event proved too complex for the witch to describe, she would reveal a visual interpretation of it somewhere in the smoke and darkness of her chamber. The technique, when deployed, apparently never failed.

Spare learned the techniques of conjuring from Witch Paterson, and although he was never able to achieve her extraordinary ability to conjure on command, Spare did later manage to bring his thoughtforms to a visible state on occasion. He described once spending many hours trying to call forth an elemental spirit after being encouraged to do so by a pair of acquaintances with a passing interest in the then fashionable occult. Initially reluctant to perform the conjuration, believing such entities to be atavistic parts of the subconscious brought into the conscious world (and thus potentially dangerous to the mental well-being of both the magician and any spectators), he eventually agreed. After a long wait, his evocation began to cause some change in the room where the three stood. A green mist became visible, and it slowly began to take a thicker, more physical form, accompanied by a choking stench. Two eyes of fire began to form in the mist, and then a hideous face. The terrified pair panicked, and Spare banished the vision, but his acquaintances were deeply affected, with one having to spend time in an insane asylum after witnessing the conjuration.[3]

At the same time as his introduction to sorcery, Spare's artistic ability also began to blossom. He attended night classes at Lambeth Art School, and at age thirteen his formal education ended so he began an apprenticeship in a stained-glass factory. While there, he attracted the attention of a couple of noble visitors to the factory who were perusing the drawings he made during his lunch hour. Impressed, they recommended Spare for a place at the Royal College of Art, an event that would launch his art career into the highest echelons at an astonishing speed. While the college itself turned out to be underwhelming, he was winning prizes of increasing renown, and his drawings were hung at the international exhibitions of both Paris and St. Louis in 1902. He worked furiously at drawing, day and night; the requisite energy seemingly gathered from his first experience of heartbreak with a rector's daughter. He drew daily late into the night and then read—Homer, the *Rubaiyat* of Omar Khayyam, and Blavatsky's *Isis Unveiled,* which gave him an in-depth tour of Theosophy and the dead gods of the Egyptian cult.

In 1904 the seventeen-year-old Spare would find himself thrust fully into the public glare. His first solo exhibition at the Newington Public Library was followed by his portrait and works being glowingly reviewed in the *Daily Mail, The Tatler,* and the popular schoolboy magazine *Chums,* among others.[4] He was recognized in the street and even pursued by journalists; an invasion of his private world that depressed him. At the Newington exhibition a work titled *Portrait of Hisself Aged 17* was displayed. This early drawing captures some of the most important elements of Spare as both artist and man. The crude and ironic misspelling in the title alludes to the narrative picked up by the press, which portrayed Spare as—not unjustly—all the more extraordinary due to his street upbringing when compared with the public schoolboys who dominated the Royal College of Art. Furthermore, he presents himself as an unhealthy-looking, sinister figure with his body pressed against that of a naked woman, who, on closer inspection, seems to have the profile of a crone—or a witch. A partially toothless skull resembling that of ancestral man floats by his leg, and under his bare foot a tube of paint is being squeezed. In spite of his wiry and devilish appearance, he is confidently balanced on a plinth, around the skirt of which are various words—most tellingly the word "Kia," which along with "Zos" would come to form the foundational concepts of Spare's magical philosophy.

Zos and Kia were entities that, to Spare, represented, respectively, the mortal, conscious, physical world and the (more complex) concept of the universal god-mind, a kind of void-state that eternally lurks behind the veil of conscious and existence, detached from any personal interaction, somewhat similar to the Chinese Tao. It would not be long before the combination of Spare's youthful brilliance and allusions to occult ideas would attract the attention of the Great Beast 666 himself—Crowley. Eleven years Spare's senior, Crowley had already made his name as a notorious occultist, and in 1907 he founded the syncretic spiritual organization A∴A∴. Spare was present from the outset and remained in the organization for five years. During that time, he expanded his concepts of Zos and Kia, and they became analogous to Crowley's Thelemite entities Hadit and the Egyptian goddess of the stars, Nuit.[5]

In 1909, Spare began work on what would become the central text in his writings: *The Book of Pleasure (Self Love): The Psychology of Ecstasy*. Within, Spare overtly references the power of combining sexual pleasure and magic. He also describes his own magical alphabet and what would become known as sigil magic, a theory that would prove highly influential on late-twentieth- and early-twenty-first-century magic. Spare believed that through visualizing a sigil or emblem, which the magician had created himself, the subconscious could be accessed and made to respond with an array of images that arise in the mind.

This idea follows from the psychological and magical theory that the subconscious mind is deaf to words, whether written or spoken, but is receptive to certain images when they are held either before the eyes or in the mind (or both) for a certain amount of time, with the operator having also successfully turned off the conscious mind. Spare formulated a technique for regularly opening this bypass to the subconscious mind that he called "union through absent mindedness."[6] The objective was to use sigils to trick the conscious mind into silence and submission so that the operator performing the magical evocation could make the transaction with the subconscious. The conscious mind, if aware of the desire of a thing, would cause the magic to fail. A sigil is created by writing down a word or phrase that represents the particular desire. Then it is simplified, duplicate letters and sometimes vowels are removed, and the magician re-forms the remaining letters into an ornamental shape. Multiple sigils are made for various desires, and each is then drawn on a card and meditated upon, then the cards are shuffled and put away for a period of time. On returning to the sigils, the operator will have forgotten what exactly each one was supposed to represent, meaning that the conscious mind cannot interfere by reading them. The magician can then concentrate on the image of each sigil, invoking it in its pure form of subconscious meaning. Spare claimed that this process could be charged further by using sex and that visualizations at the moment of orgasm were great enhancers of these powers.

Throughout his life, Spare believed he was a conduit for some universal occult force in his writing and art, but it was a force he could never identify. He did manage to identify specific magical entities at certain times, such as his process of automatic writing (a psychic technique allowing a person to produce words on a page without consciously writing them, used by Fernando Pessoa, Arthur Conan Doyle, and Robert Desnos, among others). Through this, he was able to commune with the Pythia—the ancient Greek priestess of Delphi once responsible for the ethylene-induced visions in the Temple of Apollo that so marked the history of Western civilization. The Pythia, or Pythoness, instructed Spare to build what he called the "Earthenware Virgin." This was, in fact, a phallus-shaped urn with a hole in the base whose dimensions allowed the insertion of the penis and the creation of a vacuum within. Inside the urn was the sigil of a desire that would be consecrated upon ejaculation. The vacuum expanded the penis and created a more powerful than usual orgasm—during which the magician was to potently visualize the desire and hold it in his mind for as long as possible. Spare was certain this was the method used by Greek sex magicians. He instructed that, once the ceremony was over, the magician should seal the urn and "bury the urn at midnight, the moon being quartered. When the moon wanes, disinter the urn and—while repeating a suitable incantation—pour its contents as a libation on to the earth. Then re-bury it." The process allowed Spare to, on occasion, see dense and palpable visions he called "elemental autonoma," and depictions of these familiars appear frequently in his drawing.[7]

Spare's magical pottery masturbation was interrupted by several major life events that occurred during the early 1910s: his break from Crowley, his marriage, and the commencement of the Great War. The Crowley-Spare relationship reached its conclusion in 1912 when Spare, after five years, left the A∴A∴. The relationship had become strained, ostensibly because of severe differences of opinion regarding magic. Crowley was disappointed with Spare and had been unable to initiate him fully into the order due to poor organization. He also accused Spare of being a black magician—contrary to the common conception of Crowley, he was perhaps one of the foremost campaigners *against* black magic. While Crowley dismissed notions of black and white magic, he believed that negative magic was any form of magic that was not primarily concerned with the Great Work, or Spare found Crowley's strict hierarchical system and drudging workload to be tiresome, and he thought Crowley's ceremonial magic was ridiculous. Furthermore, Crowley seems to have made sexual advances toward Spare that were rebuffed. Spare boasted of his sexual conquests during this stage of his life—including witches, dwarves, and a hermaphrodite lover—but it seems that Crowley was repugnant to him. He passed Crowley once in Piccadilly Circus, the Great Beast in heavy makeup and dressed like a male prostitute. "My God, if I had to go to all that effort to attract 'em," Spare said, "I'd give up the ghost."[8] Spare would torment Crowley at times, mocking his taste for foreign foods, once presenting him with cakes made from horse dung and dog feces, telling him they were an ancient T'ang dynasty Chinese delicacy. Halfway through the snack, Spare revealed the truth, but Crowley, never lacking a sense of humor, shrugged and continued eating, replying laconically, "I thought as much."[9]

The year before he parted from Crowley, Spare had married a woman three years his senior named Eily Shaw. The woman was already a mother, and the father of the child, a Mr. Bernstein of Golder's Green, had departed without a trace. Shaw's mother feared for her daughter's precarious position and, seated in a public house one day (itself quite a precarious position for an unaccompanied woman in 1911), she overheard Spare talking about his successful career and wealthy patrons. She suggested an introduction to her daughter, and Spare fell in love with the beautiful Shaw. She functioned as a valuable muse to Spare, but they otherwise seemed to have little in common. She feigned pregnancy to hurry him into marriage and disapproved of his unusual circle of friends, encouraging him to seek a more normal line of work. For all his boasting of his various youthful sexual conquests, it seems that Spare was quite unworldly in the field of romance. It wasn't long until both found themselves attracted to other lovers—Spare to the family's plain but voluptuous maid.

Spare had done a good job avoiding the war. There was nothing particularly unusual in this attitude, especially among Londoners, after the abattoir of the Somme had obliterated any enthusiasm for war with Germany among those most likely to go and have to fight in it. Being married kept him off the conscription list for a time, and possibly feigned flat feet helped rule him out once married men were called up. But the net for conscription was cast ever wider as the war became a hopeless attempt by both sides to bleed the other to death with unrelenting slaughter. Spare was called up to the Royal Army Medical Corps in May 1917. In later years he enjoyed recounting some of his war adventures—shielded in no-man's-land for a night by a pile of dead soldiers, coolly surviving a shipwreck after being torpedoed, stopping in Egypt to see the hieroglyphs firsthand—only none of them ever really happened. He was stationed in Blackpool, given the task of administering tetanus shots to departing soldiers, finding himself constantly at odds with his superiors over issues of impossible bureaucracy on their part, and scruffiness and a general loathing of discipline on his.

He returned from the war—or from Blackpool at least—at the end of 1918, hoping to pick up where he had left off with consistent successful exhibitions, frequent work as an illustrator, and his wife in a pleasant house in Kennington. While he was away, Shaw had left him for another man, and he was forced to give up their home. He moved to wretched accommodations on Gilbert Place, and even snuck a bed into his studio to sleep, which was against the rules. The couple never divorced, a complicated and expensive process in those days, but they never reconciled either. Even though he was aware they were mismatched, her departure and infidelity broke Spare's heart, and he spent at least a couple of years in a state of nervous anxiety and depression. Thirty-four years old, his wife having left him, and nowhere to live— but all of this seemed to fuel a burst of creative force about approximately 1920 that would remain unmatched for the rest of his life. The most important fruit of this period was *The Focus of Life,* a work in which Spare expands upon his views on sex magic outlined in *The Book of Pleasure.* Contrary to other sex magicians who focus on partnered sex magic, Spare instructs the reader that this mystical-sexual world was best accessed alone and that dispensing with any romantic collusion with another was paramount to success in "becoming one with all sensation." *The Focus of Life* also contains some of Spare's most spectacular drawings, some clearly in reaction to his heartache at the failure of his marriage—the text no less so.

Through the remainder of the 1920s, Spare scraped together an existence in a small flat in a Southwark slum, relying on the occasional investments of his benefactors. Most of the exotic objects he had collected over time were sold, and he retreated into his Kia existence, a dream world behind the veil of a reality that increasingly displeased him. He wrote *The Anathema of Zos: The Sermon to the Hypocrites* in 1924, a rant tinged with bitterness at society and fueled by his reading of Friedrich Nietzsche. *The Book of Ugly Ecstasy* came the following year and was one of the most grotesque collections of drawings in the Spare canon. Using automatic drawing techniques, Spare was recording hideous visions and nightmares of putrefying, demonic, sexualized figures from the underworld. In this period of marked solitude, not all that Spare saw was horrifying—he was, he said, constantly surrounded by his "familiars," the elemental spirits he conjured and maintained through the practice of witchcraft, and cats.[10] This retreat coincided with a succession of failures in the art world: two books, including *Zos,* failed to sell many copies and an exhibition in 1927 at the St. George's Gallery generated little interest—he had simply gone out of fashion and had become, in fact, a target for jibes in the press among those ready to move on to new pastures in art. As the charm of the occult fell temporarily away once more, Spare's esoteric content began to make him look like a crank. Modernism was sweeping aside his cobbled world of Aubrey Beardsley, Symbolism, occultism, and drawing with an unstoppable surge that brought formalist art into a period of radical experimentation, as well as a cohesive—largely socialist—political philosophy. Spare was himself a long-time supporter of left-wing ideals, an unusual case among twentieth century occultists who tended either to embrace individualism or conservatism. This all led Spare to a point whereby at the end of the decade he was weighing up various suicide methods.

What followed was not his self-destruction but rather eight years of his life in which, according to Spare, "Nothing at all happened."[11] This is not strictly true. He became a devotee of radio and developed theories of the relationship between radio waves and the occult concept of aether. In 1932 he moved out of his Southwark slum flat into new digs on York Road, Lambeth, about halfway between Westminster Bridge and Waterloo Station. The flat was above a shelter for down-and-outs, and Spare discovered this to be a valuable resource for models. He created a manifesto of sorts for his models-wanted ads, discriminating against anyone who considered themselves to have "any kind of beauty"[12] and those under forty years old. The failures of his shows in the late 1920s pushed Spare back to more realist forms of art, and he began working on paintings he termed "experiments in relativity," referencing the recent explosion of interest in the theories of Albert Einstein, following Einstein's trip to the United States in the early 1930s. The paintings were distortions of space, usually the anamorphic lengthening of women's faces—often the faces of American movie stars such as Joan Crawford in a precursory form of British Pop Art.

By 1936, Spare had moved to a larger studio in Elephant and Castle. Finally, he had the space and light required to work and display in comfort, although the violence and criminality of the borough itself shocked even the streetwise Spare (particularly a wave of cat killings) and positively terrified his visiting benefactors and art-world socialites. In this same year Salvador Dali made his first grand entrance into Britain, with a major exhibition followed by the opening of the International Surrealist Exhibition at the New Burlington Gallery. Dali gave a lecture in a deep-sea diver's suit that almost suffocated him, and the show drew thousands of visitors with a renewed appetite for dreamy, unconscious art—perhaps in response to the acuteness of the reality of 1936 and the looming war. The English tradition of painting had played its part in the formation of surrealism, with all the major surrealists fluent in the works of William Blake and the Pre-Raphaelites. This was good news for Spare, who found himself the subject of resurgent interest. He was championed in the press as an important forerunner of surrealism and was granted an exhibition under the surrealist banner late in that same year.

The year 1936 also threw up perhaps the strangest and most curious event of Spare's life when he was contacted by Adolf Hitler, who wished to commission a portrait from him. Hitler offered to fly Spare to Berlin to paint the portrait. Evidently a Spare fan working at the German embassy had sent some of his work to the Fuhrer, who was impressed. Spare declined the offer, writing, "I know of no courage sufficient to stomach your aspirations and ultimates. If you are superman let me be forever animal."[13] The idea of an official Spare portrait of Hitler is almost too tantalizing, and yet he did paint Hitler many times during the 1930s, albeit not from life and often melded into self-portraits. At this time, he also experimented with photography, attempting to photograph himself naked as Christ upon the cross as a statement, like his Hitler self-portrait, of the artist blending his reality with that of an iconic figure, something that was comfortably fifty years ahead of conceptual art ideas placing the artist as subject in photographic distortions of themselves à la Andy Warhol. Spare's attempt to immortalize himself in the form of Christ was a failure: the magnesium exploded in his face as he set up the flash, singeing his hair.

In the lead up to the war Spare seemed to be discovering purpose once more. The headline in a 1936 newspaper report proclaimed, "The Father of Surrealism—He's a Cockney!"[14] Spare began to dig into his own Cockney world, and the unique richness of the culture of East London, along with its exceptional ability to produce people of both character and a certain grotesqueness, was ideal fuel for Spare's painting. He painted down-and-outs, spivs, washerwomen, charladies, cabbies, and Woolworth's girls. There were few communities that would be so devastated as London's Cockneys by the Second World War. The bells of Mary-le-Bow fell silent in 1940 and were not rung again until the 1960s, by which time the great social upheaval of post-war London had set the Cockney dialect and culture on an inevitable path to oblivion; the pearly kings and queens, Ripper folklore, terrifying fires, gin palaces, rookeries, and, no less, witchcraft were set to become commercialized and as mythical as the medieval utopic land of Cockaigne from whence comes the demonym.

The war hit Spare personally, in an act that must have felt like a slap of revenge from Hitler. Spare enrolled as a fire watcher (having unsuccessfully tried to join up as a regular soldier to fight the Third Reich; at fifty-four and with a plethora of physical and mental ailments, he was considered better suited to the Home Guard) and was posted on top of the Collier's department store the night of May 10, 1941. Earlier in the day he'd spilled his lunchtime beer and divined the shape of a vulture in the puddle it left, and then when lighting a cigarette, he accidentally ignited the entire matchbox, burning his hand. Both of these he considered to be bad omens, and so it proved to be on the most devastating night of the Blitz. Caught among the immense destruction London suffered this one night was Spare's own studio. All his work—decades' worth—was destroyed. He was now homeless, and like many people that night he suffered several moderate injuries (although many suffered far more terrible fates), one that damaged his right arm and hand. He began living in a doss-house, dressed in an old sailor's outfit that was handed out to him. He was suffering from malnutrition, alcoholism, and extreme poverty. His mother had died and left the family inheritance to his estranged sister. He attempted to kill Hitler with black magic but could barely sustain himself physically, let alone begin the great outpouring of energy that magical work generally requires. He found comfort, as often, in the presence of animals, surrounding himself with some of the many thousands of now stray cats of the city. Reporters came and went to publish pity stories on the impoverished once great artist who carried the haunted look of a man who was rapidly being defeated by life. Yet, before the close of the war, Spare had rallied and once again found the means to draw and paint.

He, like everyone else in Britain, surfaced in a new world in 1945. It was one of rapid construction and reconstruction, a world more energetic but more complex and less comforting than the one it was replacing. Businesses now preferred a facelessness that allowed them to drive for profits in a way that the immense swath of family-run shops and firms that once covered Britain could never have managed. The world became more mobile and more impersonal, and the quality of goods declined as the thirst for quantity, and value for money, rose following the rationed war years. Spare, although pleased at the advent of the National Health Service, was not enthusiastic about the post-war world. He continued to live "like a tramp,"[15] eating his small meals of tinned fish out of a newspaper, wearing his coat indoors, and generally existing in poor circumstances in his basement flat. This lifestyle gave Spare, it seems, the will to increase his output to prodigious levels, and the themes of occultism and spiritualism returned once more to his work, including his Satyrisation (distorting portraits to resemble the god Pan) of Hollywood film stars. His 1947 comeback show ran at the Archer Gallery on Westbourne Grove, and once again Spare was attracting interest in the public and press.

Part of this renewed interest led to one meeting that proved critical in keeping the dim light of Spare's unique brilliance lit in the decades after his death. A life model for the painter Herbert Budd, a young woman named Steffi Grant, listened to Budd recount a story about Spare, with whom he had attended the Royal College of Art many years before. "A god-like creature of whom the other students stood in awe," Budd said. "A fair creature like a Greek God, curly headed, proud, self-willed, practicing the black arts, taking drugs, disdainfully apart from the crowd." Grant was intrigued, and she visited the "Greek god" in his shabby basement but was unable to contain her shock at the sight of the decrepit figure before her, living like a tramp. "That was a long time ago,"[16] Spare reassured her.

Grant bought a couple of pictures for her husband, none other than the writer, magician, Thelemic advocate, and apprentice to Crowley, Kenneth, who was already aware of Spare. The Grants were an attractive and resplendent occult couple, with Kenneth in particular seeking to forge his own path in the world of magic. He blended what he had learned from Crowley with his love of Sax Rohmer, Arthur Machen, and, in particular, H. P. Lovecraft, developing theories that Lovecraft was a kind of passive mouthpiece chosen by mysterious forces to recount truths of another world beyond our normal perception. His wife took him to meet Spare, and they instantly found a kindred spirit. The Grants, both well educated, were fascinated by Spare the raconteur and the extraordinary and often utterly fantastical life stories and conspiracy theories being put to them by the ailing artist and magician in his East London dialect. Spare, attentively, laid out the best china (the few cups that weren't cracked and tea-stained) for his guests.

The Grants managed to encourage Spare to leave his hovel and meet them in the West End, where he entertained them with the details of his array of sexual conquests. Still now, his models were occasionally "well up for it,"[17] and the old Pan was happy to oblige his "dirty" charladies. He claimed hundreds of sexual adventures, including the hermaphrodite, the dwarf, a slightly sad tale of a blind girl who loved him, his adventures with cheap and even free pre-war prostitutes, his marriage, the prosecution for adultery he was served by the wealthy husband of one mistress (Spare won the case), and his sexual awakening with Witch Paterson. Kenneth asked Spare to send him a self-portrait of when he was a young man—Spare sent him a drawing of an erect penis, with "Self-portrait, aged 18" written on it. Furthermore, he explained some of his chaotic sex magic practices, including long periods of meditation while aroused, imagining "some girl tonguing it, like," his "Earthenware Virgin," and a mysterious ritual that granted him a "grandiose" penis and took three days to get it to go back down. Even the "whores of Elephant [and Castle]" with their "very large vents" couldn't take it, he said. He remarked it was a proof of "not only psycho-somatic interaction as abstract, but as concrete."[18] It is possible that Spare was in love with Steffi—or even both of the Grants—and was enjoying his passive role in their romantic and sexual life. Furthermore, in a statement that seems to vividly encapsulate a certain Britishness, he recommended Ovaltine to the Grants as an aphrodisiac, finding that the bland, wholesome, malt-flavored beverage induced spectacular erotic dreams.

Kenneth helped Spare to formulate his ideas on sex magic, the occult, and his art. Grant had a fluidity with words that Spare sometimes lacked, and the texts Spare produced at this time show the influence of his young protégé. Grant also encouraged Spare to embrace his darker side. In the *Zoetic Grimoire of Zos* there is a tonal shift to something approaching cosmic horror. Grant also set about creating the lasting mythology of Spare, using his love of Machen, Blackwood, and Lovecraft to frame some of Spare's stories in a more horrifying, mystical way than Spare would have been able to with his plainspoken manner. Grant recounted Spare's involvement with the highly mysterious Chinese Cult of Ku. Based in Stockwell, Spare was introduced to them in the 1930s by the writer Thomas Burke, who was famous for his depictions of opium-soaked Chinese poverty, mystery, and murder in Limehouse in the early twentieth century. In Chinese magic, Ku is the I Ching's eighteenth hexagram, represented by a bowl of worms. In the cult, this bowl of worms, or sometimes venomous insects, would be left until one creature remained alive and victorious. This creature would be the Ku, and its reward would be to be sacrificed and turned into a poison or used in revenge black magic at the behest of the sorcerer. The Ku also had a sexual aspect, allowing the sorcerer to produce a shadow that, with astral projection, could solidify and then travel to a woman's bedroom and have sex with her while she slept. Rituals often involved a young and beautiful woman who would become possessed by an evil deity in a trance induced by the banging of a gong and opium and who would then have sex with the shadows in the room. Spare, it seems, was the only white man ever invited to witness these ceremonies.

Grant, now signing off his letters "Your son, Kenneth,"[19] was pressing Spare for as much information about his life as possible. Grant recorded Spare's stories and philosophy, as well as ideas that would become central to the development of chaos magic: the secrets of his sigil magic, and the Alphabet of Desire, Spare's technique of creating a set of intensely powerful personal symbols. He knew time was running out. Much had been lost in the destruction of the studio during the Blitz, and more in the increasing confusion of Spare's mind. Spare drank consistently, favoring beer, and his health was often fragile. He was rejected by the Civil List for an artist's pension, his benefactors were dying off, and he continued, as he had always resolutely done, to refuse any form of commercial art to supplement his income. He began a series of successful pub exhibitions, the informal atmosphere seemed to prove a success and brought him some financial relief—although a large portion of his earnings from the shows tended to find their way back into the pubs' cash registers.

In the early 1950s the Grants introduced Spare to another famous witch—the founder of Wicca, Gerald Gardner. The black witch and the white witch eyed one another cautiously, although they remained cordial. Spare complained to Grant later that he didn't believe that Gardner had ever attended a "real witches' sabbath" and seemed to think Wicca a watered-down, family-friendly magical order, borrowing heavily from Crowley.[20] At the same time, the Grants had begun their own magical orders, including the Nu-Isis Lodge (for lycanthropic and necromantic sorcery), of which Spare was an Honorary Member. In 1954 a conflict arose between Gardner and the Grants when Gardner accused them of having stolen a young medium of exceptional ability named Clanda. She had defected to Nu-Isis from the Gardner coven after finding the Wiccan workings somewhat tamer than she had hoped. Gardner was incensed, and he duped Spare into creating a stele and sigil that— unbeknown to Spare—Gardner intended to use against Spare's dear friend Grant. The deference shown here by Gardner to the black magician is interesting to note—the Wiccan master unable to perform his own magic as deftly and strongly as Spare. Spare, in exchange for a sacrificial check of ten shillings made out to the Royal Society for the Prevention of Cruelty to Animals, drew the stele and sigil as representations of a large winged beast that was part owl, part bat. He included instructions on how to charge and use the sigil to return the negativity he had received back to the perpetrator.

The Nu-Isis Lodge conducted a ritual centered on Clanda at the Islington home of an alchemist known as David Curwen. Curwen, a notable Islington eccentric, was reputed to have performed necrophilic rituals and once almost died after drinking liquid gold. Clanda lay naked on a huge altar in the basement of the musty, run-down old house, surrounded by two large candles. Purple-robed members of the lodge passed to and fro. Clanda lay, preparing herself to be possessed by the deity Black Isis. But this didn't happen. The room went icy cold, and Clanda had an intense astral hallucination of a giant bird crashing through the roof and dragging her away in its claws. She panicked and picked up the ritual dagger and began waving it wildly around. Grant noted that after this disaster, the walls of the basement were lightly coated with a salty and slightly slimy substance.

Spare's final days, which included the above episode, were far from the dignified stage exit of a beloved and treasured artist. Until the bitter end he remained prolific, almost obsessive. He drank only milk and took little care of his physical well-being other than drawing occasional glyphs "for health."[21] His last two shows were flops and—the Grants aside—there seemed to be a lust to knock Spare down in his final, shaky months of life. He was invited to speak on his beloved radio at last, something that thrilled him, but he was devastated to hear the result. His words had been manipulated and distorted to make him sound like a lunatic who claimed he could kill a man with magic in two weeks. The ridicule depressed him, and he spent time with his close friends only, especially his "adopted son," Grant. Austin Osman Spare died in the hospital on May 15, 1956, of peritonitis following a burst appendix.

Spare had not managed to sustain any long-term popular appeal, merely arising at moments of artistic revolt when critics looked to ground themselves in a deep narrative and motive for such change lest they, too, be left behind. The overt occult themes in his art inevitably caused the majority to shy away, and Spare in his fecundity of production was more than able to veer into kitsch and inferior work at times. His superior and meaningful art, however, is unique, skillful, and saturated with the magical philosophy he himself created. As an artist he still remains underappreciated, certainly in Britain—had Spare been French, it could have been a different story, perhaps he would have become the

Gustave Moreau of the twentieth century. In the world of the occult, however, his transformation has been more dramatic. Ten years after his death, counterculture swept the Western world, democratizing and popularizing art forms. Another ten years later the ethos of punk rock with its celebration of individualism and do-it-yourself attitude shifted the art world even further away from its classical traditions of schooling and structure. Magic followed suit. Chaos magic was given form and shape at the height of punk in England when Peter J. Carroll and Ray Sherwin formed the Illuminates of Thanateros (a neologism combining "thanatos" and "eros") and published their seminal work, *Liber Null,* in 1978, a seminal text of chaos magic. Spare is placed as the founding father and central figure of chaos magic, which dispenses with the high idealism of other forms of ritual magic and instead offers a pragmatic, syncretic, and individualistic means of understanding the power of magic. Its use of humor, sex, drugs, sigils, creative expression, both dark and light forms, and—now—the Internet as a vast magical tool have given it immense appeal in the twenty-first century. It is not inconceivable, thanks to the efforts of Grant and the formulation of his ideas by Carroll and Sherwin, that Spare's magical legacy may rise to even surpass that of his former friend, ally, enemy, and tutor, Crowley.

SELECTED WORKS BY AUSTIN OSMAN SPARE CONCERNING SEX MAGIC

Austin Osman Spare's books are available from a variety of publishers.

1913 ✦ *The Book of Pleasure (Self-Love:) The Psychology of Ecstasy*

1921 ✦ *The Focus of Life*

6

Julius Evola

(1898–1974)

The remarkable works of the radical traditionalist Julius Evola are still discussed in political circles today, even including references to his ideas in the early stages of the presidency of Donald Trump by Steve Bannon, the media executive and political strategist who was, at that time, one of Trump's advisers.[1] Evola was an influence of sorts on Italian Fascism. Though Evola was not a member of the Fascist party himself, Benito Mussolini's relationship with him was far from friendly: it was said that up until the end of Mussolini's life he would shudder at the mention of Evola's name, fearful of the magical power of the man, and make a sign of defense against the evil eye with his hands.[2]

Evola was born Baron Giulio Cesare Andrea Evola in Rome in 1898. His family were of minor aristocratic Sicilian descent and—not unusually for Italians at that time—devoted to the Catholic faith. Evola had little to say about his early years, believing that nostalgia for childhood and the normal course of emotional engagements that teenagers experience to be unworthy of discussion. He expressed a strong sense of alienation from his family, his peers, and from the modern, Christian Italy of the fin de siècle. He wrote, "I owe very little to the milieu in which I was born, to the education which I received, and to my own blood. I found myself largely opposed to both the dominant tradition of the West—Christianity and Catholicism—and to contemporary civilisation—the 'modern world' of democracy and materialism."[3]

He had an interest in adventure novels and pursuing technical and mathematical subjects as a teenager, until a sharp and spontaneous change of course led him to read the poetry of Oscar Wilde and Gabriele D'Annunzio. A ferocious appetite for art and poetry developed in Evola, and he launched an ambitious plan to write a condensed history of philosophy. This project never materialized, but the time spent in the library gave him access to knowledge about the contemporary art and literature scene. This taste for the avant-garde would flower later— after the war—into an active artistic participation. His philosophical studies in the Roman libraries introduced him to the works of two major figures in Evola's life: Friedrich Nietzsche and Otto Weininger. Weininger was a Viennese philosopher who produced a single book, *Sex and Character,* at the age of twenty-three before shooting himself dead months after its publication in the room where Ludwig van Beethoven died. In his book, Weininger proposes that all humans are a composite of masculine and feminine traits and that the masculine is best served through a chaste and active life that ought to attempt to discover a universal genius within himself, while the feminine is passive and more absorbed in the functions of reproduction. Having visited Bayreuth to see a performance of Richard Wagner's *Parsifal,* he fell into a deep depression and renounced his Jewish faith as an effeminate religion that promoted ideals of democracy, materialism, and capitalism, converting to Christianity before his death. Evola saw few better values in Christianity than he saw in Judaism, but he was deeply admiring of the passage of a kindred spirit trying to unravel himself from the binds of heavy religious and social responsibility, not unlike his own Catholic upbringing. Furthermore, the concept of a universe that is best served by a spiritual balance of masculine and feminine, developed from the ideas he found in *Sex and Character,* became a central theme in Evola's writings.

At twenty years old, Evola was a second lieutenant in the Italian artillery and witnessing the end of the Great War. He had volunteered as an enthusiastic supporter of the war, but he would write an article at this time explaining that the war should be undertaken according to "proper principles" and not "in the name of nationalist and irredentist ideologies, or the democratic, sentimental and hypocritical ideologies of Allied propaganda."[4] Evola never saw the Central Powers as barbarians threatening civilization, nor would he ever indulge in bourgeois patriotism, but saw the war as a pure revolutionary act that would see Italy shatter its stifling societal climate. However, once the treaties were signed (treaties that did not particularly represent good business for Italy when held up in the light of the nation's considerable blood sacrifice), Evola saw the war as little more than a transaction among the combatant nations. He had not experienced the "storm and steel" that marked Ernst Junger's war. Furthermore, the rapid return to normal life disgusted Evola further, such was its investment in frippery and insignificance. He returned to Weininger, took interest in the ideas of Filippo Tommaso Marinetti and the Futurist movement in art, but otherwise found himself in despair and facing the temptation of suicide.

He was saved from suicidal thoughts by a discourse on Buddha published in 1921 by Karl Eugene Neumann, one of the pioneers of European Buddhism. A relatively simple sentiment in the book hit Evola like a sudden light: again, only he who desires suicide may know of what he desires, precisely because he desires it. Evola felt regenerated following this initiatory experience, a dramatic overthrowing of his ignorance and an embrace of real freedom. This freedom sparked a period of great creative production, most especially in painting and poetry. He became associated with Tristan Tzara and the Dada movement, and his paintings were displayed in galleries throughout Italy, as well as in Geneva, Berlin, and, most thrillingly, Paris. This rage for abstraction in Evola was, however, brief: by the end of 1922 he had ceased both painting and writing. The motive for this arrest of Dadaist activity was his realization that Dada was not going to destroy itself, which it ought to have done according to Evola's understanding of its founding principles, but instead would "finish in the conventional and the academic,"[5] studied and categorized, declawed and neutered, like every other art movement, decreed safe for bourgeois consumption. Furthermore, he saw the general art mood heading toward a fashion for Surrealism that he considered regressive and uninteresting.

At this point, in 1923, Evola redirected himself toward a philosophical path, albeit a highly unconventional one with little regard for the academic world. His early pamphlet *Essays on Magical Idealism* gives a sense of Evola's thoughts, searching for a means to mix what he saw in Western philosophy and Eastern wisdom. "Philosophy," Evola wrote, "is reflection leading to recognition of one's own insufficiency and the need for an absolute action from within." It is beyond the remit of this text, not to mention beyond its physical capacity, to attempt any detailed inquiry into Evolian philosophy. It will be sufficient to note that his transcendental idealism was influenced by classical idealists such as Kant, Hegel, and Schelling, along with a strong Nietzschean current, most evidently expressed in Evola's conception of the universal state of the will to domination, obviously taken from Nietzsche's own will to power. It is his "mixture," as he put it, with more esoteric ideas that gives it its own form; the Mithraic mysteries, Buddhism, Tantra, and Eastern esotericism were expressed in his early philosophy as much as more familiar idealism. One article titled "The Path of Enlightenment According to the Mithraic Mysteries" put it thus: "Our desire for the infinite . . . our only value: a life solar and royal, a life of light, of freedom, of power."[6] Such was the basis for his conception of the Absolute Individual, a cross of Eastern wisdom and Western action—a figure who, as Evola often stated, was magical.

By 1927, Evola was under the instruction of Arturo Reghini, author of two journals on the subject of initiatic disciplines, with a tone of seriousness and scientific rigor that appealed to Evola. Tantra and the Kabbalah were discussed, as well as documents relating to the trial of the infamous eighteenth-century Italian magician, forger, and adventurer, the Count di Cagliostro. Encouraged by Reghini, Evola formed the UR Group in Rome, an esoteric association whose primary interest was in a kind of practical, active magic, in opposition to what Evola, Reghini, and the other members of the group saw as vague and passive forms of popular spiritism descended from the humanitarian ideals of Theosophy. It was a magical movement in keeping with the times in Italy, which was now of course under the assertive leadership of Benito Mussolini and his Fascist party, as well as in thrall to the vigorous art of Marinetti and the Futurists, who venerated machines, warfare, action, and masculinity. A further influence on the UR Group's fundamental magical philosophy was Roger Bacon, also known as Dr. Mirabilis, the thirteenth-century English wizard, friar, and philosopher who had proposed the equally lean and virile concept of practical metaphysics. *UR* was chosen for its root meaning of "fire," as well as being the German prefix for "primordial" or "original," as we see in Goethe's *Ur-Faust*. Tradition, and the sense of primordial, heroical-magical, and pagan order would be at the heart of the groups' activities.

Soon enough UR had expanded to a research branch in Genoa, as well as launched a bi-monthly journal titled *Krur*. In 1928 the group's activities remained closely guarded and were under scrutiny from the clergy; Giovanni Battista Montini, the future Pope John Paul VI, wrote scathingly of Evola and his "superstitious works of magic."[7]

Montini's spiritual fears were perhaps understandable, given the direct and aggressive approach to magic that the UR Group was pursuing. They first sought to define the term *magic* itself, dismissing its usual connotation of something—indeed, anything—that produces phenomenal results. Evola redefined magic as "the special formula of initiatory wisdom which obeys an active attitude, sovereign and dominatrix of all that is spiritual."[8]

What Evola specifically wanted to do with this active magical attitude was to create a psychic body that would "'graft itself, by evocation, as a true influence from above . . . to exercise, behind the scenes, an action on the predominant forces in the general milieu of the epoch."[9] This, more explicitly, was an effort by the group to formulate an egregore—a thoughtform projected into a state where it would be visible to the magicians, at least on the spiritual plane if not literally with their own eyes. The power of this group evocation would form a strong psychic body that could then be instructed and manipulated to perform works upon Western society, to shatter and break the parts Evola thought were the cause of the general sense of malaise and crisis to which the Western world had succumbed during the late 1920s. The nature of the evocations and the group's magical workings were a blend of Tantra and Roman pagan sun worship, designed at first for the individual to clear his internal fog and to also clear modernity from his mind so that he could begin to live on a higher spiritual plane, and thus be strengthened for the great psychic work.

The rituals developed by the UR Group focused on the allegorical natures of two of the four classical elements—fire and water. Fire has traditionally been considered the most magical of the elements across many traditions, likely because of its unpredictable, spectacular, and destructive nature. It is the only element that man was required to discover, since the other three are vital necessities for our momentary existence—we could live without fire (at least for a while), but our curiosity and moreover our will as a species has compelled us to try to understand and control it. With this in mind, Evola's rituals were designed to dry out the spirit through sun worship, since the material body is wet, and it is from that which the magician must depart if he is to achieve a form of immateriality. The rituals were designed to be performed at midday, under the hot Italian sun.

As did Crowley, Evola brought a rigorous scientific approach to his magic. He devised ritual forms that would begin to transfer the consciousness among different states that the magician has created through meditation and have varying degrees of materiality or immateriality. This, he said, was like in chemistry when two elements are introduced to one another under different conditions to create a third element. Evola's sun rituals were shaking up the conscious and the self in a test tube. What Evola called the "dry way" (as opposed to the "humid way," which he associated with passivity and the duality of Christian mysticism) was a highly conscious form of magic—the unconscious spiritual discovery was no good for the higher man. He must actively and assertively create his other, dried out and purified by the sun, so that this solar self might exert control and authority over the entire nature of the magician, deleting need or the desire to explore the lower self, and following a path to the supremacy of the individual. This process also took influence from space-time theories, mixing them with Hermeticism and Hatha Yoga as a means of creating this spiritual Ubermensch, who then in collaboration would create a psychic Ubermensch who might lead the world beyond modernity.

The UR Group, however, was destined to fail. The young Italian dandies, still under the Dadaist influence with green painted fingernails, monocles, and beautifully tailored suits, began to argue, especially Evola and Reghini (this mainly due to Evola's passionate and rabid anti-Catholicism, a view that was not shared by Reghini). Within two years it had ceased operations.

Throughout this magical period of Evola's life, he had been strongly under the influence of the French Theosophist, Gnostic Christian, and proponent of the traditionalist school of philosophy, René Guénon—whose works Evola came to read via Reghini. This influence was born from an initial hostility, and Evola drew first blood with a critique of Guénon's work *L'homme et son devenir selon le Vêdânta* (Man and His Becoming According to the Vedanta) in 1925. Guénon responded in kind, and vociferous critiques were exchanged between the two for the following four years—the essential dispute was Evola's strident opposition to Guénon's theory that, in terms of initiatory and traditionalist spirituality, contemplation was superior to action. However, by 1930, Evola had begun to reconsider the value of contemplation as he laid the foundation for one of his major works, *Revolt Against the Modern World,* which drew from Guénonist ideas. In the same year Guénon, despairing at a Western world that had embraced action as a political, spiritual, and philosophical absolute, removed himself from the dangerous alchemy of Europe, took

Egyptian citizenship, and converted to Islam, leading an ascetic life of contemplation.

In spite of the softening of his opposition to the contemplative, and his proclamation that attempts to label him as a Fascist were absurd, Evola was undoubtedly pleased with the political situation in Italy by 1930, where Mussolini had been in power for almost a decade. While finding much to disagree with in Italian Fascism, the fundamental desire to find another way—an active way no less—of combating the great enemies of bourgeois materialism and Marxist materialism, were enough for Evola to loosely ally himself with Fascism. Unlike these two other main wings of twentieth-century political ideology, Evola saw in Fascism the possibility of spiritual uplift, a human experience dismissed as ridiculous by Liberalism and persecuted as dangerous by Marxism. Furthermore, the symbolic and mythical references to Classical Rome made by Mussolini in his speeches and writings, as well as the Roman revival touches in Italian state art and architecture, were bound to please him. With characteristic desire to throw himself into the thick of the action, Evola launched his new journal, *La Torre* (The Tower), in which he would find expression for his political and cultural views. The subheading of the journal was "Paper of varied expressions and One Tradition." Evola employed a variety of traditionalist writers as contributors, including several former members of the UR Group, but it was one of his own articles that drew the ire of the leaders of the Fascist party. In it, Evola set out his line that the political world ought to be considered secondary to the intangible and aristocratic world of principle. He went further, stating that "insofar as fascism follows and defends these principles, in this way even we could consider ourselves fascist. And that is all."[10] Fascism, the prevailing political ideology, was being barked back into its subaltern position by Evola the aristocrat and elitist, who, furthermore, did not withhold severe criticism of a variety of party members for their lazy opportunism. The polemics in *La Torre* continued; Evola was provoking the Fascists from every angle he could reach them, and he was not beneath launching personal ad hominem assaults on editors of the state journals. Attempts were made to ban *La Torre* but proved unsuccessful, and Evola, as well as other contributors to the journal, found themselves victim to physical intimidation and threats from Fascist party members, to the point where Evola employed a team of bodyguards. The police advised Evola to cease publication for his own good, but Evola pushed onward, calling himself neither Fascist nor anti-Fascist, but beyond Fascism, directed to a purer, more virile form of Fascism without plebeian compromise. Finally, the interior minister pulled the publication of *La Torre* after ten editions, several legal battles, and five months of existence.

Evola did not waste his time complaining and instead began indulging himself in a new pastime—mountaineering. His approach to the mountain was inevitably unconventional; Evola would never debase himself by indulging in anything so vulgar as sport. The ascent of alpine peaks was a form of Nietzschean *Amor Fati,* one of the base concepts of that philosopher—quite simply the joyous love of fate, whatever it might throw at your life, and "uniting the drunkenness of adventure and of danger to an abandon confident in everything which, in our fate, is not simply human."[11] On reaching the summit, Evola found himself in a kind of ritual space that permitted magical development, which he encouraged with Scotch whiskey and his copy of the *Bhagavad Gita.* Mountains are perhaps the geological formations most associated with magic and mystery gods. Thomas Mann's 1912 masterwork, *The Magic Mountain,* explored this symbolism in the German tradition, most obviously in the chapter devoted to Walpurgisnacht, but as a consistent motif throughout—the German fascination with mountains would resurface in the 1920s with the cinema genre of *Bergefilme* (Mountain Films), sometimes cited as the only native German genre of cinema and one that would be revisited by the German master filmmaker Werner Herzog during cinema's late-twentieth-century maturity.

In Greece, Olympus is the home of the gods—since no man could ever go there, and in ancient nilotic Egypt, devoid of mountains, they were compelled to build their own. It was an Italian, though, who first broke the boundary between the low-lying world of man and the elevated mountain world of the gods. Petrarch, the fourteenth-century Florentine poet, is remembered for his sonnets and for being the first tourist; that is, the first man who traveled for pleasure. In 1336, Petrarch ascended the relatively modest alpine peak of Mount Ventoux (standing at 6,273 feet) some six hundred years before the Romantics; he did so for purely spiritual and aesthetic reasons, a strikingly unusual sensibility at a time when nature was regarded as a Satanic enemy by most Christians. Petrarch is credited—perhaps absurdly—with single-handedly delivering the Italian Renaissance with his poetry and his re-dissemination of the works of Cicero that he himself rediscovered after one thousand years of what he coined as, and we still term, the Dark Ages. Evola no doubt saw himself as a Petrarchan figure, bringing a new light onto a Europe that had once more fallen into darkness, and that light could best be gathered from Europe's mountain peaks, such as the Lyskamm, the traverse of the north face of which, at 14,852 feet, was his most impressive feat of mountaineering and places him second only to Crowley among the great magical mountaineers.

In 1934, Evola published what would become one of his most celebrated and notorious works, *Revolt Against the Modern World*. Having now absorbed the ideas of Guénon into his own philosophy, Evola presented his vision of two forms of civilization: the world of Tradition and the Modern world. While it may seem self-evident that modernity must eventually supersede tradition, Evola saw the modern world as entirely decadent, one that resulted from the fall of the "superworld" of Tradition.[12] The world of Tradition, Evola argued, was now largely invisible, its existence being far beyond living memory, and so the modern world was generally supposed to be the only viable form of civilization. The world of Tradition was one of metaphysics, as opposed to the physics of modernity, one of values rather than anti-values, and one of freedom, not of servitude and necessity. In Evola's world of Tradition there was a broad horizon of spiritual and intellectual possibility, which modernity reduced to a narrow horizon of materialism. According to

Marx, even the history in which these traditions evidently reside should be reevaluated through a lens of materialism.[13] Evola's conception of the Traditional world was concerned with nature and metaphysics, two things that are entirely absent from Marxism, being as it is exclusively concerned with society. Evola established the balancing symbolic forces of the universe as the divine masculine and feminine, representing spirit and nature, respectively. He also postulated that this fall from Tradition was necessary. It was part of nature's cycles of four ages of civilization that began in the excitement and novelty of the Golden Age. The world now had entered the decadent final age, the Iron Age, otherwise known as Kali Yuga, during which civilization—jaded and dissolute—unconsciously awaits some unknown planetary catastrophe that will wipe clean the progressive slate and reduce us back to near zero, before the build begins once more to the resurgence of another Golden Age. Evola, through a form of hierarchical elitism and imperial paganism wanted to push the world toward a resurgence of Tradition, but his ideas were not particularly well received in Italy, where attachment to Catholicism was still strong. In Romania and Germany, Evola found a more receptive audience, and he was drawn toward German National Socialism as well as Romania's Iron Guard.

In spite of this, Evola's political ideals remained marginal within the now boiling ideological cauldron of 1930s Europe. He maintained his position of pagan imperialism and decried all forms of compromise that the Italian government made with the Catholic Church. In 1934, Evola visited Germany for the first time, now under the dictatorship of Adolf Hitler. Some of his works were translated into German and found popularity among members of the Conservative Revolution. The rise of National Socialism in Germany quickly began to subvert Italian Fascism to an official line more in keeping with Nazi idealism. Seeing this, Evola began to publish works that propounded his own racial theories. In *Synthesis of the Doctrine of Race* he proposes a three-form racial ideology, concerning first the body, then the soul, and, at the top of the hierarchy, the spirit, with the last two not necessarily being tied to an individual's actual biological racial background, as defined by the racist theories of the era. Two articles published in this period clarified his racial position ("Race and Culture" and "The Responsibility of Calling Oneself Aryan"), which was to diminish the value of biological racism in favor of a "racism" of the soul or spirit. Evola hoped to engineer change toward the reestablishment of a true aristocratic spiritual elite in Italy, and throughout Europe, and his ideas were initially well received by Mussolini, who invited Evola to dine with him. In 1938, Mussolini published the infamous *Manifesto of Race* that brought Italian Fascism in line with German National Socialist racial ideologies, some fifteen years after Mussolini's rise to power. It was the first step toward the establishment of the Axis that would form one of the principal combatants of the war in Europe that would erupt in 1939, leading to Mussolini's lynching and Italy's fall.

Evola's ideals roused less admiration from the officers of the Schutzstaffel and more outright suspicion. It was recommended to *Reichsführer* Heinrich Himmler that Evola be banned from Germany and placed under constant surveillance. Himmler demurred, and Evola evaded a travel ban from the Reich. Italy's entry into the war in September 1940 was with much Mussolinian fanfare: they joined their German allies in bombing Great Britain during the Blitz and moved to occupy British Somaliland, a poorly defended colony in East Africa that had some strategic importance. However, the war would not run smoothly for the Italians, and it was not long before Churchill had identified Italy as the Axis's "soft underbelly."[14] The harrowing and bloody invasion of Italy by the Allies concluded in July 1943 with the arrest and imprisonment of Mussolini. Evola reaffirmed his view that this was evidence of that which was "inconsistent and inferior . . . behind the façade of fascism."[15] The armistice was signed on September 3rd, but Mussolini was liberated less than two weeks later and quickly removed to Munich.

After first believing himself not under threat, Evola finally accepted an offer to be flown out of Italy in a Waffen-SS uniform to the relative safety of Berlin, then to Rastenburg, where Hitler would receive Mussolini. Evola was given a mission to return to, first, Rome, then to as-yet unoccupied Naples to hide documents pertaining to the role of occult Freemasonry under Italian Fascism. He was torn between the ideal of fighting to the bitter end and a more pragmatic consideration of how to influence the political landscape after a war that was now clearly over—at least for the Italians. By the time he got to Italy, not only Naples but also Rome had been occupied by the Allies, and he narrowly escaped arrest. He fled, reaching Vienna, where he decided he would make better use of these secret documents by reforming them into a new work pertaining to the occult Masonic world called *The Secret Story of Secret Societies*. However, the Red Army was cutting a swathe through the east, and during the Soviet bombardment of Vienna, Evola's work was destroyed and he himself was severely wounded—wounds that would leave him paralyzed from the waist down for the rest of his life.

By 1948, Evola had completed sufficient physical rehabilitation in Vienna that he could be repatriated. He attended further rehabilitation in Bologna until 1951, when finally he was able to return to his apartment in Rome. Brushing aside his disability—"a purely physical bother . . . my spiritual and intellectual activity having been in no way compromised"[16]—he was pleased and surprised to discover that his intellectual stock in Rome had actually risen in his absence, particularly among the younger generation, where he discovered many groups who sought to rebuild what Italy had lost in 1943. He had expected a city in total collapse—physically and also spiritually and intellectually. Evola wrote a manifesto of radical right-wing ideals for these ideologically loose groups of young Romans who were drawn to his antidemocratic, antiliberal, and anticollectivist ideas. Furthermore, at every opportunity, Evola encouraged the growth and development of the spirit, that which he believed essential in man, and to this end he published a work on tantric yoga, *The Yoga of Power*.

Within, Evola explored his own approach to Tantra and its ultimate goal of ego-death so that the practitioner might be able to go through life without subjecting himself to the whims of the ego. Tantra as a system conforms to Evola's eternal promotion of the active rather than passive participant in spirituality. Evola proposes that Tantra is a feminine current of spiritualism, traceable to the original Mother Goddess. This view of Tantra as feminine, and therefore static and active (as opposed to dynamic and passive masculine), has been neglected in more recent Hindu interpretations of Tantra that have been heavily masculinized. He explores using pranyama, mantra, intoxicants, and sex magic as aspects of Tantra. Evola's pronouncements on women are controversial today, and often placed out of context. He believed women to be most spiritually awake when engaged with men in sexual submission, but this was a critique of contemporary masculinity as much as femininity. A true masculine force, to Evola, was virile and ought to express natural male desire. He praised sadomasochism, ritual violation of virgins, and whipping of women, as long as these were done as a means of raising consciousness. A truly virile male, spiritually enlightened and an embodiment of universal masculinity, would not have to coerce a woman into submission, according to Evola, as it would be her natural state to submit to male virility. However, Evola was extremely critical of the boorish male behavior he saw in his contemporaries, writing that "it should not be expected of women that they return to what they truly are . . . when men themselves retain only the semblance of true virility . . . men instead of being in control of sex are controlled by it and wander about like drunkards."[17] This male submission to women, then, was a sorry state of men and greatly unsatisfying for women, whose instinct was to desire the virile and dominant masculine, both sexually and spiritually, as a means of raising her own feminine power, rather than being expected to manage a world of spiritually weak, macho, and sexually frustrated males for whom they could have little but contempt.

In 1951, Evola was arrested, accused of being behind a conspiracy to reestablish the National Fascist Party as its occult leader. He spent six months in prison before being acquitted, noting at his trial that he had never even joined the Fascist party in the first place. At the same time, his book *Revolt Against the Modern World* was reprinted, and his intellectual stock continued to rise in the post-war political milieu. For the next seven years Evola was occupied in publishing articles, particularly on monarchism and antidemocracy, as well as translating works by celebrated anti-modern German writer Oswald Spengler into Italian.

In 1958 he produced one of his most important works, *Eros: The Metaphysics of Sex*. Influenced by both Randolph and Crowley (he refers to both in the text), *Eros* is an exploration of sex magic that reaches further into the metaphysical realm of sex than any other work published on the subject. Evola explains that his conception of metaphysic has two senses: first, Evola defines metaphysical in the sense of what is already familiar to us from the field of philosophy— "the search for principles and ultimate meaning. A metaphysic of sex designates, then, the study of what this means, from an absolute point of view, be it the sexes themselves, be it the relations between the sexes . . . But here the word 'metaphysic' will be equally understood in a second sense, in relation to its etymology, since 'metaphysics' means, in the literal sense, the science of that which goes beyond the physical plane." In the text Evola unites these two senses of metaphysics, in the sense that according to his rationale, the means of acquiring ultimate meaning is to venture beyond the realm of the physical. Sex, in its magical and spiritual form (which Evola described as the only real sex) is a way of recovering a primordial state that is simultaneously compatible with Tradition and is an initiatory method of enlightenment (best described in his final and reverential chapter on Randolph). Furthermore, his book *Eros* offers insight into his earlier works, seen through a loupe of magical-sexual and erotic experience as a form of (ever and always) active and impulsive transcendence.

In 1961, now at the age of sixty-three, Evola published *Ride the Tiger: A Survival Manual for Aristocrats of the Soul,* in which he expanded on his ideas to offer a guide to those who wished to stay afloat in the dissolute sea of modernity, drawing heavily from Nietzsche once more, as well as the second century Roman emperor-philosopher Marcus Aurelius. Two years after this he published *The Path of Cinnabar,* his intellectual autobiography. Cinnabar, also known as dragon's blood, is a bright red ore of mercury, renowned in the ancient world for its beauty and also for its lethal toxicity. It has also been a major component in alchemical experimentation, and practitioners of magic have long believed that cinnabar was a critical ingredient of the elusive Elixir of Life. Evola, aging and crippled, clearly did not envisage his path ending with the mere cessation of the movements of his physical body.

As the 1960s—a spectacularly un-Evolian decade—drew to a close, he published his final texts, *Fascism as Seen from the Right* and *The Bow and the Club.* He continued to edit and arrange for reprints of his earlier works, as well as accept occasional visitors, but his health was deteriorating. At 3:00 p.m. on June 11, 1974, Evola died at his work desk at his Roman home. According to his—unsurprising—wishes, he was cremated on July 11 in the ancient town of Spoleto in Umbria, late in the night, just as a Roman Pagan should be. Six weeks later his friend, the professor, writer, and traditionalist Renato del Ponte, climbed Monte Rosa in the Pennine Alps, carrying the urn containing Evola's ashes, where Evola was to be interred, as Nietzsche said, "six thousand feet above man and time."[18]

SELECTED WORKS BY JULIUS EVOLA CONCERNING SEX MAGIC

Julius Evola's books are available in translation from a variety of publishers, and the essays below are available in English within *Introduction to Magic, Volume II,* translated by Jocelyn Godwin.

1928 ✦ "Subterranean Logic," under the pseudonym Iagla

1929 ✦ "Sexual Magic"

1968 ✦ *Lo Yoga Della Potenza: Saggio sui Tantra*, published in English as *The Yoga of Power*

1969 ✦ *Metafisica del Sesso*, published in English as *Eros and the Mysteries of Love: Metaphysics of Sex*

7
Franz Bardon
(1909–1958)

Our path through the sex magic history of the Western tradition is not restricted to the far Western way; like Maria de Naglowska, many Eastern European traditions have had profound effect on the current state of Western sex magic, and one man from old Bohemia produced three great works on Hermetic magic. His books are comprehensive, taking the reader from the first moment of curiosity about the subject all the way to the level of the adept. Franz Bardon was the first to put a whole system of Hermetic magic in print, and thus liberated many people to study of their own accord—a valuable thing in times of suppression and oppression of "strange ideas." Furthermore, Bardon always emphasised the practical application of magic, and the use of sex as a magical force was paramount. So while his name may be less well known, his influence remains great.

Franz Bardon was born on December 1, 1909, in the town of Troppau/Opava, today a part of the Czech Republic but then in Austro-Hungarian Silesia. The year of 1909 was perhaps the first to begin the cataclysmic destruction of the Old World, culminating in the devastating Great War that began five years later. Notable events that surrounded Bardon's birth were mainly concerned with extraordinary technological lurches, political upheaval, and the inauguration of radical new forms of entertainment. The month of December saw the very first demonstration at Madison Square Garden of the Kinemacolor, the first process of displaying motion pictures in color, while the Brickyard at Indianapolis got its first bricks. Almost every day saw some kind of landmark advance in glider technology as the steps toward powered flight became faster and faster, and airships began to appear in the night skies, causing panic and wonder among rural people on a scale not seen since the mysterious celestial apparitions of the Middle Ages that appear so frequently in pictorial records of that epoch.

Austria, which would play a central role in both forthcoming World Wars, was a particularly fertile and febrile environment. While Bardon was drawing his first breaths, Adolf Hitler was sleeping in freezing flophouses in Vienna, getting by on casual labor and the occasional sale of a watercolor painting, losing himself in the operas of Richard Wagner and cultivating rage at the injustice of his life, which would later be concentrated on the Jews. Notoriously, he referred to the one Jewish boy in his school class who had inspired his racist ideology, and that figure was likely Ludwig Wittgenstein. Wittgenstein was two years Hitler's junior, but they were in the same class due to Hitler being held back a year and the academically brilliant Wittgenstein being moved forward one year. In 1909, Wittgenstein was in Manchester studying aeronautics, but his appetite for philosophy had been sparked—like Evola—by reading Otto Weininger's *Sex and Character*. Thirty years later Hitler and Wittgenstein would find themselves opposed on the deadliest chessboard in human history.

A reminder of the importance of Hitler's role in twentieth century history is unnecessary, but Wittgenstein was also deeply entrenched in the political death struggle of the midcentury; he was partly responsible for the British cracking of the Nazi Enigma code, one of the single major factors of the war shifting away from Nazi ascendancy to British and Allied supremacy, and he was also implicated as the éminence grise, along with 3rd Baron Victor Rothschild in the Cambridge spy ring, whereby Kim Philby and four other Soviet spies and members of the prestigious Cambridge Apostles society at the University of

Cambridge were convicted in 1951 of passing nuclear and state secrets to the KGB during the 1930s and 1940s.

Where Hitler and Wittgenstein find common ground is in their mystical and active utilization of the hermetic tradition—Hitler in his oratory and Wittgenstein in his writings on the philosophy of language. Central to Hitler was his extraordinary ability to take hold of the single mind of the mass as one, through powerful oratory and spectacular ritual. At the same time, Wittgenstein's theories of language were influenced by Arthur Schopenhauer's idea of the "unity of will," which is to say a universally shared will among all living things, that Wittgenstein translated into language theory by dismissing the idea of "mental privacy." All of which, whether Hitler, Schopenhauer, or Wittgenstein, were ideas formed from the foundational writings of Hermes Trismegistus (Hermes the Thrice-Great), the legendary author of the *Hermetic Corpus* and he who gave his name to the Western tradition of Hermeticism—the magical specialty of Franz Bardon. While Bardon and Wittgenstein would not have any direct interaction in life, Bardon would, however, find himself facing the magical wrath of Hitler at the height of his powers.

Bardon was the first child of Viktor Bardon, a textile factory worker, and his wife, Hedwika. The Bardon family would produce eleven more children after Franz, although only four others would make it to adulthood, his sisters Stephanie, Anna, Marie, and Beatrice. Aside from these documented details, not a great deal is known about Franz's early life. His life until the age of fourteen appears to have been that of an ordinary Czech boy in an ordinary working-class family, growing up in a mid-size, predominantly German Roman Catholic town. The only point of particular curiosity was his father's strong interest in Christian mysticism and Hermetics, a longstanding tradition in Western esotericism that purports to follow the teachings of the mythical prophet Hermes Trismegistus, author of the *Hermetic Corpus*. The book is a body of work that explains there is one true theology that is present in all religions, and this theology was passed down to man by God in ancient times. Hermetics is a kind of unified field theory of magic, and this sense of practical application of the spirit and cosmological rationale became especially appealing during the Renaissance (Isaac Newton being a prominent Hermeticist), when Europe's great minds sought to apply astrology, magic, and alchemy to the hard sciences in an attempt to create an understanding of our universe that was both physical and metaphysical.

Devoted in study and practice, Viktor called upon Divine Providence to send him a guru, one who could guide him through his spiritual life. Remarkably, this guru was sent to Viktor in the form of his own son, Franz. At the age of fourteen, Franz went through a dramatic change of character, which was remarked upon by all of his schoolteachers. Young Franz began to display capacities for clairvoyance, with a particular knack for discovering the whereabouts of drowning victims in Opava's eponymous river, a tributary of the River Oder. Furthermore, the young guru began to study herbalism in his spare time outside of school, and then later outside of his job as an apprentice sewing machine mechanic. Before long, Bardon was locally well known as a sage and a mystic, and he began devoting more of his time to receiving residents of the town who turned to him for all manner of problems. To allow himself more freedom on his path toward becoming an adept, he began earning money performing stage magic under the name Frabato, a moniker formed from Franz, Bardon, Troppau (the German name for the town), and Opava (the same, in Czech).

The shows were somewhat typical of the era's popular magical performances. Frabato dressed in the classic magician's attire of formal tuxedo, but the psychological impression of hierarchy and authority given by this outfit was tempered with his generally kindly and smiling disposition. He explained the powers of suggestion, auto-suggestion, and what he understood as the forces of animal magnetism—a vital, animalistic energy given off by all people in different strengths but which nevertheless could always be trained and would give that individual greater self-control and spiritual, psychic power. In one recorded example[1] of his act, he asked for three members of his apprehensive audience to stand up and join him on stage. After some coaxing, an attractive blond woman stood up, prompting Frabato to note that the so-called weaker sex were usually the first to make the brave step up to the mysteries of the illusionist's stage. Immediately, a young man followed, piqued by this suggestion of male timorousness, and finally an old woman completed the necessary trio. The three stood around Frabato's blue-clothed table and were instructed to place a personal possession upon it. The blond woman placed her silver wristwatch, the young man put down his wallet, and the old lady unhooked her necklace and added it to the pile. Frabato announced that he would give a demonstration of psychometry—that people, due to their animal vital energy, always leave traces of energy within objects with which they have come into contact. Frabato, with his clairvoyant gifts, could see these energies, even if thousands of years had passed and many others had come into contact with the objects. He picked up the wristwatch first and held it to his forehead, taking his time to read the energies. After a short time, he pronounced to the young woman: "You seem to seriously doubt my abilities, otherwise you would certainly not have come on stage with a watch that you borrowed from your sister. I am able to see that you wear it quite often without her knowledge, since she works in Berlin. This watch was a confirmation gift from an aunt who died in an accident, and that is why she does not wear it anymore. It would certainly cause some ill-feeling if she knew that you wear the watch." The woman's face turned red in embarrassment, confirming Frabato's account of the life of the watch. The young man now tried to snatch his wallet back, but Frabato was quicker, and he gave him the same treatment—telling him he would not be happy with either of the two women he was currently deceiving with plans of romance and marriage. "I should not like to live near you," the young man said, sheepishly reclaiming his wallet, and adding, "I should not feel safe with my own thoughts." Finally, he came to the old woman's necklace. Frabato revealed that the necklace had once belonged to a French aristocrat who went to the guillotine during the Terror and has since brought all of its owners a degree of misfortune, including the old woman, whose husband was killed during the Great War, leaving her to struggle on a small military pension and forcing her to twice pawn the necklace. This account caused the old woman to weep as she had her life's misfortunes read back to her.

The three were then sent out with two neutral observers, and Frabato asked the audience what kind of emotional reaction each object should elicit from its owner. The watch was given laughter, the wallet tears, and the necklace—since it seemed to have brought misfortune to its owners—should provoke the owner to throw it away violently. Frabato performed the necessary magical transference to each object, then left the room with two audience members to guard him, so as to waylay any suspicions of hypnotism. On returning to the room, the young woman picked up her watch and began laughing hysterically, causing the audience to join in. The young man pocketed his wallet and began to sob, while the old woman, of course, flung her necklace across the stage, already perturbed by the reactions of the other two. A young man got up and returned the necklace to her, much to her relief. The audience, in wonder by now, rushed the stage, and Frabato sat them down one by one to diagnose their medical ailments. Frabato then finished his show, telling the audience they had all received a great boost to their animal vitality and that their conditions would improve accordingly.

On one occasion in his early celebrity, a young woman named Marie came to him to ask his advice on which of two suitors she should choose to marry. She showed photographs of the two men to Bardon (who was himself a keen photographer) and asked him to divine which was the better man for her. Bardon asked what qualities Marie found attractive in a man, and she answered by saying that she would prefer to marry someone who looked and spoke like Bardon—and so he was able to give the answer easily: she should marry neither of these men and marry him instead. His suggestion worked, and they were married.

Bardon refused to have children, which he thought would get in the way of his important work spreading knowledge of Hermeticism. Eventually, they reached a compromise on the matter: Bardon agreed to have a child with Marie, on the condition that she take care of its upbringing. In 1937 their son, Lumir, was born, one month prematurely. Before heading to the maternity ward in Opava, Bardon consulted a local witch who informed him that his child would be a girl, but Bardon replied with certainty that it would be a boy. Lumir was born with a deformed foot, and Bardon personally attended to its care, using forms of daily massage and herbal remedies to correct the deformity. Lumir attested as an adult that no one could guess which foot had been deformed at birth. Later, the couple would also have a daughter named Marie (after her mother), who suffered from respiratory problems that Bardon also successfully treated with a combination of herbal remedies, massage, and magical workings.[2]

Bardon's primary work was the production of a system of Hermetics that emphasized practical application above theory. The tradition of Hermetic magic has long suffered from intellectual and theoretical saturation. Like Crowley, Bardon sought to clarify his subject so that it might attain a broader appeal in a world where straying from proscribed religion no longer posed a violent threat to one's existence. He put particular emphasis on training the body, on the grounds that a fit and healthy body was apt for the rigors of spiritual and magical enlightenment. Bardon himself suffered from several ailments, including an underactive thyroid and problems with blood pressure. He had, he claimed, produced a magical working that alleviated high blood pressure, but in experimenting on his own body he managed to give himself low blood pressure and the associated problems of lethargy that came with it. To counteract this, he consumed vast amounts of coffee and smoked sixty cigarettes a day (neither of which, surely, conformed to his teachings on maintaining optimum physical health).

Bardon wanted to provide a democratized means of introducing Hermetic principles to others who may not have access to an adept instructor. To this end he began, in the 1930s, to compile the writings that would form the basis of his three great works, *Initiation into Hermetics, The Practice of Magical Evocation,* and *The Key to the True Kabbalah.* The publication of these works led many late-twentieth-century magicians to consider Bardon to have been the greatest magical teacher of all.

It was perhaps ironic, then, that Bardon found himself (like Naglowska) submerged in a part of twentieth-century history that was anything but enthusiastic about diverse esoteric traditions rising to the surface. In 1938, German encroachment into Austrian and Czechoslovakian territory began. In March, Anschluss saw the annexation of Austria into the German Reich, and in October the Czechoslovakian region of the Sudetenland was taken by Germany. Following his appointment as German Chancellor in 1933, Hitler had begun outlawing a variety of magical orders, partly due to suspicions of Freemasonry and partly, it seems, due to the Nazi hierarchy's own mixed feelings about the occult, which veered from fascination and co-opting to paranoia and suppression. The O.T.O. was outlawed, as was the Fraternitas Saturni (The Fraternity of Saturn), a German magical order of which Bardon was allegedly a member. The Fraturnitas Saturni was formed following the Weida Conference in 1925, at which various magical orders met to consolidate support for Crowley as the world teacher and head of the O.T.O. However, the conference was ill tempered, and many of the German representatives withdrew their support for Crowley and would not accept Thelema as their central doctrine. This schism led one group of Crowley supporters to establish the Fraturnitas Saturni, which took *The Book of the Law* as central to its teachings and proclaimed Crowley to be a great prophet, but they put themselves out of his jurisdiction and would not answer to him or members of the O.T.O. The Fraturnitas Saturni instead developed a reading of *The Book of the Law* and Thelema that was independent of Crowley's teachings and more rooted in Luciferianism and astrology, as well as diverging from the O.T.O. approach to sex magic, which was fundamentally concerned with the power of transgression. The Fraturnitas

Saturni gave sex magic more scope, and, in line with Luciferian teachings, saw the power of sexual energy as a means of magical charge, one that could be dangerous if wielded incorrectly. When the Fraternitas Saturni was outlawed in Germany in 1936, most of its members fled the country to escape arrest, but Bardon remained. Following the full occupation of Czechoslovakia in 1939, Bardon began instructing all of his magical students and correspondents to destroy his letters once read as a means of protection against Nazi spies. He was already known to both Hitler and Heinrich Himmler (Himmler being the most devout occultist and pagan among the Nazi high command) as a powerful magician who had a considerable following in Czechoslovakia, Austria, and Germany.[3]

Bardon's connections to esoteric orders informed him that Hitler was himself, in fact, connected to two magical orders. The first, the Thule Society, was relatively uncontroversial, albeit allegedly an off-shoot of an order of Tibetan black monks who wished to use the society to counteract the threat of Communism to Tibet. The Thule Society was formed in Munich in 1918 by the occultist, political activist, spy, and writer Rudolf von Sebottendorf and was named for the mystical and mythical northern country in the legends of ancient Greece. The society's volkish, romantic, and occultist pagan ideals attracted both aristocrats and disillusioned German soldiers looking for others who opposed the armistice of 1918 and the subsequent German revolution. It became famous primarily as being the financial benefactor of the nascent Nazi Party, and many figures who would rise to prominence during Nazi Germany were also members of the Thule Society in 1918. Rudolph Hess and Hans Frank were certainly members, but the list likely extended to Alfred Rosenberg, Julius Lehmann, Gottfried Feder, Dietrich Eckhart, Karl Harrer, and Hitler, all of whom at the very least gave speeches at Thule Society meetings.[4]

Hitler's other occult connection was altogether more sinister and shadier—the Freemasonic Order of the Golden Centurium, also known simply as the 99 Lodge. In spite of its official title, the 99 Lodge was not a Freemasonic order and had no degrees or formally established hierarchy of realization among its members. It was founded in Munich in 1840 by the city's wealthiest and most powerful citizens and was populated by ninety-nine male members.[5] Perhaps unsurprisingly, the lodge was entirely cloaked in secrecy and never openly acknowledged. It was a magical-mystical order, and its objective was the evocation of the most powerful, dangerous, and darkest of demonic forces to assist the lodge in the most difficult magical workings—death curses, vast material gains, warfare, power, and money. Whichever demon was called would serve as the one-hundredth member of the lodge—Astaroth the Bull-god; Belial "the wicked one" and the Devil himself; Asmodai the lust demon and King of the Nine Hells; or mars-daimon Bartzabel, a spirit of Mars in geomantic magic (a once popular form of divination and one of the seven forbidden arts of Renaissance Magic). Every five years the lodge would meet on June 23 and the ninety-nine would each draw out a ball from a ballot box. Ninety-eight of the balls were white and one black. He who drew the black ball would be forced to take poison at that lodge meeting as a sacrifice to the demonic forces with whom they were magically allied. Furthermore, the material possessions of the sacrificial victim would be transferred to the 99 Lodge's funds. Should a member die between these five yearly meetings, then no sacrifice would be necessary. The place would be taken by a new member the day following the ritual. The members were initiated into mastery of black magic and bound by oaths and pacts of blood and mind, among one another and with the lodge egregore. Most tellingly, there are accounts that the 99 Lodge made use of forms of telepathic combat, especially through the Tepaphone, an instrument for magical warfare that Bardon claimed the members of the 99 Lodge used to try to murder him when he rejected their offer to join them. It seems that Bardon may have been the Tepaphone's inventor, as he was able to describe it in technical detail, as well as asserting that the Fraternitus Saturni were in possession of one as well. It was a kind of lantern with extremely complex optic lenses that allowed glass slides to be placed in front of a light source, all of which was bound with copper coils and fueled with ethyl alcohol. Sigils would be drawn on the slides and the object containing the energy of the target (as usual, hair, flesh, bodily fluid, a photograph, etc.) would be put onto a copper plate—all of which supposedly worked like a Tesla coil and could transmit energy wirelessly, in this case negative energy designed to disrupt an enemy's nervous system or general physical or psychological well-being.[6] In the 1970s another member of the Fraternitus Saturni, Guido Wolther (also known as Master Daniel) gave another account of the Tepaphone that corroborated that of Bardon. However, Wolther disputed Bardon's claim that the 99 Lodge was in possession of one, saying that had they used one, even a magical being as strong as Bardon could not have survived. Furthermore, he revealed that one of the grandmasters of the 99 Lodge was taken to Buchenwald, but according to SS paperwork, "disappeared," and that rituals performed by the SS (notably the *ordenjunker,* or "noblemanorder") were similar in style and appearance to the rituals of the lodge, albeit with very different intentions.[7]

Given the nature of the 99 Lodge and its location, it seems improbable that Hitler would not have been high on their list of potential invitees in 1930, or perhaps 1925. Whether or not he was previously or currently a member, the 99 Lodge was a major point of contention between Hitler and Bardon, and the Nazis had Bardon in a vise. Finally, one of Bardon's students, Wilhelm Quintscher, was interrogated by the Gestapo, and they found in his possession many letters from Bardon, which proved the adept's involvement in the Fraternitas Saturni—Quintscher had failed to follow his master's instructions to destroy his correspondence.[8] Quintscher and Bardon were immediately arrested and taken away to be questioned. Both denied any involvement in magical orders, but under torture, Quintscher's resolve broke and he screamed a Kabbalistic formula at his torturers that caused them to fall paralyzed and relent the flogging, but this also proved that they were both more than mere dabblers. In revenge Quintscher was taken away and shot. Bardon was spared and taken to Hitler personally. Hitler offered him a high position in the Nazi regime if he would collaborate with him in destroying his enemies with telepathic and magical combat. Furthermore, Hitler implored Bardon to reveal the locations of the other ninety-eight members of the Freemasonic Order of the Golden Centurium (suggesting that either Hitler certainly was not a member or that the lodge kept their identities largely secret from one another). Bardon denied all knowledge, and was thus sentenced to spend the next three and a half years in prison, where he would have iron balls chained to his ankles and would have to endure un-anaesthetized surgery.[9]

In 1945, Bardon was sentenced to death by the Nazis, but the prison he was confined in was bombed and Bardon was pulled from the rubble by some of his Russian fellow inmates. In secret, he returned to Gillschwitz, a suburb of Opava/Troppau and the home of his wife, children, and mother-in-law, and went into hiding. In September 1944, Czechoslovak troops liberated the first Czechoslovakian town from German occupation, beginning a battle for the country that would continue until May 1945, when the Prague uprising overthrew the Germans in the city and returned it to Czech control, just one day before the Soviet Red Army arrived. This period was the bloodiest of the war for Czechoslovakia, which had been relatively peaceful overall. Bardon and his family hid for two weeks in the cellar below his mother-in-law's house as the change of governance of Opava/Troppau took place, concealed among the stores of carrots and potatoes. His young son, Lumir, was drafted into local resistance and collected black powder and detonators, twice injuring himself in minor explosions that burned his face and hands, wounds that Bardon was able to treat with his herbal medicines. Once the new Czechoslovakian government had been established, the Sudeten Germans—Czechoslovakians of German ethnicity—were forcibly expelled from the country into Germany. Bardon was an ethnic German on his father's side, but his mother was Czech, and so he would have been given an exemption on these grounds. Almost two million ethnic Germans were forced from their homes and sent to Germany, often subjected to violence, rape, and murder as a frenzy of reprisal took hold of central and eastern Europe.

After the war Bardon was made director of Knight's Hospital in the town, which—like so many places—was suffering from a severe lack of trained doctors. Bardon bought a house in the center of town not long after this, although his wife refused to give up her farming business in Gillschwitz, and moreover did not want to leave her mother alone. Bardon, equally, had no desire to continue the farm work he had undertaken during his stay there, so the couple began life apart, although Bardon visited twice a week and often took Lumir to the theater or cinema. It was at this time that Divine Providence instructed Bardon to complete his works of literature on the subject of Hermetics, and he produced the manuscripts for his three books in the years following the war.

More political upheaval would pose further problems for Frabato. In 1948 the Soviet Union supported a Communist seizure of power, essentially creating a Soviet puppet state with nothing more than a sham democracy lain over it. Bardon was arrested in 1949 on grounds of charlatanry for his occult practices and celebrated healing powers and once again sent to a forced labor camp. On release, he reassumed his position at the hospital and continued to provide his own spiritual and medicinal practices at his nearby home. He used his clairvoyant powers to attempt to locate Hitler and proclaimed that he had escaped Berlin and undergone extensive plastic surgery to disguise his appearance—a legend put forth by many and that will prevail until the end of history no doubt.

Bardon published his first book, *Initiation into Hermetics,* in 1956. In March 1958, however, he attracted the attentions once more of the Communist regime and was arrested and imprisoned on charges of providing illegal medicine. In July of the same year, while awaiting trial, Bardon died of what was recorded as pancreatitis. The events surrounding his death are mysterious, and the regime destroyed all of Bardon's possessions, with nothing being returned to Marie. Marie later claimed that Bardon—rather strangely, even by the standards of his life—had committed suicide by bacon, asking her for large quantities of his favorite kind to be brought to him in prison. Bardon, she reasoned, knew well how dangerous the consumption of bacon is for someone suffering from pancreatic illnesses and wanted to end his own life rather than face what the Communists had in store for him. His other works were published posthumously, and all were translated into English by the 1970s, including his magical autobiography, *Frabato the Magician,* largely compiled by his secretary, and *Franz Bardon, Questions and Answers,* his lecture notes compiled by Dieter Ruggeberg.

Bardon today, although less known than some of the other figures in this book, is perhaps the most respected magician of the modern Western occult, and his serious and practical approach to initiation, most especially the emphasis he placed on the great powers and dangers of sex magic, are of great importance in the field. The reincarnation of Hermes Trismegistus, Lao-tzu, Mahum Tah-Ta, and Shambhala landed this time in the heat of the greatest war humanity has ever known and placed him right in front of one of its principal protagonists, the alleged black magician Adolf Hitler, and Bardon prevailed—just about.

SELECTED WORKS BY FRANZ BARDON CONCERNING SEX MAGIC

Franz Bardon's series of initiatory books is available almost exclusively from Merkur Publishing.

1956 ✦ *Der Weg zum wahren Adepten,* published in English as *Initiation into Hermetics: A Course of Instruction of Magic Theory and Practice*

1971 ✦ *Frabato the Magician*, published posthumously in English

8

Jack Parsons
(1914–1952)

There is a crater on the dark side of the moon called the "Parsons Crater," named for the American rocket engineer, chemist, rocket propulsion pioneer, and Thelemite John Whiteside Parsons. Perhaps it's a stretch, but surrounding the crater are five smaller cavities spaced quite neatly so that if one were to draw connecting lines between them, a near-enough equilateral pentagram would be formed. A coincidence of passing amusement, perhaps, but when considering some of the dramatic headlines that followed Parsons's death, such as "Ventures Into Black Magic By Blast Victim Revealed" and "Slain Scientist Priest In Black Magic Cult," it should be clear how deep the symbiosis between magic and physics ran in Parsons.

Parsons was born in Los Angeles on October 2, 1914. His parents, Marvel H. Parsons and Ruth Virginia (née Whiteside), had moved to California from their native Massachusetts the previous year. The irresistible attraction of sunshine and prosperity called them, like millions of others, since the gold rush of the 1840s had opened up California to Americans. Both were in their early twenties and had been married barely a year when they made the move—although the motive was not only sunshine but also Ruth's frail physical and psychological state following the stillbirth of their first child. Los Angeles would be a place for her to regenerate, and since both Marvel and Ruth came from prosperous middle-class backgrounds, some of the more testing obstacles before them were smoothed by a financial security. They moved into a large house just off Wilshere Boulevard on what was then Romeo Street but is now S. Catalina Street in Koreatown (Juliet Street still exists, a block west). L.A. was then an unremarkable midsize city, but with the installation of its first aqueduct in 1913 it was destined to experience a population and culture explosion of astonishing scale. During the years of the Great War, rich and poor, the adventurous, eccentric, and criminal arrived in L.A. in droves. The city bloated, incorporating surrounding districts, such as Hollywood, that attracted the attention of a band of New Yorkers with an interest in shooting cinema year-round in the clement weather. The steady Protestant nature of the town, once famous for beef and little else, was swept away by a wave of obscure religious sects. Christian Science, Theosophy, Spiritualism, secular utopians, various Eastern religions, Marxists, and others set up camp in L.A. Racketeering was big business as the Anti-Saloon League struggled to contend with the waves of vice coming to the city under blazing neon lights. Brothels sprang up opposite churches in an awkward arrangement of urban convenience. This particular aspect of L.A. would have a devastating effect on the Parsons family.

Just after Parsons was born (at birth he was named after his father as Marvel Whiteside Parsons), his mother, Ruth, discovered that her husband had been regularly visiting prostitutes. She forced him to move out of their home and never spoke to him again, refusing to respond to any of his remorseful letters pleading for clemency and for the chance to see their son. She maintained an unbroken silence, filed for divorce (publicly exposing her husband as an adulterer when he'd begged she give another reason), and changed her son's name to John—or Jack, as the common diminutive—and he never really got to know his father. Marvel, publicly humiliated and deprived of his son, eventually moved back to Massachusetts. The house on Romeo Street was abandoned, and Ruth moved Jack and her parents to a property in exclusive, wealthy, and liberal Pasadena.

Parsons grew up an only child, spoiled and waited on by an army of servants in their wooden mansion. It was literature that filled his solitary days, and he developed particular fascination for Norse and Greek mythology, the legends of King Arthur, and, perhaps most importantly, the novels of Jules Verne. Reading Verne's 1865 tale *From the Earth to the Moon,* which tells of a group of explosives experts and former American soldiers, not unlike the Knights of the Round Table in their demeanor, blasting themselves into space with a 900-foot cannon, sparked an interest in Parsons for any form of literature to do with space travel. In 1926 he became an avid reader of the new magazine *Amazing Stories,* a publication that is credited with cementing science fiction into the popular imagination of America.

Until the age of twelve, Parsons was relatively isolated from the furious explosion of the city of L.A. as it tripled in size to become the fifth largest city in the United States by the mid-1920s. He was mollycoddled and schooled at home, free to experiment with his own furious explosions as he began to build crude bottle rockets and launch them into the sky. After that he attended a local high school where his love of sci-fi magazines, chubbiness, affected English accent, smart clothes, and dyslexia made him a prime target for bullies. He seemed able to take care of himself, however, and one incident, in which Parsons was caught beating one of his tormentors, ended in him receiving a bloody nose from the schoolyard monitor, Ed Forman, in a straightforward attempt to bring his charges to order. Forman was two years older than Parsons, and from a much poorer family. He was tall and athletic, but also suffered from dyslexia. As is often the case with schoolboy fights, the initial violence opened a passage to friendship, and they became the very best of friends. Forman offered protection and credibility to Parsons, while in return, Parsons shared his superior knowledge of myths and his advancing understanding of rocketry—as well as his mother's generous lunch money. Forman's father was an engineer, which gave them access to important materials, and the two set out through their teenage years with one objective: to put a rocket on the moon.

His enthusiasm for blowing up things out in the desert and his distinct lack of enthusiasm for his schoolwork and sports teams led his mother to take drastic action to set her son on a more conventional path. He was sent to the Brown Military Academy in San Diego. For a sensitive, curious, and generally solitary child, this environment would prove to be a form of hell. Bullied mercilessly from the outset, Parsons had the shrewdness to blow up the school toilets, finding himself expelled and back in Pasadena, where he could resume his experiments and friendship with Forman.

Rocketry at this time was very much a niche pursuit; governments and corporations were still blind to its vast possibilities in the 1920s. The Soviet Union and United States had a rocketry pioneer of note each at this time. The Russian Konstantin Tsiolkovsky solved many theoretical problems of rocketry, including how to formulate rocket fuel that allowed a rocket to gather enough speed quickly enough to overcome the pull of Earth's gravity. In the United States, Robert H. Goddard launched the first successful liquid-fueled rocket in 1926 and was soon launching rockets that achieved speeds of 550 mph and altitudes of 1.5 miles. Both men were ridiculed as eccentric hobbyists, and both are now considered the forefathers of modern rocketry.

Parsons was one of the few who shared the beliefs of Tsiolkovsky and Goddard. However, the economic crash of 1929 hit the family hard, and when his grandfather died in 1931, Parsons was forced to drop out of Pasadena Junior College (where he studied chemistry and physics) and get a job to help support his family and fund his future university education. He found employment at the Hercules Powder Company, one of America's largest explosives manufacturing plants, at Pinole, near San Francisco. He earned a good salary of $100 per week, but the work was tough and dangerous. He pushed around four-ton carts of dynamite and was exposed to nitroglycerine. There were explosions and accidents on a regular basis, and at least one worker died per year at the plant. He described this isolated place as like "a vision of Hell," especially at night as molten slag oozed and red licks of flame burned against the darkness.

Parsons, now more than six feet tall and strong, was a good worker, and his intelligence set him apart from the others. He befriended the chief chemist and through him extended his knowledge of explosives, often by stealing materials with which to experiment. He was offered a promotion, but he turned it down in the hope of being offered a place at university—which he received at Stanford, to study chemistry.

While Parsons was away, Forman had also found work with Hercules, but in the L.A. plant where they built the shells and guns into which the trinitrotoluene, commonly known as TNT, would eventually be stuffed. The machining skills Forman learned here meant that he and Parsons were now able to build metal rockets in place of wooden ones. However, these experiments proved limited, and as Parsons read more about experiments being conducted by the American Interplanetary Society, he realized that the skills needed to emulate their recent advances were beyond him. To get the help they needed, Parsons and Forman decided to take a direct approach. They walked straight onto the campus of the California Institute of Technology, known as Caltech, and asked for it. In the mid-1930s, Caltech was transforming itself from a respectable young university— once known as Throop University—into a modern lyceum of science. Once an engineering school, Caltech was transformed by the arrival of the astrophysicist George Ellery Hale in the first years of the twentieth century. He believed that astronomy, the oldest of the sciences, was a discipline like philosophy and saw in it a direct link to the ancients of Greece, Mesopotamia, Egypt, and Babylon. He conversed with woodland elves and considered himself a sun worshipper, and Hale tried to reinstate the same reverence for celestial objects that led the pagans to revere the sun as a god—only Hale wanted to do it with the largest telescopes on Earth. In 1908 work finished on his first sixty-inch reflector telescope, which had been dragged by muscle up Mount Wilson, overlooking Pasadena. The lodgings at the foot of the telescope were decorated with the mystical symbols and hieroglyphs of ancient Egypt, a reminder to the men observing the stars that they were joining a mystical as well as scientific tradition that began in prehistory.

By the 1930s, Caltech could boast luminaries such as Edwin Hubble, Thomas Hunt Morgan, Linus Pauling, Charles Richter, J. Robert Oppenheimer, Niels Bohr, Werner Heisenberg, and Albert Einstein wandering through its campus. Parsons found a sympathetic ear among the bustling young men in sports jackets and cream slacks with set squares tucked under their arms: the graduate student Frank Malina. Malina was a student of the mathematician and aeronautics expert Theodore von Kármán, and an associate of Bill Bollay, who had recently given a seminar on rocketry that had inspired Parsons and Forman to make the visit. Rocketry remained an eccentric and, one might even say, occulted subject among most scientists of the time. The Swiss astronomer Fritz Zwicky, who theorized dark matter, ridiculed the idea of rocket propulsion in space, believing that a rocket could not function in a vacuum. It seems incredible, but Zwicky was not alone in his apparent ignorance of Newton's Third Law, evidently believing that a rocket engine pushed against air to generate motion, rather than the simpler—and accurate—belief of Parsons that the rocket would react to the action of the expulsion of heated gases.

Parsons and Forman asked Malina to help them design a liquid propellant rocket engine. With the blessing of von Kármán, the three plus Bollay set out to start experiments. Von Kármán gave the group a veneer of formality by allowing them to operate through Caltech's Guggenheim Aeronautical Laboratory (GALCIT), but their level of funding was zero. They spent two-and-a-half years blowing things up on campus, earning themselves the title "The Suicide Squad" due to the craziness and danger of their experiments. Finally, in 1938, von Kármán suggested that Malina head to Washington and give a report to the Army Air Corps research committee, who had expressed an interest in rockets as auxiliary means of propulsion for aircraft. Malina filed the report and came back with their first government grant of $1,000. About $250 of this was immediately given to the university to pay off repairs that had to be made to buildings damaged by wayward rockets, and the Suicide Squad were sent out into the Arroyo Seco canyon to carry on their experiments. While there they were closely watched by the FBI. Communism was still fashionable among undergraduates at Caltech, and with the recent influx of Europeans fleeing the German regime the FBI were keen to keep a close eye on any possible combination of explosives and left-wing radicals. While Parsons at this time had Communist sympathies, he was led to an altogether more arcane system of belief, one that, while not a political threat, was capable of inciting absolute terror in some segments of society.

Parsons began reading the works of Crowley approximately 1935, which was also the year he married Helen Northup, who he had met at a church dance. Crowley fascinated Parsons, not least because Crowley (who majored in chemistry at Cambridge) had been able to present a set of spiritual beliefs that were wholly compatible with physics; Crowley was even able to explain the deep mysteries that existed in the quantum world as part of a magical system. It's perhaps unsurprising that physicists are often, on a personal level, deeply drawn to the mystical and metaphysical, in spite of a professional adherence to rationale and the scientific method. Parsons, already an outsider in physics, saw no reason to pursue conventional spiritual fulfillment, either.

In 1939 he joined the Hollywood Agape Lodge of Crowley's O.T.O. Here he attended a gnostic mass, a ceremony that Crowley had written for the O.T.O. that was loosely based on the Catholic and Orthodox Christian masses. However, unlike either of those, the gnostic mass was designed to sexually charge the atmosphere of the temple. The formal and beautiful ceremony is lit by candles and decorated by veils and hieroglyphs, while white-robed initiates oversee. A female deacon leads the congregation through the Gnostic Creed, standing before the altar of incense, from which plumes of frankincense and abramelin burn. She announces a belief in Chaos, Baphomet, the Sun, and Babalon, among others. A naked virgin then enters and makes a snake dance around the altar of incense that represents the awakening of the kundalini serpent that, according to Hindu philosophy, is coiled around the base of the spine and can bring spiritual enlightenment and supernormal powers once awoken. She then approaches the Tomb (an upright coffin) and tears down the veil surrounding it with her ceremonial sword, bringing the priest to life by the power of Iron, the Sun, and the Lord. The priest then carries the virgin to the high altar, and the congregation kneels before her in adoration. The priest then invokes Crowley's trinity of Thelemic deities: Nuit, Hadit, and Ra-Hoor Khuit. The priest opens the veil of the high altar with his lance, and the virgin kisses it eleven times. Then the cakes of light are presented—containing meal, red wine, honey, oil of abramelin, olive oil, and menstrual blood. The virgin impales a cake upon the lance and lets out an orgasmic scream. The congregation then takes a cake and a goblet of wine before the ceremony closes with the priest giving the benediction that the congregation be blessed and enlightened, and that they be able to follow their True Will.

Parsons took the name Frater T.O.P.A.N. (an acronym of the Latin *Thelemum Obtentum Procedero Amoris Nuptiae,* or "The obtainment of will through the nuptials of love"), or Frater 210 for short, and his wife, Helen, was dubbed Soror Grimaud by the O.T.O.

Over the years, Parsons made it across the Great Abyss and into the higher echelons of the O.T.O.'s seventh degree and beyond. The adept at this stage was required to display an ability to know certain self-evident truths about the universe and is, in some sense, reborn. This rebirth is what engenders sexual magic as a prerequisite for further enlightenment and the attainment of the Godhead. In the seventh degree, the practitioner performs a masturbation ritual in which the phallus is adored as Baphomet (the idol most important to the Knights Templar), as well as swearing a vow of chastity—although the interpretation of this is perhaps not the same as the Christian equivalent. The eighth degree involved the adept anointing the anus with a mixture of saliva, semen, and vaginal fluid, then taking this mixture from the anus as an elixir to further anoint the chakras, and then being consumed. The ninth degree was devoted to vaginal, heterosexual intercourse, and the mixing of the fluids, including menstrual blood, which both partners would then consume via a kiss after the man had taken them in his mouth through cunnilingus. The ninth degree also contains extraordinary instructions on the creation of a homunculus; that is to say, a small humanoid creature. After some astrological matching, and, as the order stresses, some clarification of what this involves to both parties and their consent, the couple begin to copulate continuously, especially at times astrologically favorable to the working. The copulation should be performed in a temple, and both should be adepts. Once impregnation takes place, the woman is withdrawn and taken away to a specially prepared location in a great desert. Magical circles are drawn around her dwelling, and she performs various banishing rituals five or six times a day to keep her mind and environment pure. The woman is not to leave the circle at any time, and she must inhale continuously the incense of the appropriate spirit, while meditating constantly to focus her magical power. At the quickening (traditionally considered the beginning of the life of a child, but here the beginning of its spiritual life—often at between fifteen to twenty weeks), the banishing rituals can stop, and the woman then feasts to the reception of the spirit. Afterward, the woman spends the rest of the pregnancy in magical evocation of the deity, and the birth is delayed or provoked so that the child gains a desirable astrological rising sign. The child is immediately dedicated, purified, and consecrated to the planets, elements, and astrological sign. If all has been successfully conducted (and the O.T.O. warn that this happens about once every one hundred thousand years) then the result will be a "perfect human form," a miniature spirit who will serve its parents with its immense power, knowledge, and might. The tenth degree is also to do with impregnation, although this time merely for the creation of a magical successor and the process of bringing God into the pregnancy. The final degree, the eleventh, is perhaps the most complex. To Crowley, the final frontier was passive anal homosexual intercourse—but this is perhaps to do with his religious and fiercely homophobic upbringing—to a gay man, passive anal intercourse may not seem remotely taboo. But Crowley also made use of anal intercourse to uncover a more universal taboo, which is the use of excrement in a sexual ritual, wherein all the body's fluids (blood, saliva, vaginal fluid, semen, and feces) could be mixed within the anal cavity, where the membranes would allow this potion to be absorbed into the blood supply. He also spoke of the "Child of such a love" as a "bodiless creation of a divine nature." Crowley dreamed of producing one of these children a year, "a mass of blood and slime."

As Parsons made his way through the degrees of the O.T.O., the United States braced itself for war, a situation that meant considerable increases in the amount of money the government was willing to spend on rocket research. In fact, President Roosevelt sanctioned a staggering 800 percent increase in defense spending in 1940 as the United States began to supply their British friends with weapons and ammunition to assist their single-handed fight against the Axis powers. Parsons's experiments began to advance into discoveries that would shape the entire history of rocketry. He made the first ever American jet-assisted take-off (JATO; the group used the word *jet* to avoid the stigma attached to rocketry) in August 1941 using a solid fuel, which further intrigued the military who saw potential in the capability to launch airplanes with rocket assistance if they had to take off over a short distance, such as on an aircraft carrier. Further funding and tests followed this successful flight, and Parsons set about making himself useful to the war effort by developing a more stable liquid fuel. As he launched various combinations of gasoline and red fuming nitric acid, he would ecstatically recite Crowley's "Hymn to Pan" as the rockets launched in fiery bursts and exploded in the heavens, to the apprehensive amusement of observers. The group came upon the correct combination, and, withstanding one explosion that could have killed them all, were now able to propose the sale of sixty JATO engines to the US Army Air Corps. To do this, Von Kármán advised the GALCIT group to create a company, and Parsons, Forman, and the others formed the Aerojet Engineering Corporation in 1942.

The sale of the engines made Parsons a rich man, and he invested some of his wealth in renting a house that would be able to accommodate his Thelemic activities in comfort. He settled on property at 1003 South Orange Grove Avenue in Pasadena. The house was enormous and was built by the philanthropist Arthur Flemming in the style of a Swiss chalet. It had ten rooms in the main building, plus a three-roomed coach house in the yard, a swimming pool, and twenty-five acres of private gardens and allotments where animals were kept and slaughtered for both food and blood rituals.

Frater T.O.P.A.N. and his wife, Soror Grimaud, began welcoming members of the Agape Lodge to their home to stay and indulge in magical learning and experimentation, and pitch in with the $100 per month for rent. Parsons filled his room with his collection of ceremonial swords and daggers, a copy of the Stele of Revealing, and a statue of Pan. He built a chemical lab in the garage, leaving his battered old Packard to the elements; entertained guests with science-fiction readings in his kitchen; and conducted fairy hunts through the grounds to entertain the children of his O.T.O. friends. One of the first experiments Parsons undertook was to seduce his wife's sixteen-year-old sister, Sara Northrup, whom he called Betty, who had also joined the lodge, and the O.T.O. authorities encouraged their sexual exploration. In response, his wife began an affair with one of the many lodgers in their home—the head of the Agape O.T.O. lodge, Wilfred Smith. In spite of this friction, one of the principal O.T.O. teachings was that jealousy was a base emotion unfitting for the enlightened, and tensions seem to have simmered down quickly, and all four remained friends. Smith became a father figure to Parsons, and Helen stayed on at the house where her husband and younger sister had fallen in love.

Well before the sexual revolution of the 1960s, free love and sexual experimentation, as well as drugs and magic, were the norm in the big wooden Pasadena house, which became known as "the Parsonage." Parsons's long-time associate Frank Malina's wife, the abstract artist Liljan Wunderman, recalled years later that it was, "a big, big thing, full of people. Some of them had masks on, some had costumes on, women were weirdly dressed. It was like walking into a Fellini movie. Women were walking around in diaphanous togas and weird make-up, some dressed up like animals, like a costume party."[1] The guests included practicing witches, science-fiction authors (including a young Ray Bradbury), Thelemites from the lodge, and even physicists blowing off steam on leave from their hard work on the Manhattan Project.

The neighbors were horrified at the orgies, chanting, and attempts to evoke the Antichrist, and the police were called several times, once due to a naked pregnant woman jumping through fire in the yard. Parsons's respected position and wealth made it easy for him to deflect the attentions of the local Pasadena cops, but all the while the FBI were building a meticulous file on their wayward rocket scientist.[2]

Parsons began to find his dual commitments to the O.T.O. and rocketry increasingly difficult to maintain. Always a drinker and smoker of marijuana, he was now experimenting with cocaine, peyote, mescaline, opium, and amphetamines on a regular basis. He voluntarily sent much of his money to the lodge and directly to Crowley himself, but even Crowley was growing concerned at the behavior at the Agape Lodge. He believed that Smith's leadership had led the lodge down a path of debauchery and was in danger of sullying the name of his new religion, which as far as the Great Beast was concerned was exclusively designed to guide its members through the Great Work and not to orgies and taking drugs for hedonistic pleasure. Parsons tried to defend his mentor, but Smith was removed and Parsons elevated to standing head of the lodge. At Aerojet he often showed up hungover and was beginning to incur resentment among his sober-minded colleagues who saw his eccentric lifestyle as impacting negatively his more important work developing rockets for the war effort. A pacifist, whose sole goal in rocketry was the exploration of space, Parsons was increasingly psychologically affected by his contribution to destructive weaponry. Aerojet's budget was increased again, but this time it came at the cost of major structural reorganization. Employee wages were cut, and the former loose and outlaw collective was obliged to conform to government expectations. Board members, including Parsons, were exempt from the wage cut that caused anger among the employees. Zwicky, who had once ridiculed Parsons's theories of rocket travel in a vacuum, was appointed as head of research. Von Kármán was replaced by the lawyer (and later recognized as the first ever practitioner of space law) and Andrew G. Haley as chairman, who proved a brilliant but ruthless administrator. The new order at Aerojet, and some of the older order, did not look kindly on Parsons's seduction of the company secretaries with promises of naked fire dances in his mansion home. At the Parsonage he had managed to upset senior Thelemite Grady McMurty by getting his fiancée pregnant. The older members of the lodge were unimpressed by a perceived overemphasis on sex and polyamory, but his leadership proved popular with his younger congregation, and he turned out to be a charismatic orator. He set up a poetry journal in honor of Crowley called the *Oriflamme,* but Crowley was unimpressed, still considering Parsons's drug use to be more debauchery than a means to enlightenment. Crowley then had a change of heart about Smith after an astrological reading led him to believe that Smith was the incarnation of a god, but both Smith and Parsons were growing weary of Crowley's ego and unpredictable nature. Relations between Smith and Crowley broke down, and Smith left the O.T.O., heading to a meditative retreat with Helen and their newborn son. Parsons resigned in protest at Smith's treatment but withdrew his resignation after a letter of appeasement from Crowley.

The military, now fully engaged in the war against Japan and Germany, was ordering 20,000 JATOs per month from Aerojet. The group, still led by Von Kármán, Forman, Malina, and Parsons, expanded and renamed themselves as the Jet Propulsion Laboratory, or JPL for short. The demand was more than JPL could cope with, and in December 1944, Haley negotiated a deal to sell 51 percent of the business to the General Tire and Rubber Company to help production. The company was now under the direct command of the army, and several employees of JPL said they would only agree to the sale if Parsons and

Forman were removed from the board. Zwicky and Malina in particular objected to Parsons's continued presence. Partially, this was due to a contempt for the rogue methods he continued to employ in his research, wild and unsafe experiments interspersed with dangerous entertainments where Forman and Parsons would shoot the ground at one another's feet with pistols and try not to flinch. But, as Parsons became accustomed to greeting visiting scientists and government officials at his home half naked with a snake wound around his torso, Zwicky in particular raised moral issues about the magician in their midst. "We told him all the time, I mean, all these fantasies about Zoroaster and about voodoo and so on, this is okay; we do that too in our dreams," Zwicky said. "But keep it for yourself; don't start impressing this on poor secretaries. I mean he had a whole club there you know."[3] Parsons was offered $20,000 for his share in JPL, and he had little choice but to take it and leave behind his years of research.

He and Forman started a chemical manufacturing company called the Vulcan Powder Company, as well as the Ad Astra Engineering Company through which they would continue their rocketry experiments with the aim of achieving space flight. Already under suspicion as a threat to national security due to, as was written in his FBI file, "black magic rituals," "probable bisexuality," and his entourage of radicals and undesirables, Ad Astra was forced to fend off an FBI investigation after Manhattan Project security agents discovered that Parsons had acquired something known only as "x-metal" (that was, in fact, natural uranium) from a top-secret government project. They were acquitted, but the FBI would return.

He threw himself more passionately into magic than ever before. The disputes with Crowley led him to begin experimenting with various other forms of magic including witchcraft and voodoo, desperate to see more tangible evidence of the success of his workings. His intensity worried even his magical friends, one writing to Karl Germer, who was second only to Crowley in the O.T.O. hierarchy that "our own Jack is enamored of witchcraft, the houmfort, voodoo. From the start he always wanted to evoke something—no matter what, I am inclined to think, so long as he got a result."[4]

It might be speculated that the entity he was striving to evoke came to him in a strange but unmistakably human form, and a highly negative one at that. In 1945 a young man named L. Ron Hubbard appeared at the Parsonage, and Parsons took to him enthusiastically. Hubbard, who would go on to found the Church of Scientology, was at the time a science-fiction writer, but he seemed to stoke suspicion in his literary peers for the fervor with which he told his tales and his insistence that they were true stories being relayed through him. Charismatic and good looking, Hubbard reveled in the environment of free love, seducing a large number of the women at the Parsonage, including Betty, Parsons's girlfriend. Parsons was put out by this, but Hubbard cited Parsons's own beliefs on sexual liberty and Parsons was obliged to swallow his jealousy. He remained fascinated by Hubbard's charisma and magical ability, writing to Crowley that Hubbard had "an extraordinary amount of experience and understanding in the field. From some of his experiences I deduce he is in direct touch with some higher intelligence, possibly his Guardian Angel . . . He is the most Thelemic person I have ever met and is in complete accord with our own principles."[5]

Nevertheless, the emotional trauma of Betty's sexual relationship with Hubbard led Parsons further down a path of black magic, which began to worry the other members of the house, who believed that Parsons was allowing dark energy and demonic forces to run loose through the property. Parsons became fascinated by disembodied voices, orbs, paranormal activity, poltergeists, and ghosts, including one occasion that brought howling banshees to the windows of the Parsonage during the night, leaving Forman traumatized by the event for the rest of his life. Aware of Parsons's susceptibility, Hubbard and Betty played elaborate tricks on Parsons to feed his belief in the paranormal.

Taking the responsibility upon himself to fulfill one of Crowley's prophecies, in 1946, Parsons decided to embark on an eleven-day ritual that he called the Babalon Working.[6] Wanting to restore good relations with his friend, Hubbard insisted on coming along as the scribe, and Parsons agreed due to his belief in Hubbard's exceptional abilities of visualization. The first part of the ritual began on January 4, and they continued incantations and waving of talismans for eleven days. The objective of this part of the work was to evoke the Thelemic goddess Babalon, or the Scarlet Woman, in human form. Prokofiev's "Second Violin Concerto" and Rachmaninoff's "Isle of the Dead" played as Hubbard at the altar induced sexual frenzy in Parsons by intoning "Her mouth is red and her breasts are fair, and her loins of full of fire"[7] and other similar things. Using forms of the notorious Enochian magic, Parsons masturbated onto prepared sigils while Hubbard scanned the astral plane and made notes of any magical phenomena he perceived. Banishing and invoking rituals were performed, pentagrams of earth drawn in the air with consecrated daggers, archangels visualized, sigils were doused with animal blood, and Parsons ejaculated onto magical tablets to charge them. What he wanted from Babalon was, in his own words, that "she will come girt with the sword of freedom, and before her kings and priests will tremble and cities and empires will fall, and she will be called BABALON, the scarlet woman. . . . And women will respond to her war cry, and throw off their shackles and chains, and men will respond to her challenge, forsaking the foolish ways and the little ways, and she will shine as the ruddy evening star in the bloody sunset of Gotterdammerung, will shine as a morning star when the night has passed, and a new dawn breaks over the garden of Pan."[8] On the third day he wrote to Crowley, "The wind storm is very interesting, but that is not what I asked for."[9]

Back at the Parsonage, strange occurrences were bewildering the guests. On the seventh day, the sleeping household was awakened by seven large poundings on the walls, but no source was discovered, although a smashed lamp was lying on the floor in one of the unoccupied rooms. One member of the group had a candle knocked out of his hand and was left with his right arm paralyzed for a day in an apparent magical attack. On another night, Parsons had to take his magical sword and banish a muddy yellow light that was stalking the house in the form of a man, which he believed to be Wilfred Smith, expelled head of the O.T.O. Agape Lodge. Finally, on the eleventh day he returned home and discovered that a new tenant had arrived at the house. It was a beautiful young woman with red lips and flame hair named Marjorie Cameron. She, an unemployed illustrator, had little-to-no knowledge of magic and had come to the Parsonage looking for interesting people and a place to stay. She was perplexed at the immediate hubbub upon her arrival, as the entire commune recognized her as Parsons's Scarlet Woman incarnate. He wrote to Crowley, delighted: "I have my elemental! . . . She has red hair and slant green eyes as specified."[10] Parsons and Cameron began an intense magical and sexual relationship.

In February, Parsons and Hubbard went out to the Mojave Desert for two days to complete the second part of the working, also inspired by Crowley, but this time by his novel *Moonchild,* in an effort to create their own moonchild, a magical entity drawn down from the astral plane. In the desert they aimed to use magic to fertilize a woman (seemingly at random) in an immaculate conception, meaning that nine months later a Thelemic messiah would be born as the embodiment of Babalon. Parsons saw it as a scientific attempt to use magic to warp the standard boundaries of four-dimensional space and time. In the desert Parsons, with the help of Hubbard, received a psychographic transmission from a magical entity in a manner similar to that experienced by Crowley with his demon Aiwass years earlier. The text transcribed by Hubbard formed the "Liber 49," which he meant to become the fourth chapter of Crowley's *The Book of the Law,* the founding text of Thelema spoken to him by Aiwass. On hearing of this Crowley wrote, "Apparently Parsons or Hubbard or somebody is producing a Moonchild. I get fairly frantic when I contemplate the idiocy of these louts!"[11] This was not the reaction for which Parsons had hoped.

Nevertheless, he believed the working to have been a complete success. He had the Scarlet Woman, and now he needed only to wait for the birth of the messiah. He sold the Parsonage, staying on in the coach house with Cameron, and relinquished the leadership of the Agape Lodge. Euphoric at the role Hubbard had played in his successes, he agreed to invest his life savings of $20,000 in a joint business venture—to buy three yachts in Miami, sail them through the Panama Canal, and sell them on the West Coast for a considerable profit. His friends advised Parsons against this risky undertaking, but he went ahead anyway. Hubbard left for Miami with Betty and all of Parsons's money and set sail. Realizing he had been duped, Parsons followed them there and found them at a harbor. Hubbard and Betty fled in one of the yachts they had purchased, but Parsons threw himself into a violent and emotional magical working designed to invoke the demon and Mars spirit Bartzabel. The wind picked up and forced the yacht back to shore. Parsons confronted the pair, but Betty threatened to report Parsons to the police for statutory rape, as she had still been underage when their sexual relationship began. Confounded, Parsons lost his friend and magical partner, his girlfriend, and all of his money in one fell swoop, as well as a good deal of his dignity with Crowley branding him a "weak fool" and pointing out that Hubbard and Betty had deployed a "confidence trick" and were "obvious victim prowling swindlers."[12] Though he was already married, Hubbard married Betty (whom Crowley denounced as a vampire). He would use his wealth to found Dianetics and Scientology. When questioned in 1969 by an article in the *Sunday Times* about Hubbard's involvement with the occult, the Church of Scientology released a statement claiming that Hubbard was an agent of the naval intelligence sent to rescue Betty and destroy Parsons's black magic order.[13]

Parsons, now thirty-two, finalized his divorce from Helen and married Cameron on October 19, 1946. Cameron developed catalepsy, which is characterized by rigidity of the body in a form of seizure and a trancelike state in which all sensation and consciousness are temporarily lost. Parsons encouraged her to smoke marijuana to ease her anxiety and introduced her to the techniques of astral travel so she could gain stronger control over her subconscious. They moved to a house in Manhattan Beach, and he took a job working on the Navajo Missile Program for North American Aviation. He gave occasional talks on rocketry and was called as an expert consultant in various legal trials. Magically, he was more private. Though they remained in touch, Crowley had denounced Parsons for his erratic behavior and in the winter of 1947, Cameron traveled to visit Crowley in England to defend her husband. Crowley died before she arrived, and she suspected that she was followed during her travels.

Cameron's suspicions were not unfounded. In March 1947 the Truman Doctrine had been announced to Congress by President Harry S. Truman. It was a piece of foreign policy in which the United States pledged to support global resistance to Soviet expansionism and is often cited as the outbreak of the Cold War. This had ramifications on the domestic front as the House Un-American Activities Committee began earnest investigations into the lives of those perceived to have communist sympathies or subversive lifestyles. Parsons was high on their list of targets. He had his security clearance revoked, effectively ending any opportunity for him to work in rocketry in the United States on the grounds of his sexual perversion and previous association with communist groups at Caltech. Under questioning, Parsons denied being a communist but took the opportunity to denounce Frank Malina, who had forced him out of his own company. Malina, too, had his clearance revoked.

Parsons was reduced to pumping gas, working as a car mechanic, and bootlegging nitroglycerine. Under the strain, his relationship with Cameron deteriorated, and she traveled to Mexico, where she stayed in an artist's commune. He regained an enthusiasm for the occult, hiring prostitutes with whom to perform sex magic workings. He had an astral projection that took him to Chorazin, a ruined city in Galilee, where, invoked by Babalon, he believed he had come to embody the Antichrist and thus completed the final part of the Babalon Working. He wrote a book titled *The Book of the Antichrist* in which he prophesied the overthrow of Abrahamic religions within nine years. Cameron returned from Mexico; they argued violently, and Parsons began divorce proceedings.

Parsons was offered a job though the American Technion Society to work on the rocket program for the newly formed state of Israel. Parsons was intrigued, not least because his astral travels had recently led him to the country. The Red Scare began to close its net on American society, and Parsons hoped to emigrate to Israel to work on their rocket program. Before he could go, he was dragged in once more by the FBI on suspicion of espionage and selling state secrets to Israel, while the company that hired him was blacklisted for links to the Soviet government. He was acquitted in 1951 by the US Attorney, but the FBI responded by making the revocation of his security clearance permanent.

Broke and desperate for cash, he formed a company to make pyrotechnic effects and explosive squibs for the Hollywood movie industry and took a job once again manufacturing chemicals. He managed to reconcile with Cameron, and they moved to a house right next to the former Parsonage. They began throwing parties again and wrote poetry together. They were the subject of endless police attention and FBI surveillance so they planned to move to Mexico, where Parsons hoped to work on the Mexican rocket program, which he believed might offer him a way into Israel where he and Cameron could settle down and he would be able to develop his rocketry in peace.

On June 17, 1952, he received an urgent order for a batch of special effects explosives for a film, and he set about creating them in his home laboratory. He and Cameron were due to leave Pasadena for Mexico on the following day. While Parsons was working in the laboratory, there was a huge explosion. It tore off his right arm, broke his legs and left arm, punctured a hole in his face, and removed part of his scalp. When he was found Parsons was still conscious, but he could not be saved. He died from his injuries in the ambulance on the way to the hospital, aged thirty-seven. His beloved mother, upon hearing the news, took a fatal barbiturate overdose.

Parsons's death went down in the official records as an accident. According to the police report, he had dropped volatile chemicals, causing an explosion that triggered a chain reaction of further explosions of the other chemicals stored in his lab. While Forman accepted this explanation, others protested strongly that such an amateurish mistake was extremely unlikely in the safety conscious and experienced Parsons. An unused syringe of morphine was also found at the scene, which the police suggested was evidence that he was intoxicated. Upon reviewing the scene, a colleague from the Bermite Powders Company insisted that the blast could have only come from beneath, suggesting an assassination. Other friends, including founder of the Agape Lodge, Wilfrid Smith, believed that his death was a suicide, citing longstanding depression. Cameron was convinced that Parsons was murdered by anti-Zionists opposed to his potential engagement by the Israeli government. Others speculated that eccentric billionaire Howard Hughes was responsible, in revenge for Parsons's theft of documents during a brief employment at his aviation company. Other more esoteric theories abounded that he was attempting the creation of a homunculus—or that he had taken a step too far into black magic and finally received his comeuppance. Strangest of all was the suggestion that Parsons's death was the fulfillment of a premonition for seven years in the future he had made just after the Babalon working: "Babalon is incarnate upon the earth today awaiting the proper hour of her manifestation. And in that day my work will be accomplished and I shall be blown away up on the breath of the father even as it is prophecied."[14] In fact, the explosion happened six and a half years after the 1946 working. His ashes were scattered by Cameron in the Mojave Desert, where he had done so many of his experiments. She spent many years trying to communicate with him on the astral plane and would go on to cultivate a remarkable magical life of her own.

To this day JPL—now an important part of NASA—is often referred to as "Jack Parsons Lives" among its employees. His contributions to rocketry are among the most significant in American history, although this fact has not always been fully recognized by the scientific establishment. His contributions to magic are more secure, and he is revered as one of the most important figures in Thelema. Kenneth Grant, who had apprenticed to Crowley and supported Spare's work, noted that immediately after the completion of the first part of the Babalon Working, an era known as the "Flying Saucer Trap" commenced, where sightings of UFOs (including many above the Parsonage) spiked enormously: "Parsons opened a door and something flew in," said Grant.[15] Parsons's legacy is one of a great voyager of both outer and inner space.

> *I hight Don Quixote, I live on peyote,*
> *marijuana, morphine and cocaine.*
> *I never know sadness, but only a madness*
> *that burns at the heart and the brain.*
> *I see each charwoman, ecstatic, inhuman,*
> *angelic, demonic, divine.*
> *Each wagon a dragon, each beer mug a flagon*
> *that brims with ambrosial wine.*[16]
>
> JACK PARSONS

SELECTED WORKS BY JACK PARSONS CONCERNING SEX MAGIC

Jack Parsons's writing is not widely published at this time but can be found online.

1946 ✦ *Freedom Is a Two-Edged Sword*

1946 ✦ "The Birth of Babalon"

9

William S. Burroughs
(1914–1997)

Crowley is not the only figure included in this book to appear on the album cover of *Sgt. Pepper's Lonely Hearts Club Band*. While Crowley stares ominously down from the back left, a slim-faced figure peers out from the center, partly obscuring Marilyn Monroe. He is looking down his nose in the direction of comedian Issy Bonn and Beatle George Harrison.

His appearance, as with many others on the album cover, further cemented his place as an icon of the counterculture, although William S. Burroughs's place in this particular history was already assured, Beatles or no Beatles. Upon his death, obituaries concentrated heavily on the rebellious events of his life, his supreme hipness, and his unrelenting assault on, by that time, safely dead and buried social mores. It ought to be noted that Burroughs was, above all, a writer and major contributor to the canon of American literature. There are plenty of books available discussing his literary legacy, but he was just as important a figure in the history of the modern occult as he was in literature.

Burroughs was born February 5, 1914, into a wealthy family in St. Louis, Missouri. Both of his parents, Mortimer Perry and Laura Hammon Burroughs (née Lee), were of English ancestry, and his mother claimed descent from the commander of the Confederate States army, Robert E. Lee. His paternal grandfather invented a popular adding machine, and his father inherited the business, forming the Burroughs Adding Machine Company in 1904, which quickly became the largest of its kind in the United States.

The Burroughs were happily married and seemingly devoted to one another and their children, and the household employed a gardener, maid, cook, and nanny. The family nevertheless kept at a distance from the WASP bourgeois society of St. Louis, unimpressed by the affectations and pretensions of that social class—while they themselves were disdained as lacking sophistication. Billy, as they called their youngest child, was met with particular wariness, being gangly, pale, and morbid as well as suffering from various sinus problems, a penchant for high jinks and general uncouthness. He withdrew from his schoolmates who had shunned the oddball figure who was set among them, and he yielded to his natural state of introversion. He formed an especially close bond with his Welsh nanny, Mary Evans.

Versed in the folk witchcraft of Wales and various curses, Burroughs got his first taste of the occult from "Nursey," as he called his nanny when throwing a screaming fit demanding to be with her on her days off. She taught him a simple curse that he kept for the rest of his life: *"Trip and stumble, Slip and fall, Down the stairs, And hit the wall,"* and Burroughs claimed that she was able to cause a fire to light by simply saying, "It will be lit."[1] Evans gave Burroughs his first taste of opium, he claimed, and then, many years later in the depths of a long process of psychoanalysis by Dr. Federn (a student of Sigmund Freud), Burroughs remembered something else about Nursey. His recollection was vague and scattered, but Evans had taken four-year-old Billy with her on a day out to meet her boyfriend, a veterinary surgeon. The setting was unclear; Burroughs remembered a wood, perhaps, and some words, "Come on Billy, it won't hurt you," a slap to the head, a dream that Nursey threatened to pull out his eyes if he told on her, his brother asking him if he should tell.[2] The boyfriend, with his pants down had screamed. Burroughs had bitten the boyfriend's penis, after being forced to perform oral sex on him. A couple of months later, Nursey was sent away, never to be spoken of again. Billy was indifferent to the news.

He attended the John Burroughs (no relation) School in St. Louis, where his interest in writing developed, and he wrote his first piece of fiction, *Autobiography of a Wolf,* identifying himself as the tragic wolf who was, in the end, mauled to death by a bear. In 1929 his mother sent him to a prestigious high school in Los Alamos, New Mexico, where boys were encouraged to exercise their adventurous spirits in a progressive educational atmosphere. The family had astutely sold their shares in the Burroughs Adding Machine Company for almost $300,000 just before the Wall Street Crash, and Laura wanted her son to attend a school in a drier climate to help his sinuses. The Ranch School in Los Alamos seemed a perfect fit, specializing in transforming frail and slender rich boys into society's next virile generation of eminent men. Burroughs hated it, although he excelled at shooting, chemistry (in spite of almost blowing his left hand off in one experiment), and literature. He was again isolated and became a troublesome student, once throwing a homemade bomb through the window of his principal's office (it failed to detonate). In March 1930, just after his sixteenth birthday, his mother came to visit and took Billy and a friend into Santa Fe, allowing the boys to wander about the city. He stopped outside a pharmacy and told his friend he wanted to get some chloral hydrate—otherwise known as knockout drops—"to see what it's like."[3] The chemist asked why he would want such a thing, and Billy said, deadpan, "to commit suicide." A few days later, Billy was seen by his schoolmates being stretchered hurriedly across the sports field after taking a near fatal dose of the drug. Once recovered, he found himself in serious trouble with his father and principal, but it was an important first endeavor into the world of psychically altering substances.

He had also fallen into obsessive love with another boy at the school, who he convinced to masturbate with him under a sheet, but who thereafter turned against Billy in a campaign of cruel bullying. Heartbroken and persecuted, he wrote down the details of his lust and trauma in a journal that was then discovered, turning his life into a living hell; homosexuality was still, of course, a serious crime in pre-war America. He appealed to his mother's pity and convinced her to allow him to finish school at a college preparatory high school in St. Louis. All he'd learned at Los Alamos, he said, was a hatred of horses: "A dying artefact."[4] Curiously, in 1943 the school was requisitioned by the military at the suggestion of Robert Oppenheimer, who remembered Los Alamos as a place of extraordinary peacefulness and beauty. The Manhattan Project would unfold in Burroughs's old classrooms, and the serenity would be shattered by the Trinity test on July 16, 1945—the day even demons realized that it was they who ought to fear humanity, and not the reverse.

Burroughs enrolled at Harvard in 1932, and he found it no more enlightening than any of his previous educational institutions. He seems to have lost his troublemaking streak, and he spent his time there in the background, joining no clubs or societies, and again finding himself the outcast among the energetic and healthy East Coast prep school boys who dominated the place. He took an interest in Communism, which was fashionable at the time as half the world sank into economic depression and the surrealist movement in Europe embraced the ideals of Marx. In his English studies he took particular interest in the Romantic-era English writers Thomas de Quincey and Samuel Taylor Coleridge, both notorious for their use of opium as a generator of artistic output. Otherwise, Burroughs moped quietly about the lack of sexual experiences on offer and sat in his room playing with his .32 revolver and pet ferret.

In 1936 his parents sent him to Europe for a year where he planned to study medicine in Vienna, but suffering from syphilis and unenthused by the state of Austria following the Anschluss with Hitler's Germany, he returned to the United States with Ilse Klapper, a middle-aged Jewish woman he had taken as his wife in an act of benevolence, allowing her to settle in New York and escape the simmering anti-Semitic atmosphere in Germanic Europe.

Burroughs continued studying psychology at Harvard and Columbia for four more years, leaving in 1939 without completing a class. He had his first real love affair with Jack Anderson, a sadomasochistic entanglement with Burroughs firmly in the "maso" role as Anderson taunted him by bringing other lovers home and letting Burroughs hear them having sex through the thin walls of their shared apartment. In response, Burroughs cut off the tip of the pinkie finger of his left hand to demonstrate to Anderson the ferocity of his passion. The incident prompted his mother to commit him to the Bellevue psychiatric ward. Later this episode would provide him with an escape from service in the Second World War—Burroughs enlisted in the US Army following the bombing of Pearl Harbor but was rejected from the officer class. His mother used this previous episode of mental illness to secure a disability discharge for her son, meaning he would not have to join the war as regular infantry.

Burroughs moved to Chicago, where he worked briefly as an exterminator, then in 1942 to New York, where he began to gain confidence and write more. Here he met the other two heavyweights of the Holy Trinity of the Beat Generation: Allen Ginsberg and Jack Kerouac. He moved in with Kerouac and Ginsberg, mentoring the younger men and introducing them to psychoanalysis. He also began a love affair with their other housemate, Joan Vollmer. Burroughs and Vollmer shared a mutual appetite for narcotics, and they both became heavy users of morphine, heroin, Benzedrine, and alcohol. Both fell afoul of the law due to their addictions: Burroughs was sentenced to go home for four months, while Vollmer was sent for a stay in Bellevue after a series of benzo-induced psychotic episodes. At the end of 1946, Burroughs rescued his lover and took her to a Times Square hotel where, in a blaze of drug taking, they conceived a child, William Burroughs Jr.

Burroughs and Vollmer began to live an itinerant lifestyle, moving between continents, staying ahead of the authorities, searching for new drug experiences. Burroughs now had a monthly $200 stipend put in his account by his family (equivalent to about $3,000 today), meaning he was free to live without the albatross of employment around his neck.

In 1949, Burroughs invested some of this newfound wealth in his first practical experiments with something that is part sex magic, part occult science—he built an orgone accumulator. The concept of orgones was developed by Dr. Wilhelm Reich in the 1930s. Reich coined the word *orgone* as a portmanteau of the German words for *orgasm* and *organism*. Orgones, according to Reich, are a form of biological energy that can be harnessed and used to beneficial effect by removing electrical blockages in human beings and thus enhancing sexual energy. The orgone accumulator is an ordinary box big enough for a man to sit inside on a chair: a layer of wood, a layer of metal, and another layer of wood gather orgones from the atmosphere and hold them captive long enough for the human body to absorb more than a usual share. According to Reich, orgones are vibratory atmospheric atoms of the life principle, and people get cancer because they run out of orgones. He built orgone accumulators and began to ship them to the United States, but before long his message of sexual liberation (he is credited with coining the phrase "the sexual revolution") won him an army of enemies in his own field of psychiatry, as well as in politics. His business was shut down, and he was persecuted by the authorities, winding up in prison where he died in uncertain and controversial circumstances in 1956, aged sixty.

Burroughs's orgone accumulator was put together on a farm in Texas. It was an eight-foot-high wooden box lined with galvanized iron. Inside was an old ice box, and the participant would get inside wrapped in a towel and pull a lever to bring down a steel sheet. It was essentially a kind of Faraday cage, which was used to block electromagnetic fields. After a while Burroughs, or whomever he invited to try it, would exit, "usually with a hard-on." He testified that it had a "definite sexual effect."[5] He also built a handheld version of the accumulator that he put directly on his penis and found that it could bring him to orgasm without any other movement on his part—an invention he attributed to a party trick for which Jean Cocteau was notorious. Cocteau would strip naked at a party, lie down, and make himself ejaculate without using his hands, merely by force of will. In Kerouac's seminal (no pun intended) novel *On The Road,* Kerouac, in the guise of Sal Paradise, visits Old Bull Lee (a character modeled after Burroughs) and witnesses him injecting heroin and using his orgone box: "Say, why don't you fellows try my orgone accumulator? Put some juice in your bones. I always rush up and take off ninety miles an hour for the nearest whorehouse, hor-hor-hor!" This was his laugh when he wasn't really laughing.

Burroughs and Vollmer found their way to Mexico (after a drug bust that left Burroughs facing hard time in the notorious Angola prison in Louisiana), where Vollmer's frustration at Burroughs's lack of sexual interest in her led her to drink heavily. Off heroin, his libido returned, and he was much more interested in the cheap and plentiful Mexican boys. Mexico suited Burroughs in other ways, too: gun laws were almost nonexistent, the police had little interest in bothering a wealthy white man about anything other than the occasional paltry bribe, and morphine was readily available at rock-bottom prices.

In 1951—some three years before Aldous Huxley published his ground-breaking treatise on the entheogenic power of psychedelic drugs, *The Doors of Perception*—Burroughs and a college student he had befriended named Lewis Marker left Mexico City for Puyo, Ecuador, on a quest to discover the miracle drug yage, or as it's more commonly known in the modern Western world, ayahuasca. The expedition failed in its primary objective, but Burroughs returned determined to uncover the secret of the mysterious Amazonian drug. In Mexico, however, he discovered Vollmer in a state of advanced Benzedrine addiction and alcoholism, and she had apparently been having an affair. She began to be openly antagonistic toward Burroughs, mocking him in front of their friends. One evening, after heavy drinking and drug taking, she challenged Burroughs to shoot a highball glass off the top of her head in the style of William Tell. An overconfident Burroughs agreed, and missed, killing his twenty-eight-year-old common-law wife after shooting her in the head.

Even the lenient Mexican police couldn't ignore a domestic homicide, and Burroughs spent two weeks in jail while his lawyer worked on coaching witnesses and bribing officials, trying to get Burroughs off the hook for murder. The couples' two children, William Jr. and Julie, were sent to live with the Burroughs and Vollmer grandparents, respectively, and Burroughs reported to Mexico City jail once a week for a year while the case was being resolved. His prominent lawyer then shot and killed a trespasser on his land and was called to face murder charges himself, prompting Burroughs to drop everything and flee back to the United States. Fortunately, the state of Louisiana hadn't filed a warrant for his arrest for the drug charges that had caused him to leave in the first place. Burroughs was so traumatized by the events that he considered it the catalyst for his entire writing career, as well as the moment that his mystical conception of the universe took on a new and dark shade: "I am forced to the appalling conclusion that I would have never become a writer but for Joan's death . . . so the death of Joan brought me into contact with the invader, the Ugly Spirit, and maneuvered me into a lifelong struggle, in which I had no choice except to write my way out."[6]

Junk-sick and distressed, Burroughs set out once more on his quest for yage in 1953. His adventures began in Panama (where he was held up awhile to "have his piles out," staying at the aptly named Hotel Colon), and he had the good fortune to meet a fellow Harvard man, the renowned botanist and expert on hallucinogenic flora, Richard Evans Schultes. Schultes, although dubious about his unconventional companion, agreed to set out on the 1,000-mile trek to Colombia with Burroughs in search of ayahuasca. The adventure was recorded by Burroughs in letters he sent back to Ginsberg, published in 1963 by Lawrence Ferlinghetti as *The Yage Letters*.

Schultes had tried ayahuasca, but he reported only experiencing mild hallucinations and no visions. He also told Burroughs about the Indian belief that the entheogenic concoction (the Greek word *entheogenic* meaning literally "generating God within") allowed the user to contact the spirit world and communicate with it. Schultes sent Burroughs alone along the Putumayo River to Mocoa, where he met the *brujos,* magicians who would prepare the oily, bitter, black liquid. In the hut of an old brujo, Burroughs drank down the ayahuasca preparation and very soon doubled over in a wave of intense nausea accompanied by ferocious flashing blue lights around him. Barely able to stand, he dragged himself outside to vomit violently. He found it impossible to come down off the drug and had to take barbiturates for relief of the effects. He was not deterred, however, and decided to take it again, in a smaller dose. In spite of the ill effects, which he described as "an insane overwhelming rape of the senses,"[7] he believed he had discovered the drug for which he'd always been looking. "This is the most powerful drug I have ever experienced," he wrote to Ginsberg. "There is a definite sense of space time travel that seems to shake the room."[8] His subsequent trips were more serene and gave him the access to the god-space in his mind for which he had hoped. He also contributed an important piece of knowledge to the Western understanding of the composition of ayahuasca, learning from one brujo that a plant called chacruna needs to be added to the preparation of the ayahuasca vine. The chacruna functions as an activator for the dimethyltryptamine (DMT) in ayahuasca, releasing the full potential of its hallucinogenic properties. Another ingredient, harmeline (once known as telepathine due to its supposed power to induce telepathy), is an alkaloid present in the human pineal gland, or third eye (according to Blavatsky). The hallucinations can include intense out-of-body experiences, astral travel, sexual experiences, and atavistic memory surges allowing the user to access a sort of common phylogenetic experience shared by all humans. In fact, what is so curious about the ayahuasca experience is the frequency with which users report very similar visions and states, something not common at all with other psychedelics that tend to be highly individualized. Ayahuasca's deep interaction with the pineal gland, considered more acute than any other drug, perhaps has the capacity to bring the user to a primal state of serenity and loss of conscious awareness that is shared across the genome (as Freud proposed was theoretically possible). Practitioners of modern magic will perhaps recognize, if not the effects, then the theoretical objectives of achieving this state, as through the use of meditation, ritual, and evocation (or invocation) of apparent demonic entities. A magician may equally find themselves confronting visions gathered from some profound and atavistic part of the subconscious.

Returning home with a suitcase full of yage, Burroughs headed straight for New York City and Ginsberg, intent on introducing him to the drug and commencing a perfect spiritual and sexual romance. Ginsberg, while keen to try ayahuasca, was a hardened New Yorker and had little time for Burroughs's medieval romantic ideals. They parted ways and Burroughs left New York following the publication of his first novel, *Junky,* with no particular destination in mind. He ended up in Tangier in 1954, which was a designated international zone since 1923 (the years of WWII apart) and administered jointly by Spain, France, and Britain. The perfect storm of Eastern exoticism and Western liberalism meant the city became a magnet for assorted British and American writers, spies, and artists. It was also notorious as a hive of male homosexual activity, and the city lived under a largely French legal culture—France having no prohibitions against male homosexuality between 1791 and 1960. At first Burroughs found the local men aggressive and uninteresting and not to his taste, and he felt the same way about the local hashish. But he soon adapted, finding a steady and handsome young Spanish lover named Kiki and becoming hooked on Eukadol, which fed him paranoid hallucinations that frequently left him lying hysterical on the floor of his room after rereading something he had just written.

In Tangier he worked on a collection of writings he called *Interzone,* some commercial travel articles, and the passages of prose that would come to form *Naked Lunch,* his most acclaimed work. Burroughs struggled to make any friends in Tangier and didn't find Kiki or the procession of young Spanish boys who visited his hotel able to provide the intellectual companionship he craved. He did meet two men who would become important friends in later life—one of his literary idols,

Paul Bowles, and the English artist and writer Brion Gysin, whom Burroughs would call "the only man I ever respected."[9]

For now, though, Burroughs remained just another client at Gysin's popular restaurant, 1001 Nights, famous for its employ of the musical group the Master Magicians of Joujouka, who would prove a great influence upon Brian Jones of the Rolling Stones, among others.

In 1957 his loneliness was alleviated by the arrival of Kerouac and Ginsberg in Tangier. They had come to help edit the unwieldy manuscript for *Naked Lunch,* but Kerouac was repelled by Tangier and unsettled by Burroughs's erratic behavior and returned to the United States. Ginsberg found a boyfriend and helped his friend slog through the editing, enthused by the writing Burroughs had produced.

Once the editing was finished, Ginsberg then left for Paris, and Burroughs returned to his disheveled state: "I lived in one room in the Native Quarter of Tangier. I had not taken a bath in a year nor changed my clothes or removed them except to stick a needle every hour in the fibrous grey wooden flesh of terminal addiction. I never cleaned or dusted the room. Empty ampule boxes and garbage piled to the ceiling. Light and water long since turned off for non-payment. I did absolutely nothing. I could look at the end of my shoe for eight hours."[10]

Eventually, Ginsberg was followed to Paris by both Burroughs and Gysin, and all three—among other notables including Gregory Corso, Peter Orlovsky, and Harold Norse—ended up staying in a "class 13" (the lowest) flophouse hotel at 9 Rue Gît-le-Coeur in the 6th arrondissement, which became known as the Beat Hotel. The rent was cheap and sometimes payable in artworks, and residents were allowed by the proprietor Madame Rachou to decorate their rooms as they pleased. It was here in the spring of 1958 that Gysin came across what he thought of as a Dada technique, the cut-up. Slicing into some newspapers that he'd put down to protect a table while preparing a drawing, he realized that applying this technique to writing would emulate the way painters were forming new images. Cut-up consisted of cutting out bits of text from a linear narrative and rearranging them selectively to form an entirely new, surreal narrative. He inducted Burroughs into this new technique, and Burroughs then applied the technique to *Naked Lunch* in an act that would revolutionize the artistic meaning and value of American literature.

Gysin and Burroughs considered cut-up to be both a psychological and magical technique. Burroughs explained that it represented the cut-up experienced in every day modern life: "As soon as you walk down the street . . . or look out the window, turn a page, turn on the TV—your awareness is being cut: that sign in the shop window, that car passing by, the sound of the radio . . . Life IS a cut-up."[11] Furthermore, Burroughs explicitly stated that he was open to seeing cut-up as a form of mediumship, saying, "Cut ups often come through as code messages with special meaning for the cutter. Table tapping? Perhaps."[12] Burroughs felt able to destabilize language, which he believed was a kind of virus, and could access a more profound nature of language, an objective of both medieval magicians and Spare. He thought of cut-up as overthrowing the "once upon a time" convention of narrative and introducing "once in future time"[13] as a kind of scrambled prophetic dream. *Naked Lunch* has become notorious—among other things—for having forecast such late-century phenomena as AIDS, radical Islam, liposuction, LSD, the crack epidemic, and autoerotic asphyxiation. (Though Naglowska was teaching the erotic and magical powers of hanging in Montparnasse more than thirty years before Burroughs arrived, Burroughs brought it to a far more prevalent erotic current than ever before, with this famous scene in *Naked Lunch:* "Green sparks explode behind his eyes and sweet toothache pain shoots through his neck down the spine to the groin, contracting the body in spasms of delight. His whole body squeezes out through his cock. A final spasm throws a great spit of semen across the red screen like a shooting star.")

Burroughs, now clean thanks to his discovery of apomorphine, regained his sexual energy once more, and this time he was able to apply it to trance states and magical workings. The Beat Hotel was a magical place, with all the inhabitants experimenting with mirror scrying, rituals, and conjuring. Gysin built his Dream Machine, a cylinder of carefully cut card surrounding a lightbulb and set upon a turntable. As it spins, the Dream Machine projects patterns of light onto the closed eyes of the user, creating visions and light play upon the canvas of the eyelid. As Gysin described it: "one sees all of ancient and modern abstract art with eyes closed."[14]

Burroughs used the machine to generate images that he then wrote down, forming a large part of his writing in that period. Later, Kurt Cobain also became an avid user of the Gysin Dream Machine; Gysin had hoped to see one in every living room in America in place of a TV set, but this proved rather ambitious.

In a trance, Gysin managed to give his friend a little psychic relief, telling Burroughs that it was the previously mentioned "Ugly Spirit" that caused him to shoot low and kill his wife. Burroughs came to believe in a more traditional form of dark magic, whereby an individual could become possessed by an external force, as opposed to the modern conception whereby all forces, whether dark or light, are generated within.

Naked Lunch finally found a publisher (the infamous Olympia Press in Paris) after great effort from Ginsberg to bring the novel into print, and, in 1960, Burroughs moved to London where he managed to stay clean for several years. He took journalism jobs to supplement his income while his reputation as a dangerous avant-garde writer slowly grew across university campuses. There he met L. Ron Hubbard, who had founded Scientology a few years before, and discovered they shared an interest in the life and works of Crowley. Burroughs briefly joined the Scientology movement, but he quickly saw through Hubbard's scheme. It would prove more useful to him as a money-spinner when he began writing exposés on Scientology for *Mayfair* magazine (a British *Playboy* equivalent) than it would as a form of spiritual enlightenment. He also developed his interests in the occult, studying Mayan and ancient Egyptian civilization, as well as medieval magic, Thelema, and the O.T.O. Much of what he learned here would resurface in his later writing, such as *Cities of the Red Night and The Wild Boys,* which contain detailed descriptions of orgiastic gay sex magic rituals.

About this same time, Burroughs agreed to take responsibility for his thirteen-year-old son, William, who was living out the early part of a life that would be beset with tragedy and addiction. Burroughs brought his son to Tangier in an attempt to rebuild the relationship with his son. On this trip, Burroughs met and befriended Timothy Leary, the psychologist and advocate of psychedelic drugs, even though he remained skeptical of Leary's unscientific methods. On this visit, Burroughs, Gysin, and the eighteen-year-old English actor Michael Portman attempted to perform the six-month-long Abramelin ritual. Gysin, Burroughs, and Portman were no more successful than Crowley had been in his attempt at Boleskine, although Portman became a fanatical devotee of Crowley and later in life took to scourging himself with a studded leather belt screaming, "Victory to Aleister Crowley!"[15]

Burroughs introduced his son to marijuana, but after young William was victim to several sexual assaults by the natives of Tangier, he sent him back home again. Their relationship never recovered, and William ended up despising his father. He suffered a mental breakdown in his twenties, believing he had shot his best friend dead (the friend survived), and his life plunged into a spiral of severe alcoholism. At a dinner with his father in 1976 the twenty-seven-year-old began heaving blood uncontrollably and was diagnosed as suffering from cirrhosis of the liver. He happened to be in one of only two hospitals in the United States that performed liver transplants in 1976, although the survival rate was below 30 percent. William was fortunate, and the operation was a success, but he continued to drink, and in 1981 he stopped taking his anti-rejection drugs and died, aged thirty-three.

By 1966, *Naked Lunch* had made Burroughs famous, and the long-running obscenity trial sparked by the book (the last of its kind in the United States) had ended in his favor, after attracting heavyweight authors such as Norman Mailer to speak in his defense, and a swathe of media coverage. While in London, Burroughs undertook some more magical experimentation, some of it quite unconventional. Burroughs was a fan of Dion Fortune's *Psychic Self Defense,* and utilized it to protect himself from his great fear—demonic possession. He also maintained a dream diary throughout his life that he was able to use to master dream control and astral projection techniques. He had always believed in what he called a magical universe and also followed Crowley in seeing a world in which all action is fundamentally motivated by will. Furthermore, he believed in and had witnessed the powers of curses and possession. He and Gysin both reported witnessing powerful black magic in Morocco, Burroughs saying, "Now anyone who has lived for any time in countries like Morocco where magic is widely practiced has probably seen a curse work. I have."[16] Burroughs saw not only a magical universe, but also a universe that was at war and in which dark and light forces clashed violently. Those placed in the field of battle were wise to struggle against being overwhelmed by either side, of any shape of terrifying psychological and spiritual forces. He decided to demonstrate his abilities as a magician in what may be one of the first acts of anti-gentrification in London's history. Already annoyed at what he considered an expensive, conservative, and increasingly enfeebled Britain ("Swinging London" had done nothing but irritate him), he launched an astonishing magical attack against a coffee shop in Soho. To be precise, it was the Moka Bar, London's first ever Italian espresso café, opened in 1953 to great interest among the city's wealthy and cosmopolitan circles. By 1972 coffee shops were springing up all throughout Soho, and Burroughs began to feel as if his home territory—previously a seedy land of "Dilly Boys" (male prostitutes), dandies, hookers, radicals, and starving artists—was being invaded by the bourgeoisie. Rents and utilities were driving upward and face-lifting Soho, and Burroughs, following an altercation with "a snarling counterman,"[17] decided the Moka Bar must pay.

To accomplish this retribution, he used a magical technique that blended Crowley, North African curses, and his own cut-up magic; something he had previously deployed successfully against the Church of Scientology. He calmly tape-recorded and photographed the mundane events of a morning in the café, then returned the following day to play back the tape and place photographs of the previous day around. His theory was that the superimposition of yesterday's events on top of the present would "pull them out of their time position."[18] The tapes were magical weapons with which he could attack the "control system" of the vicinity, transferring the power of the normal passage of present time to himself, as he became a local god, able to manipulate and disrupt. It seemed to work: "They are seething in there," he wrote in the "Vaduz Archive," a vast collection of his notes and journals. "I have them and they know it." In October of the same year, the Moka Bar sold and became a Queens Snack Bar.[19]

About this time, he was visited at his flat on Duke Street by a young musician who went by the name Genesis P-Orridge. "Tell me about magic," was P-Orridge's first question to the man who had, at this point, become known as the godfather of counterculture. Burroughs poured them both a large glass of Jack Daniels and put on the television. An episode of *The Man from U.N.C.L.E.* was on. He flipped between the channels and then used his Sony tape recorder to play back prerecorded cut-ups of other television shows. P-Orridge later said, "I was already being taught. What Bill explained to me then was pivotal to the unfolding of my life and art: Everything is recorded. If it is recorded, it can be edited. If it can be edited then the order, sense, meaning and direction are as arbitrary and personal as the agenda and/or person editing. This is magick."[20]

Burroughs moved back to the United States once and for all in 1974, first heading to New York to teach for a while at the behest of Ginsberg, who was worried about Burroughs's drug consumption; then in 1981 he moved to Lawrence, Kansas. There he was able to indulge himself once more in some of his other passions: cats, snakes, and weapons. He slept with his revolver and always carried a custom-made sword cane. In spite of this, the opportunity to take stock led Burroughs to fall into a period of deep despair and depression as he surveyed the wreckage of his personal life. He began painting, developing a technique of shooting cans of spray paint with his shotgun so the contents spattered onto a canvas. Between 1981 and 1987 he published his first novels since 1971, the *Red Night Trilogy*, which received mixed reviews. Burroughs went through a kind of spiritual awakening during these years as he tried to haul himself out of depression and regret. While remaining as acerbic and sepulchral as ever before, he developed a warmth and generosity that had been absent for many years. He surrounded himself with younger musicians and artists including Patti Smith, Michael Stipe, Nick Cave, and Cobain (who enthusiastically tried out Burroughs's orgone box) and seemed to gather something from their energy—while they, of course, learned a great deal from the wild old man in a three-piece suit. He collaborated with the filmmaker Gus van Sant, who later filmed a short based on Burroughs's Do Easy magical method of making life's small movements as efficient and precise as possible.

In 1991 he required triple-bypass surgery, an event that caused him to quit smoking and, evidently, contemplate death. In spite of his earlier proclamation to Ginsberg that death was "a gimmick. It's the time-birth-death gimmick. Can't go on much longer, too many people are wising up,"[21] he seemed to want to make peace with himself. In 1992 he went back to his childhood home with Ginsberg and five other friends to perform a magical ritual designed to exorcise the Ugly Spirit once and for all. They dug a hole with a fire pit in the middle and prayed for several hours as they sweat the evil out of their bodies—even putting the hot coals in their mouths to swallow the evil spirits and presumably pass them out later. He considered the operation a success, and in the following year he was initiated into the chaos magic organization the Illuminates of Thanateros.

He filled his last years with cats and journal entries (as well as somewhat uncharacteristic appearances in TV commercials for Nike and the Gap, Inc.). He continued to rail against the same thing he'd been railing against from the outset—the eternal depths of man's ignorance. But he also seems to have learned a kind of compassion, perhaps imbibed from Eastern philosophy, an understanding that ignorance is, in fact, the greatest suffering. He died of a heart attack, aged eighty-three, on August 2, 1997. His final journal entry read: "Love? What is it? Most natural painkiller what there is. Love."[22]

SELECTED WORKS OF WILLIAM S. BURROUGHS CONCERNING SEX MAGIC

William S. Burroughs's books are available from a variety of publishers.

1961 ✦ *The Soft Machine*

1981 ✦ *Cities of the Red Night*

1985 ✦ *The Adding Machine: Selected Essays*

10
Marjorie Cameron
(1922–1995)

The death of Parsons in 1952 was far from the end of Marjorie Cameron's magical life, and Babalon, as Parsons had dubbed her, was still grieving for her husband following his suspicious passing, when she propelled herself into a unique place among the American artistic and cinematic avant-garde of the mid-twentieth century.

She was born in Belle Plaine, Iowa, on April 23, 1922. The Camerons were an archetypal lower-middle-class small-town American family: her father, Hill Cameron, had a decent job as a machinist at Belle Plain's major employer, the Roundhouse, a steam train repair company. Her mother, Carrie, was born a Ridenour, a German-Dutch family of old Iowa stock. Marjorie was raised partially by her tuberculosis-stricken and dogmatic Catholic aunt Nell, who insisted that the Camerons' first-born child be given a suitably religious name, which she hoped might guide the girl toward a conventual life as a bride of Christ. The young couple acquiesced to Nell's demands and Christened their daughter Marjorie Elizabeth. Within a year of Marjorie's birth, Nell had died of tuberculosis and the young girl was given the aunt's former room as her own. The haunting presence of her pious aunt gave the imaginative young girl plenty of fuel for nightmares and unpleasant hallucinations. She complained of ghostly white horses riding through her room at night and believed that she could see Hell at the bottom of a well that sat in the backyard of her maternal grandfather's house. Belle Plaine was a small, prosperous, and close-knit community. The clapboard houses were attractive and comfortable. The schools were well maintained, the streets leafy, and even the advent of the Great Depression did little to dent the fruits of a hardworking, Christian, and altogether pleasant little town. This utopian state of affairs, as H. P. Lovecraft, David Lynch, and other artistic luminaries of the American Century noticed, somehow concealed a deep, intangible horror. The sensitive, as Cameron was, could do little but help notice this peculiar sensation of the weird that lurks under the surface of small-town middle America.

Cameron was an average student, although she excelled at drawing and painting. Aloof, yet popular, naturally good looking with red hair and pouting lips, free thinking, artistically minded, growing up in a dull environment where prohibition meant that even the release of juvenile experimentation with alcohol was near impossible, it would not be long before this particular recipe had Cameron in, as they used to call it, "trouble." Sexually aware at a young age, she was caught masturbating at the age of nine by her father, who responded by beating his daughter. By fourteen Cameron was sneaking out of her room at night to meet boys, running around the local cemetery, fulfilling her macabre and sexual fascinations at once. At fifteen, in terror, she confessed to her mother that she was pregnant. Carrie performed an incredibly dangerous but evidently successful home abortion on her daughter, keeping the incident secret from Hill Cameron and the local community.

When Cameron was seventeen her father took a new job at a munitions factory in nearby Davenport, profiting from the booming armaments industry as the United States geared up for its entry into the Second World War. Although hardly a metropolis, Davenport was a midsize city of about 70,000 inhabitants in 1940 when the Camerons arrived, a significantly larger place than the 1,000 or so population of Belle Plaine. The new environment was stimulating for Cameron, but as she went through her final year of high school, she was involved in a tragic event that revealed her passionate and dark sides. Her best friend, with whom Cameron had experimented romantically and sexually, killed herself following the death of her boyfriend. Cameron, traumatized by this, took an overdose of sleeping pills in an attempt to also end her own life, but it proved unsuccessful. Managing to graduate, she found a job as a display artist at the local department store, but perhaps motivated by the anguish and instability of her teenage years, in 1943 she joined the US Navy as the nation threw itself full-tilt into the most catastrophic conflict in human history.

While it goes without saying that women were not considered for active service by the 1940s US Navy, Cameron claims to have found herself operating in a very active role indeed on one occasion in her war service. After boot camp, she impressed her senior officers and was assigned work drafting military maps for the Joint Chiefs of Staff in Washington D.C., where she worked as the sole female in an office of men. Her artistic qualities utilized, one of Cameron's other attributes caught the eye of her superiors: her striking looks. Pale, slim, redheaded, and with bright blue eyes, she had also spent a large portion of her youth carefully studying the great Hollywood movie stars of the 1930s, saying, "Joan Crawford taught us how to walk into a room."[1] Her sex appeal was of military use, and she was deployed to seduce a man suspected of being the paymaster of the German American Bund, an organization founded in 1936 to promote National Socialism among German Americans. The identity of the suspect remains unknown, but Cameron was to bring him to a hotel where she would extract information from this figure in a honey trap. While it is impossible to speculate who exactly the US Naval Intelligence wanted to track, the position of paymaster for such a large and politically controversial organization narrows the field considerably, and it later became known that Walt Disney was not only a regular attendee of the Bund's meetings but also an alleged financial backer. Disney, known for his womanizing, would likely have found the advances of the twenty-two-year-old Cameron difficult to resist, but there Cameron never gave any further account of the event.

By the end of the war Cameron had become a conscientious

objector, dismayed at what she believed was a war being fought on behalf of vested interests. She was traumatized after being assigned a role in which she had to sort through the blood-spattered uniforms of dead American soldiers so that they could be re-appropriated for propaganda films; she would often find letters and mementoes giving the uniforms' former owners a stark reality. When her younger brother James, a tail gunner, was injured, she went AWOL, returning home to visit him in the hospital. When she got back to D.C., she was court-martialed for desertion and reassigned to a naval barracks, an experience she found depressing as she fell victim to bullying by a superior female officer jealous of Cameron's popularity with men—she began to fantasize about murdering the officer. In another harrowing experience, she was put on a troop train on a four-day ride to Washington D.C., the only female aboard among hundreds of survivors of the Guadalcanal Campaign, one of the bloodiest the Americans endured during the war. The losses suffered by the US Navy fighting the Japanese at Guadalcanal were hushed up so as not to damage public morale. Those on the train with Cameron, she recalled, were like shells, unable to look at her, with many simply staring silently at the ground for the duration.[2]

At the end of the war she was surprised to discover that her court-martial conviction had been erased from her record, and she was given an honorable discharge. Following this, a seemingly mundane shift in her father's career path would lead to the encounter that would radically alter her life and provide her with both an outlet for her artistic ambitions and a means of beginning to understand the complex fascinations of the sexual and paranormal worlds she had held since childhood. Hill Cameron was offered a job at Parsons's JPL, and so Cameron went with her family to their new home in Pasadena, California. Her plans were to join a boyfriend named Napoleon in New York, where they hoped to start a small advertising business together. Before she managed to organize her move to New York, she befriended a couple of people who were living in a huge mansion belonging to a "mad scientist" in the wealthiest part of town. The mansion was, of course, the Parsonage, and the mad scientist was Jack Parsons. Her curiosity was truly piqued, and Cameron was invited to come and visit so she could meet Parsons. In January 1946, she showed up with a bag of records and made herself at home, playing them on a record player, with no idea at all of what was really happening at the Parsonage. Parsons poked his head in, took a look at the visitor, and left again. On her next visit, Parsons proclaimed that he had found his elemental, the summoning of the Scarlet Woman had been a success, and that Cameron was the embodiment of Babalon, mother of harlots. Now unleashed, the elemental spirit Babalon's mission was to shatter the sexually repressive chains with which Christianity had bound the Western world for nearly two millennia. The first step in achieving this was for its physical form, as Cameron, to embark on an intense, sometimes fractious, but unrelentingly sexually powerful relationship with Parsons, and Cameron was more than willing. They spent two straight weeks in Parsons's bed—an antique piece of furniture that once belonged to Cesare Borgia.

Parsons was not the only resident of the Parsonage who instructed Cameron in her magical development. She became friends with Jane Wolfe, the silent movie star who had also been with Crowley at the Abbey of Thelema in the 1920s. She was inducted into the O.T.O. and began practicing sex magic, informed by the rituals of Thelema, with Parsons, although she still remained more curious about Thelema than devoted to it.

Cameron and Parsons married in October 1946 at San Juan Capistrano, and in the winter of that year, she traveled to Paris where she intended to pursue her artistic development by enrolling at l'Académie de la Grande Chaumière, the more radical and less structured rival school to the École des Beaux-Arts, and a school that has produced, among others, Balthus, Serge Gainsbourg, Alberto Giacometti, and Louise Bourgeois. She also intended to visit Crowley in England to plead her husband's case following Crowley's denouncement of his wayward O.T.O. prodigy. Before she could get there, the Great Beast had already died. On the voyage over, Cameron became convinced that secret service agents were keeping her under surveillance, looking to find out what business the young wife of an unruly rocket scientist might have traveling alone to Europe. The subsequent encirclement of Parsons by the authorities, and their possible direct role in his demise, demonstrate that Cameron's concerns were likely not entirely due to paranoia.

She found Paris "extreme and bleak"[3] and claims to have witnessed the ritual head shaving of a woman accused of *collaboration horizontale* (prostitutes and other women who had their heads publicly shaved for having had sex with the Nazi occupiers during the Vichy government). She befriended Juliette Greco, still a young café singer but who would go on to become a superstar of the bohemian left bank, friend of Jean-Paul Sartre and Boris Vian, drinking partner to Orson Welles, and Miles Davis's lover and smoky muse. Uncertain about Paris and still concerned she was being shadowed, she gave up on the idea of art school and fled to Lugano in Switzerland, staying at a convent. Things took a turn for the worse here, and Cameron described her experience as a "psychotic episode"[4] in which she found herself disheveled and naked in her room, growling at a mirror like a wolf. She telephoned Parsons and asked him to wire her some money so she could come home, her great adventure having been somewhat disastrous. On the way back, she was once again convinced that a tall, blond American man was following her every move.

At home, the House Un-American Activities Committee had just fired up, and Parsons's previous association with communist groups at Caltech ensured his name was on their watchlist. The Parsonage was raided by the police on several occasions, and the stress was taking its toll on Parsons, the other residents, and on Cameron. The stress was severe enough for her to develop catalepsy, as was detailed in the chapter on Parsons, and Parsons guided her into being able to use her seizures for astral projection.

Parsons was also anxious for Cameron to invest more time in her magical education. He instructed her in Gnosticism, tarot, and the Kabbalah and gave her stacks of literature including the works of Crowley and James Frazer's *The Golden Bough,* though he never told her the full extent of her role in the Babalon working. Their marriage was becoming fractious at times, particularly when Parsons was absent for long periods with work. Continuing to pursue art, Cameron stayed for a time in an artists' community in San Miguel de Allende, Mexico, where she first met artist and filmmaker Renate Druks. Cameron and Parsons had agreed the marriage would be sexually open, but both struggled to contain occasional bouts of jealousy, although things were generally more harmonious when they were in one another's physical presence, and it seems the sexual component remained very much alive.

Parsons was growing paranoid that his immense Babalon working had unleashed forces that were beyond his control. He wanted to pass on its secrets to his wife, as he feared he would be "blown away" once the work of Babalon was begun in earnest on this Earth.

After Parsons's shocking death, and her mother-in-law's subsequent suicide, Cameron headed straight to San Miguel de Allende. Harrowed by grief and fear for her future, she performed a blood ritual for the first time, gashing her arm in an attempt to shock herself into an altered reality in the hope of contacting Parsons in the beyond. She befriended a couple of young artists and set about Crowley's Bornless Ritual, his variant on the ancient Greco-Egyptian preliminary Invocation of the Goetia. Driven near-mad with grief, she was throwing all her magical and emotional energy into this complex ritual in the hope of contacting Parsons in the afterlife. The basic purpose of the ritual is to form a strong bond with heavenly powers so as to be well reinforced before beginning contact with the demons of the Goetia. To Crowley and the followers of the O.T.O., the heavenly power in question was the Holy Guardian Angel. From this ritual, Cameron received a new magical identity: Hilarion, also the name of one of Crowley's own Scarlet Women. Prior to his death, Parsons had begun using Hilarion as an another name for the entity Babalon, as well as being an intended feminine counterpart to his own magical identity of Belarion. Though she was not yet aware of her role as Babalon, it is strange and fitting that Cameron would adopt it then.

After two months in San Miguel de Allende, Cameron returned to Altadena, California, following an incident where she rode naked into a church on a white stallion in an act of blasphemous defiance—which led to her arrest and being forced to leave the town. Now in the darkest despair, she attempted suicide in an abandoned Altadena house she'd been living in. She recovered in the hospital and then moved in with a friend. Here she began a more earnest practice of witchcraft and the black arts, setting up an altar in her room. She finally opened Parsons's black box of secret papers and read through many of his old letters and writings, and in doing so she discovered the true nature of her role in the Babalon Working and that Parsons had really believed she was the embodiment of the goddess. He detailed the acts of sex magic he had performed in his mind while having sex with Cameron, and it was here she learned that he wanted to create a moonchild with Cameron.

Four months after Parsons's death, Cameron moved in with a new lover, Leroy Booth, but by the end of 1952, Cameron had moved back out again to squat in an abandoned house in Beaumont, a small village near Palm Springs. Just after her departure, Booth and his housemates were arrested for marijuana possession, following several raids on the property that were mainly inspired by the mixed-race makeup of the housemates (Booth was African American), which violated housing rules of the era. Alone again in this almost-deserted village, Cameron reached a high-point in her magical life. She lived without electricity and running water, but the night sky was perfectly clear, and she stayed up late UFO spotting, while in the day she disciplined herself into strict rituals and workings. She realized that she could succeed where both Crowley and Parsons had failed and that fulfilling the Babalon Working was her destiny—she was Babalon incarnate.

Her first step was to establish a sex magic group in Beaumont that she called the Children. Her boyfriend Booth was among its number, as were several old figures from the Parsonage. She divided the group into racial orders, and assigned them tarot suits: she and the other white women were the suit of Pentacles, while the four black men of the group were Wands, for example. On the solstices and equinoxes she organized sex magic rituals for the group. Her objective was to fulfill her responsibility in creating a moonchild with Parsons, and she believed the child should represent Horus, who she saw as a multiracial deity and the path by which humanity could save itself, by becoming a single race. Drawing from the section of Parsons's magical notes titled "Wormwood Star," she performed sex magic with the four members of the Wands suit—Booth being one of them. Before each ritual, she consecrated her star of Babalon, and then worked herself into a meditative state while having sex. She used astral projection to meet Parsons on the astral plane and envisioned herself having sex with him before repeating Crowley's magic word "Abrahadabra!" at climax, this being the word Crowley reserved for the completion of a great magical work. Sure enough Cameron fell pregnant. Her beautiful friend Joan Whitney moved in with her after returning from Paris where she'd worked as a model for Chanel, and Cameron was glad for the company, although Whitney declined to participate in the rituals, not wanting to have Cameron tell her who she was to have sex with or not.

The group also used the peyote they gathered from the mountainside in the rituals, and Cameron began attending lectures about psychedelics, including one by British writer Gerald Heard, who was at that time working with Aldous Huxley, just prior to the publication of *The Doors of Perception*. Cameron learned about the practices of Native Americans who used peyote to contact spirit beings, and she realized that peyote was a means to thrust herself onto the astral plane, with the added bonus that peyote often has a strong aphrodisiac effect—the ideal accompaniment for ritual sex magic. She also found herself artistically inspired, and she produced a drawing titled *Peyote Visions,* a self-portrait in which Cameron is on all fours, her head thrust up with a snake-like tongue flicking from her lips. Her breasts are full and veined, her buttocks are distortedly huge, and she is being penetrated by a muscular humanoid peyote cactus-alien hybrid. In 1957 the work was displayed by her friend, the celebrated California artist Wallace Berman, at the Ferus Gallery, leading to his arrest and conviction for obscenity, following a raid by the L.A. Police Department vice squad (this was several years before Burroughs would experience his own obscenity trial triggered by his book *Naked Lunch*).

However, the peyote and somewhat reckless magical workings began to have a severely negative effect on her already fragile state of mind. She began to be consumed by paranoid delusions, terrifying and eventually tiring her friends with conspiracies and conceptions of her own grand destiny. She claimed she would one day, as Babalon, lead the men of Africa, Asia, and India in a race war that would wipe out white Europeans. She was subject to an array of auditory and visual hallucinations even when not taking peyote, she saw UFOs and believed them to be the first signs that the almighty violence of the final part of *The Book of the Law* was imminent, and she believed her body was a kind of cosmic aerial through which she could pick up interstellar communications. She visited her family and beset them with zealous evangelism in efforts to convert them to *The Book of the Law,* but when they resisted, she accused her brothers of incestuous desire toward her and her mother of conducting affairs behind her father's back. Her mother physically threw Cameron out of the family home and banished her.

She continued to push herself into ever more radical forms of magical training, including going out into the desert for weeks at a time with just her dog and a strange sex doll that she'd developed a romantic attachment to for company. She'd spotted this doll in a store in Palm Springs while she looked for a pair of hiking boots and had noticed the resemblance to her own apperance, albeit nude, large breasted, kneeling and wearing a polkadot headscarf. Out in the desert, under the haze of peyote, she'd fallen somewhat in love with her reticent ersatz twin. Furthermore she came across a tree with the letters MCHB carved into the trunk—to Cameron this signified "Margorie Cameron Hilarion Belarion": her own name plus the magical names of both Parsons and herself. She slept under the stars, wondering how her life had become so tormented. She wore an amulet that Parsons had given her at all times, knowing that it contained deadly poison, her escape from this plane of existence should it all become too much.[5] After returning from her sojourn in the desert, she visited a psychic medium who told her that someone had burned nine black candles during her birth and put a curse on her, and she realized this was her aunt Nell. She replaced all the black candles on her altar, choosing green ones instead, and believed that the psychic had been able to finally lift the curse—from here on, things would improve, she decided, and the first bit of good news was that Booth was soon to be released from prison after serving time on narcotics charges.

However, things were not running smoothly in other facets of her life at all. In 1953, now aged thirty-two, she miscarried her moon-child and then discovered that the other moonchildren created by the Children—two further pregnancies from the Pentacles and Wands sex magic matching—had been terminated by the mothers. Cameron was furious and devastated that her magical family had been taken from her, and she headed back to Altadena to move in with Booth once again. Not long after she arrived, she and Booth were arrested and charged with violations of the racially discriminatory rooming house ordinance laws, and while under arrest she attacked a female police officer who was trying to remove her magical and poisonous amulet, a fracas that made the front pages of local papers.

Homeless once more, she did now experience some much-needed good fortune, which came via her friend, fellow witch and member of the Children Renate Druks. Druks was familiar with the strange homosexual underground scene of L.A., in which the occultist Samson de Brier was a notorious figure, a Wildean, openly homosexual dandy, whose own story was dramatic enough: Born in China, De Brier's father was stabbed to death by a spurned lover, he made his way in the glamour and decadence of the silent era, and was by the 1950s the orchestrator of some of the most spectacular parties California has ever seen. One attendee of these parties was filmmaker and occultist Kenneth Anger, and through Druks he was introduced to the infamous Scarlet Woman. "I've been waiting to meet you for a thousand years," Anger said as he was presented to Cameron.[6] Anger's project was to make a cinematic re-creation of one of De Brier's most wonderful parties that had been titled "Come as Your Madness" and had inspired some truly spectacular costuming, much of it appropriately egomaniacal L.A. re-creations of pagan gods and goddesses. The centerpiece was Anaïs Nin, the famed writer and former lover of Henry Miller, who had come draped in animal furs as a kind of sexual Salammbo. As at the party, Anger's vision was to make Nin the lead in his film, but as soon as he met Cameron, his mind was changed and he decided to side-line Nin and replace her with Cameron, much to Nin's irritation. The two women did not get along, but Cameron's dark and evil presence was overpowering, and she won the battle to become Anger's muse. *Inauguration of the Pleasure Dome,* taking its title from Samuel Taylor Coleridge's opium-infused poem "Kublai Khan," was a spectacular and radical piece of filmmaking for its time, a cascade of color and symbolism projected on a triple screen, featuring Pan; the Great Beast Crowley (played by De Brier, as were Shiva and Nero); a bare-breasted Cameron as Kali, Ganymede, Lucifer, Lilith; and a whole cast of darkly magical and pagan entities at a masquerade where Pan is the prize. Hecate's wine is drunk by the guests, but Pan's cup is poisoned and the rites begin, with Cameron rising as the Scarlet Woman as the film reaches its climax. The black magic (according to the press) or Thelemic (according to Anger) film was met with cautious and bemused praise from film critics, but with almost unequivocal fury and dismissal by Thelemites. Anger found himself berated by followers of Crowley after one screening, telling him it was sacrilege and that the Great Beast would have despised it.[7] Anger stood firm in his defense of it as a Thelemic film, and he became a devotee of *The Book of the Law*—receiving support from Crowley apprentice Kenneth Grant, whose own story wove into Spare's and Parsons's lives as well, and who was by then the likely heir to Crowley's disputed mantle. Grant wrote to Cameron proclaiming her the true incarnation of Babalon, and later he met Anger.

Following this success, Cameron got a job making clothes through her friendship with Wallace Berman and continued making art. She then met her second husband, Sheridan Kimmel, whom she called her "tomb-mate."[8] Kimmel was a WWII veteran who had served as a tail gunner in the Pacific until a serious shrapnel wound to his skull cut short his war. Traumatized, the remaining inoperable shrapnel shifted around in his skull, causing mood swings and suicidal thoughts. However, he was handsome, funny, sensitive, and artistically inclined, as well as fascinated by the occult, aliens, sexual experimentation, and peyote; a kindred spirit for Cameron, no doubt. He had a reputation as a risk taker and of being something of a loon, taking Benzedrine and driving his car at breakneck speeds through the dark desert being one form of entertainment in which he indulged. But it seemed that Cameron had at last found some happiness, and love again, after years in the wilderness.

She became pregnant—now for the fourth time in her life—and Sherry, as Sheridan was called, was delighted at the prospect of fatherhood. However, his assumptions were hasty, as it turns out he was not the biological father. A more likely father was one of the Jacobi twins, regular attendees of De Brier's parties. They were blond Italians who had an almost cartoonish resemblance to gods of the ancient world, with curls, chiseled jaws, and rippling torsos; Anger claimed that Cameron's child was the result of a sexual encounter with *both* of the twins at the same time.[9] The baby was born healthy on Christmas Eve 1955 and named Crystal Eve Kimmel, with Kimmel on the birth certificate as the father.

The demands of motherhood were almost too much for Cameron. Needing to escape the terrifying responsibility, she frequently left Crystal with friends, the experimental artist Wallace Berman and his wife, Shirley. Furthermore, Kimmel was prone to jealous rages, particularly at the mention of Parsons, and he destroyed Parsons's magical diary as well as the journal Cameron had kept of her first marriage.

The couple managed to stay together through Kimmel's various stints in psychiatric hospitals, but the marriage was on the rocks and they would separate in 1960. Before this, Cameron was the subject of a short film by Curtis Harrison called *The Wormwood Star,* which focuses on Cameron's Wormwood Star ritual as well as her artwork in a dreamy, ritualistic glimpse into her own private world of magic and painting. This was followed by *Night Tide,* Harrison's feature debut, in which Cameron plays a sea witch in his tale inspired by the sirens of Greek mythology, alongside a first starring role for Dennis Hopper.

In 1962, Anger returned from a stay in Paris, which coincided with his own emotional breakdown and a stay in a psychiatric hospital there. Cameron and Anger had been writing to one another, and she regretted not running away to Europe with Anger earlier. She was delighted at his return, and she moved in with him, although her increasing desire for a romantic and sexual relationship with Anger began to cause tension. Anger, at the same time, was distraught to discover how much of both her own art and Parsons's writings she had destroyed, claiming they would live forever on the astral plane, and that it was not Cameron but her magical identity, Hilarion, who was responsible for the destruction, having been told to do so by Parsons himself, who spoke to her through a photograph she meditated on, telling her to burn things. Her feelings toward Parsons were wild and volatile—heartbreak, tenderness, and love mixed with hatred and a belief that he had intended to burn her to death as a ritual sacrifice. Anger brought home a young gay man he'd picked up on Venice Beach one night, and Cameron flew into a fury when Anger noted how much the boy looked like Cameron. She attacked Anger in a rage, and he threw her out. He decided that the boy, whose name was Prince Little, was an elemental he had conjured and related to the eponymous hero of Antoine de Saint-Exupery's *The Little Prince,* a copy of which he had bought that very day. He took Prince Little out into the New Mexico desert by bus and performed a sex magic working dedicated to the Roman god of war, Mars, that climaxed with a great meteor shower above the two men that night.

Cameron was back out on her own once more, living in the desert for six months, then heading back to live with her parents once more, as her aging father approached death.

As the 1960s progressed, Cameron continued to produce art and did her best to carry the torch for Thelema as the order went through multiple crises, particularly following the death of Germer. The Thelemites had also requested that Cameron transfer Parsons's magical diaries and texts to them in copies, following various incidents where parts had been lost, stolen, or destroyed. Cameron refused, only granting Jane Wolfe access to the tapes and documents, which were by now at the point of being worn through. Kimmel also continued to pursue Cameron, heartbroken and psychologically devastated, he deployed increasing violence and emotional blackmail against Cameron, but she turned away from him, not allowing Kimmel to see their daughter at Christmas and refusing to respond to his agonized pleas. Kimmel died in 1966 of what was officially recorded as a brain hemorrhage but was in all likelihood an overdose, intentional or otherwise. Cameron also began making her own LSD at this time, but like many pioneers of sexual liberation and drug use, the arrival at the promised land brought a great sense of disappointment.

The 1960s explosion of freedoms with sex and drugs seemed to Cameron and many others to be removing any sense of transcendence and the mystical from both and replacing them with thrills, pleasure, and escapism. She began to withdraw. Failing to land a role in Harrison's follow-up feature film, she concentrated on Crystal and discovered the benefits of t'ai chi. The family moved to Santa Fe, New Mexico, then back to Joshua Tree, California, before settling among the sex shops, petty crime, and adult movie theaters of Genesse Avenue, West Hollywood. She devoted herself to her family, a grandmother by the end of the 1970s, and took on a parental role as Crystal struggled to bring up her children alone. She met Genesis P-Orridge during the 1980s and then veered toward Wicca, dressing as an archetypal white witch in long white robes and wild white hair, playing a Celtic harp and smoking joints, as well as taking an interest in the New Age best-seller *The Mayan Factor* by José Argüelles. She always retained her belief in Thelema and *The Book of the Law* as her primary spiritual guide, however. The end of her life was not filled with great happiness, and she was far from the almightily powerful dark witch she had seen herself becoming; the Scarlet Woman seems to have departed long before the end, but she had the love of her daughter and her granddaughter Iris, in whose arms Cameron died from a brain tumor on July 24, 1995, at the age of seventy-three.

In the twenty-first century there has been a steady increase in Cameron's artworks—in spite of her having destroyed so many of them in fits of amphetamine-induced madness, as she described it. Her writings, important to her artistic works, have hardly been published, and there remains a great body of work to be discovered by those who seek inspiration from the true incarnation of the Wormwood Star. Scott Hobbs, director of the Cameron-Parsons foundation, says that he hopes one day to see a feature film of her life produced, with Tilda Swinton playing Cameron. With the 2018 CBS show *Strange Angel* about Jack Parsons having seen some success, perhaps it is time for his magical coconspirator to have her own life brought to the screen.

SELECTED WORKS BY MARJORIE CAMERON CONCERNING SEX MAGIC

Neither Marjorie Cameron's writings nor artworks are widely published at this time. The exception is the collection below of love poems and illustrations available in limited release from Fulgur Press.

1951 ✦ *Songs for the Witch Woman* with Jack Parsons

11

Anton Szandor LaVey
(1930–1997)

It was the pinnacle of what Anton LaVey later termed "Phase One Satanism," which was nevertheless the vision of Satanism that was etched in the popular memory at that moment: theater, blasphemy, nudity, and the Black Pope himself, in his peaked zucchetto that sprouted two baby goat horns, plus a black cape and large pendant bearing the inverted pentagram. Behind him, a naked young woman lay on an altar. Next to her was LaVey's young daughter, Zeena, in a red riding hood. This was the first Satanic baptism, and it took place at 9:00 p.m. on Tuesday, May 23, 1967—otherwise known as the Second Year of our Satanic Lord. Down in the ritual chamber of the Black House at 6114 California Street, San Francisco, television crews, photographers, and journalists bustled in with attendant Satanists to document the scene, a sensation in the national press, and just what LaVey wanted.

Anton Szandor LaVey was born on April 11, 1930, in Chicago to an ordinary middle-class family who left Chicago for the Bay Area of San Francisco not long after his birth. His birth name was Howard Stanton Levey, and he was known as Tony to his parents and peers through his childhood. Howard was soon dropped from his name, and at age ten he added Szandor as a middle name, after hearing his grandmother's tales of his Hungarian relatives, as well as the great battles the Hungarians once fought against the Turks and the Russians.

Like many boys of his time, at least the ones afforded an upbringing largely free from religious pressure, he developed an interest in the hugely popular pulp magazine *Weird Tales,* publisher of Clark Ashton Smith and the first Cthulhu stories of H. P. Lovecraft. He read *Dracula* and *Frankenstein,* as well as William Hope Hodgson; his interest in the macabre, the uncanny, and the horrific was developing as he entered his teenage years.

He witnessed San Francisco celebrating its glorious rebirth, which came after the devastation wreaked by the earthquake of 1906, and was consummated by the opening of the now iconic Golden Gate Bridge during the World's Fair of 1939–1940; the ten-year-old LaVey was among the first group to walk across it. Even during the Depression, the city had thrived—famously not one bank in San Francisco failed— and the particular mixture of wealth, architectural beauty, and a growing sense of artistic freedom would culminate in a period of radical self-expression in the city some twenty-five years later, and LaVey would find himself right in the center.

LaVey took little interest in the formal education offered to him by his school. He instead taught himself hypnotism and become fascinated by the life of Basil Zaharoff, a Greek arms dealer sometimes also known as the "Merchant of Death." Zaharoff's mundane business affairs were extraordinary enough—he sold the first Maxim guns and then later some of the first submarines, both of which would completely change the complexion of modern warfare. But it was his Machiavellian methods that were most interesting to LaVey. Zaharoff lived a seeming amoral existence, making fortunes from governmental vanity, stupidity, and bloodlust. He provided weapons to multiple opposing sides during conquests, and even manipulated national governments to declare war on a rival nation or two as part of a political strategy to increase popularity at home, before then providing weapons to both sides of the conflict. He sold faulty equipment that had been rejected by major powers to smaller nations as a means of increasing prestige. During the arms race of the 1900s, Zaharoff, through his company Vickers, supplied and encouraged both Britain and Germany to spend staggering fortunes on improving their navies. He also built a large business empire by acquiring sometimes national-scale arms manufacturers at relatively cheap prices, something he attributed to his sexual prowess and ability to seduce powerful women, all of which drove LaVey's admiration for Zaharoff higher and higher. Here was a man who could expose the frailties of what seemed like entities of almighty power—governments, militaries, global business—by simply outwitting them and preying on their basic lack of intelligence and fundamental vanity, with sex thrown in as an alternative resort.

Leaving school early and encouraged by what he'd learned from Zaharoff, LaVey knew the most important thing was to avoid following the mundane paths of his classmates. He joined the circus, which seemed to offer adventure and freedom, and worked as a roustabout. He soon took the opportunity to become a cage-boy for the lions and tigers, where he learned to train them. He would take his own dinner into the cages and eat with the lions so as to be accepted as one of their own. He built a good rapport with the big cats and was put in charge of them during performances. He understood the lions well, but nevertheless one session of playtime with an overexuberant lion who pounced on him for a gentle bite and claw proved almost fatal for LaVey. In the meantime, he had learned to play the steam calliope, which would open up his next adventure.

In the late 1940s, LaVey left the circus and went on the road with the carnival. His skills on a keyboard proved useful as he would play the musical accompaniment to the educational shows about sex shown to adult audiences at the carnivals, usually presented by a buxom young woman. LaVey played the calliope, the Wurlitzer band organ, and the Hammond. From the carnival performers he got his first taste of magic, learning the tricks of the illusionists and how they deceived people; the trick being to remember that most people *want* to be deceived—all it takes is a guide.

Still only eighteen years old, he took a job at the Mayan Burlesque

Theatre on South Hill Street, L.A. (still in operation with its original 1927 décor intact, albeit now as a nightclub) playing organ for the strippers. Carnival work dried up in the winter, but LaVey could rely on his musical skills and sense of theater to keep himself afloat. The burlesque houses also proved a source of revenue to others who were experiencing longer career winters, and the young Hollywood hopefuls would strip before the soused clientele, many of them dozing off in the smoky low light, while they waited for their big break in the movies or theater. One such young woman, a curvaceous and very pale blonde, went by several stage names, but her birth name was Norma Jean Mortensen, and she had just been dropped from her contract with Columbia, after completing one low-budget musical, *Ladies of the Chorus*. Columbia had added a few important characteristics to the young actress's appearance; they raised her hairline and dyed her hair platinum blond, hoping to push her more in the alluring direction of Rita Hayworth than the girl-next-door roles for which she had been typecast until then. They also helped her fix her stage name, calling her Marilyn Monroe. Monroe experimented with this slow, seductive style as she danced for the drunks at the burlesque house, to LaVey's organ accompaniment. LaVey noted that the women who really believed they were doing this only until something better comes along tended to adopt the slower style of removing their clothes, while the women who didn't aspire to anything more than the burlesque houses preferred to pull off the clothes quickly and give the punters what they wanted.

LaVey was, as might be expected, more aroused by what remained tantalizingly hidden, occulted even. Monroe, now reveling in her more liberated role of seductress, was equally fascinated by this dark and mysterious organist. It was not long before their making eyes at one another during her dances exploded into a sexual affair that would mark LaVey, at least, for the rest of his life. Their affair was brief and physically intense. LaVey knew how to bring out a woman's naughty side, and he was rapt in lust for Monroe. Pale and plump thighs became something of a permanent fetish for LaVey, and his taste in women following her was generally for a classic

Hollywood blonde, as seen in many of his most significant later lovers and wives. It wasn't long before Monroe was gone and had become the lover of Hollywood agent Johnny Hyde, who would pay for her jaw implants and rhinoplasty and set her on the track to a degree of fame and stardom unknown to almost any other person who has ever lived.

During their short-lived romance, LaVey and Monroe moved into a cheap motel on Washington Boulevard together and would drive home from the theater in Monroe's Pontiac convertible or take the train along Venice Boulevard. Monroe enjoyed a little danger in her sex, and they would have sex on the train, in the back of the car, in abandoned buildings—anywhere there was a chance they might be caught or watched. Monroe was as disdainful of organized religion and Christian morality as LaVey, and she had a huge thirst for learning, so would sit up listening to LaVey talk on his research into the occult, fascinated by the dark side. Their astrological compatibility was spectacularly geared toward sexual chemistry and intellectual understanding, if perhaps displaying two emotionally different creatures.

LaVey remembered Monroe as confused and depressed at this time, the loss of her contract having been a major blow. He also refutes the many claims that came later about Monroe's willingness to give out sexual favors to advance her career during this lost period of her life, saying that studio bosses would buy her dinner, take a photo and—at worst— masturbate while looking her over. "Not that kind of girl,"[1] LaVey would say, as one of the very few people from that time who would know. After barely a couple of months, LaVey left her for another woman, and Marilyn was gone—something he would quickly regret when he reflected on their strong sexual and intellectual bond. Later, in death, she would transcend her image and become a new kind of goddess, and LaVey would claim her as a Satanic goddess, perhaps harking back to the flawed, fleshly, sensual, troubled, and brilliant goddesses of ancient Greece, in opposition to the Christian veneration of a pure and serene virgin.

LaVey experienced something of a gloomy period himself around the time he left Monroe, and decided to leave L.A. and return to

San Francisco. He continued to work as an organist at strip shows, although in June 1950 a new menace appeared on the horizon—the draft for the Korean War. Having no desire to be conscripted, LaVey managed to enroll as a student at the San Francisco City College studying criminology, in spite of not having completed high school. Also at this time, LaVey was attracted to the cause of radical Zionism. The violent strategies used by militant Zionists were drawing comparison to those deployed by the National Socialists just a few years before. LaVey was fascinated when he met battle-hardened fighters for the Israeli cause, many of whom were ex-convicts from Europe, had bullet wounds from all kinds of conflicts whether military, political, or criminal, and several of whom had followed a career path that seems absurd to our revised view of twentieth-century history but was not entirely unusual among Jewish soldiers at the time: fighting for Germany in the Great War, often winning medals, taking part in the German revolution, fighting against Germany in Spain, then forming a mutually uneasy alliance with Nazi Germany during the 1930s with the shared objective of ejecting the British from Palestine. Now many of them, having left Europe for the US, were engaged in running guns for Israel. LaVey assisted with packing boxes marked "Menorahs" that were filled with German and Japanese weapons collected as war booty by American soldiers and which were then piled onto ships in the dead of night and set sail for Israel.

Through the early 1950s, LaVey had a comparatively mundane life: he married a woman called Carole Lansing, and in 1952 they had a daughter, Karla. LaVey found work as a photographer for the San Francisco Police Department (SFPD), photographing crime scenes. The daily exposure to suicides, murders, traffic accident deaths, botched robberies, and women and children slain in all kinds of circumstances eradicated from LaVey's mind any lingering idea of a benevolent God. By 1955, LaVey had gathered sufficient proficiency in hypnotism and spirit-cleaning people's homes to quit his job at the SFPD and become self-employed doing something he loved. This also afforded him more time to develop his ideas on magic and spirituality and to increase his knowledge of the occult.

In 1956, LaVey, now earning good money in self-employment, bought a small family home at 6114 California Street in the Richmond District of San Francisco. He was originally in the area to view another property but convinced the real estate agent to let him take a look around the old shotgun cottage across the street. The property had already been bought by the agency, but LaVey discovered that the current proprietor was a mystic and had herself held séances in the house LaVey could not ignore this synchronicity and so he offered her more than the agency had agreed to pay, and a deal was done.

He learned that the house had been built by a Scottish sea captain in 1887 (although public records list its date of construction as 1905) with ballast timbers from one of his ships. Neighborhood folklore told that the wife and child of the sea captain mysteriously disappeared after six years, and then he himself left the house, never to return. It had also functioned as a brothel, belonging to a well-known madame called Mammy Pleasant, a fact that pleased LaVey greatly. His first task was to paint the exterior of the property with black submarine paint, to match his usual attire, his black 1949 Citroen, and the black leopard named Zoltan whom a friend had smuggled into the United States from Israel as a gift to LaVey.

The neighbors were, at first, disconcerted. But they soon found LaVey charming and personable, and moreover extremely curious to hear more about the history of the house, especially the various anecdotes about ghost sightings there. In 1906 a ridiculously oversized fireplace had been added, built from flagstones dislodged from the docks of San Francisco during the devastating earthquake that year that killed three thousand San Franciscans and destroyed 80 percent of the city's buildings. The flagstones, huge and the color of iron, had been transported to San Francisco from England, where—it is said—they once formed part of a Roman temple. This fireplace, built from stones of pagan mysticism, would become the notorious altar for LaVey's rituals.

The magic of the ancients and the sexual energy of the old brothel would provide the perfect foundry for him to forge his magical-sexual Church of Satan. In a final confirmation that his new home was in the perfect neighborhood, he discovered that the telephone landline prefix number given to the area was to be 666.

LaVey began to throw informal gatherings of select friends, giving lectures on esoteric topics, and staying up late into the night. Journalists were soon attracted to the house and visited to report on the strange "Black House," as it was now known, where the owner kept tarantulas and a leopard, and LaVey was happy to give them a tour, showing the old trapdoors and secret passages the house contained. By 1960, his marriage to Carole was over, as he had fallen in love with a beautiful seventeen-year-old named Diane Hegarty after she began attending LaVey's gatherings, which he had now given the title of Midnight Magic Seminars. Hegarty moved into the Black House and became the in-house sorceress and enchantress, as well as hosting the seminars that were attended by around two dozen regular visitors, mostly comprising educated professionals. She gave birth to LaVey's second daughter, Zeena, in 1963. Hegerty also helped to raise the family's new pet, a lion named Togare who was bought after Zoltan met the sad fate of so many city felines: he was killed by a passing car.

Practical evenings were also arranged to complement the seminars given on the occult, extra-sensory perception, haunted houses, black masses, and homunculi. One such event was a banquet evening hosted by the LaVeys where the delicacy of the Fiji Islanders known as *puaka balava,* meaning "long pig" and referring to human flesh, was served. Hegarty prepared the meat with triple sec, fruit, yams, grenadine, and beans, as demanded by the recipe. The meat was provided by a regular attendee of the seminars, a physician who had smuggled an amputated thigh out of the hospital where he worked. Other oddities were served at the banquet, including caterpillar hors d'oeuvres.

The increasing popularity and local notoriety of LaVey and his gatherings gave him the idea to formalize the meetings. On Walpurgisnacht, an important traditional date in the Christian calendar falling on April 30, 1966, LaVey and Hegarty announced the formal creation of the Church of Satan in a ceremony at the Black House. It was Satanic Year Zero.

Walpurgisnacht is also known as Saint Walpurga's Eve and is particularly important among Christians of Germanic, Finnish, and Slavic Europe, marking a day when they prayed to ward off evil. Saint Walpurga, an eighth-century English nun, was believed to have the power to ward off evil spirits, most especially the greatest menace to the bodies and souls of the Middle Ages and the Renaissance: witches. The night of Saint Walpurga has always been observed on April 30, due to the strong pagan tradition of worshipping nature and spring that had occurred for many centuries on the first day of May. May Day remains a public holiday and a time for folkloric festivals in many parts of Europe, including the UK, and in recent times has become synonymous with radical protests against global capitalism and government. The Christians rationalized that since the pagans seemed to draw so much energy from their May Day celebrations, the preceding night must be the time of year when witches gather to do their most evil work, guiding the souls of men and women away from God and into nature, festivity, sex, and devilry. The myth developed that witches gathered atop the highest peak of the Herz mountain range (known as the Brokken) on the night before May Day, ready to do their annual evil. Christians would, then, that same night, pray to Saint Walpurga for her protection, as well as light bonfires and clang pots in an effort to scare away the witches. To LaVey, this was the perfect date to formally give birth to the Church of Satan before his own coven of witches, as spring, too, was born.

On that San Francisco night in 1966, a group of well-heeled men and women congregated in the antechamber, a small room before the ritual chamber, of the Black House, waiting for the clock to run down towards midnight. As the hour approached, they were called in to the ritual chamber. Silently, they moved into the pitch-dark room. After a moment, an organ began to play Wagner, Bach, and old Christian hymns, mixed in with sound effects from horror movies. The lights were raised just enough for everyone to see the altar and those who would be performing the ritual, including, of course, LaVey himself, dressed in his black cape with pointed cowl. Two figures in black cloaks stood beside him, while a naked woman reclined on the stone mantle-piece, flanked by two more naked priestesses. The music from the organist continued a little while as the congregation took in the scene, as well as the coffin, taxidermy animals, and black walls with red ceiling. After a while LaVey rang a bell nine times to signal the start of the ceremony proper: *"In nomine Dei nostri Satanas Luciferi excelsi!"* ("In the name of our lord Satan, the high Morning Star.") LaVey then proceeded to go through his Satanic litany, evoking the infernal names, calling the demons into the chamber, readying them to listen to the desires of those congregated. One by one, each of the congregated whispered their greatest desire, whether for lust, love, power, success, money, or freedom, into LaVey's ear. As the high priest, he acted as a conduit for their desires into the world beyond.

By the following February, the media had whipped into a full frenzy about the happenings at the Black House. The Satanic wedding ceremony of journalist John Raymond and New York socialite Judith Case drew a vast crowd that had to be dispersed by the police, amid claims that a lion could be heard roaring somewhere within. LaVey made the front page of the *Los Angeles Times,* and the media dubbed him "The Black Pope."

LaVey's Church of Satan, the first religious organization to openly venerate Satan in human history (we live in times where some of LaVey's ideas have become morally intolerable), was a highly syncretic religious system. The first and most striking tenet of the church was that it is atheistic. This was not the Satanic worship of the Templars, in which both God and Satan were believed to be real. In this case, Satan is an ideology for a godless society, and this was appealing to the particularly liberated environment of 1960s California, a place that had become fatigued with wholesome piety. *Satan* was taken in its literal Hebrew form, meaning "adversary." A Satanist is encouraged to be a skeptic; to embrace a form of Nietzschean positivism, joy in life, and the natural world; to be stridently individualistic; to understand the benefit of pride; and to be, broadly speaking, enlightened. Satanism embraces an extremely liberal stance on many things, most notably sexuality, in which consensual sex among any number of people is considered not only acceptable, but admirable. Satan, then, is a model for a reasoned way of living in the world and not a deity to be worshipped.

The church itself had its foundation in a core group that LaVey had collected earlier in the 1960s known as the Order of the Trapezoid. It is here that LaVey formulated his more profound and complex spiritual philosophy, accompanied by fellow members of the order Kenneth Anger (the filmmaker with whom Cameron was also associated), the Baroness Carin de Plessen, Dr. Cecil Nixon, Russell Wolden, and Donald Werby. The outer Church of Satan was built up around this inner circle and from its first incarnation was designed to be sensational, theatrical, and newsworthy, while at the core, the occult of the occult, was the Trapezoid.

The blasphemous pantomime that excited the media, however, was little more than that. LaVey used the inner sanctum of the Trapezoid to begin constructing a form of magical practice that went beyond merely provoking America's straight-laced Christian social order. He began to develop his own magical system, one that—unlike many of the others discussed in this book—requires no faith, is dependent on rationale, is atheistic, and enforces compliance with the only true regulations imposed upon an individual, the laws of nature. This was expressed in the first Satanic baptism, performed on his daughter Zeena, and the ceremony was designed to venerate the natural instincts that were already in her and those that would develop in time as Zeena grew into a woman. Furthermore, LaVey formulated specific methods for cursing, a channeling of emotional energy to be directed at an entity deserving of a negative charge. Again, the ceremony was subject to great interest from reporters—now from the world over—and photographs of three-year-old Zeena looking slightly bewildered but at ease with the attention being lavished upon her, stand in stark contrast to the fear-inducing waterboarding methods used in Christian baptism rites. Later in 1967, LaVey performed an official US Navy funeral for one of its officers, Edward Olsen, who had been killed in a car crash while on leave. Dutifully, the Navy sent a guard of honor, and Olsen's coffin was draped in the star-spangled banner as rifle volleys were fired and black-clad Satanists cried, "Hail Satan!" to mark his departure into the beyond. In a short time, Satanism had grown to become a mainstream religious order with ten thousand members claimed.

One of those members was an authentic American deity, albeit one who had recently been discarded from the pantheon that was Hollywood and had found herself adrift in a decade that no longer wanted anything more from her than opening shopping malls in mid-size towns—Jayne Mansfield. Like LaVey, Mansfield was also notorious for overthrowing accepted aesthetic considerations of home décor, and homing in on one symbolic color, which in Mansfield's case was pink. Her Pink Palace on Sunset Boulevard (which sadly became a victim of unsentimental property development in the early 2000s, as did the Black House) was certainly more luxurious than LaVey's relatively modest abode. The heart-shaped bathtub and pool, the fluorescent pink lights, and a fountain that squirted pink champagne are hardwired into Hollywood's eternal mythology from its Golden Age. But by the 1960s, Mansfield's "dumb blonde" archetype, with a forty-inch bust and ear-piercing squeal (a personality expertly crafted by Mansfield, who had a reported IQ score of 149), was under assault. The sex symbol was taken to its most absurd and cartoonish extreme by Mansfield, but she nevertheless retained the aura of the uncanny goddess, an emotionally supernatural being with a hypnotic hold over men and women alike, embodying the long heritage of Hollywood sex symbols that included Monroe, of course, but also Jean Harlow, Lana Turner, and the foundation screen goddess Theda Bara. By the time Mansfield asked to be introduced to LaVey in late 1966, she had been repackaged by second-wave feminism and the National Organization for Women not as a goddess but as a victim of male objectification. Mansfield, presumably, was not consulted—but Hollywood, always hypersensitive to the modes of its market, moved quickly to usher out the deadwood and bring in new role models for women. Mansfield was thus reduced to burlesque shows, mall openings, and easing her pain with severe alcoholism.

An old Hollywood adage about Mansfield was that her private life out-rivaled any of the roles she played. Married three times, she had five children and an extraordinary list of lovers that included (like Monroe) both John and Robert Kennedy, and almost her entire adult life she had been of relentless interest to reporters wanting to put her scandals under the microscope. It was not surprising, perhaps, that she sought refuge in the cloaked world offered by LaVey. At the time of their meeting, Mansfield was involved in a bitter divorce lawsuit with her third husband, film director Matt Cimbar, who was trying to obtain custody of their children on the grounds that Mansfield was an unfit mother. Furthermore, Mansfield found herself romantically involved with her attorney, Sam Brody, who emotionally blackmailed her into a possessive and violently jealous relationship on the grounds of being the only one who could keep her united with her children.

Brody was instantly jealous of the warmth developing between LaVey and Mansfield as she became a full-fledged Satanist, and his suspicions of a love affair between them were not unfounded, but the encounter between LaVey, Mansfield, and Brody led to a series of events that have become a fundamental part of both occult and Hollywood lore. It began, so it is told, with Brody picking up a candle from LaVey's altar at the Black House and criticizing it as hokey. LaVey took offense and sternly advised Brody not to touch anything on his altar. Brody responded with sarcasm, asking, "Are you going to put a curse on me?" To which LaVey warned, "You'd be well advised not to ridicule powers you're hopelessly incapable of understanding."[2]

While Mansfield was tied to Brody, her relationship with LaVey developed, and LaVey recognized in her what he considered to be a natural Satanist, soon making her a priestess, and inducting her in sex magic rituals designed to invoke compassion and lust, as well as the Shibboleth ritual, a purge for frustration and anger. When Mansfield's young son Zoltan was mauled by a lion in a bizarre incident at a local amusement park, LaVey conducted a mountaintop ritual with several members of the church designed to save the boy's life, and Zoltan recovered from his critical condition, after which Mansfield vowed her everlasting gratitude to LaVey. Although LaVey found the force of nature that was Mansfield to be suffocating and overwhelming at times, a genuine affection existed between them, and she looked to LaVey for protection, her "sorcerer on call," as he termed it.[3] To this end, LaVey realized that the most negative force in Mansfield's life was Brody. Furthermore, the volatile Brody had begun to make threats against LaVey, screaming down the telephone that he would expose him as a charlatan. By now LaVey had had enough of this psychic vampire and saw these insults as casus belli. According to Blanche Barton, LaVey's wife in his later years and head of the Church of Satan after his death, following that telephone conversation in January 1967, LaVey performed a destruction ritual on Brody. He evoked infernal beings and burned Brody's name on a piece of paper, insisting that Brody be dead within a year.

In the months that followed, Brody wrecked his car on two occasions, resulting in a broken leg from the second incident. LaVey's curse had swung twice and missed. Furthermore, Mansfield's sixteen-year-old daughter, Jayne Marie, filed battery charges against Brody and her mother, putting herself into protective custody—evidently not something that would have assisted Brody's attempts to keep Mansfield and her children legally together.

In the early hours of June 19, 1967, LaVey was at his desk working (he was a night owl, naturally), clipping up a German newspaper that had run a story featuring photographs of LaVey laying flowers on the grave of Marilyn Monroe. In doing so he noticed that on the reverse of one of the photographs was a picture of Mansfield, and LaVey had unconsciously cut through that picture in a way that severed her head from her body. LaVey was momentarily distressed to see what he'd done. At about the same time—2:00 a.m.—on the US 90 toward New Orleans, Mansfield, Brody, and her three youngest children, Zoltan, Mickey, and Mariska, were being driven by a friend, Ronnie Harrison. Mansfield was scheduled to appear on television in New Orleans later that day. Driving too fast, at night and in the fog, Harrison slammed the car right into the back of a slow-moving tank truck that had been partially obscured by the anti-mosquito pesticide it was spraying. The car's chassis continued on under the truck, while the upper part of the car was crushed like an accordion as it impacted the rear of the tank. Mansfield, who was sleeping, Brody, and Harrison were killed instantly. All three of the children, low enough down in the backseats, escaped miraculously unharmed.

Initial reports suggested that Mansfield had been decapitated, which gave a horrifying precision to LaVey's actions on the night his curse seemingly took full effect, albeit with the magical irony of also claiming Mansfield herself and the entirely innocent Harrison. But it transpired that detectives on the scene had merely seen her giant blond wig and initially believed it was her head—her body was discovered intact.

After her death, LaVey decided to rent the Pink Palace and move into Mansfield's old home. The intention was to return to Hollywood full time, now that his celebrity had grown, all those years after his time there playing organ at the Mayan. In his months there he worked as a consultant on a horror film and made contacts in the movie business, not least the Rat Pack, of whom Sammy Davis Jr. would join the church, but LaVey soon found that the heat and insincerity of Hollywood was not to his liking at all, and so the Church of Satan returned to its birth town of San Francisco.

These setbacks aside, the next few years saw the rise of the Church of Satan. *The Satanic Bible,* published in 1969, became an instant bestseller and has remained in print ever since, and furthermore its availability was not limited to obscure occult bookstores, but it was for sale in supermarkets across America, alongside *The Godfather, Portnoy's Complaint,* and *The Day Kennedy Was Shot.* LaVey's next book, *The Compleat Witch,* followed in 1970, and 1973 saw the publication of *The Satanic Rituals,* a compendium of black magic rituals as practiced through history. LaVey's reestablishment of the Satanic archetype—now molded in his own form—at the center of popular culture was proving a success. The spirit of the time was becoming fatigued by the hollow and self-righteous ideals of the hippie movement, and LaVey, who had declared himself an enemy of hippie idealism and egalitarianism, provided a seductive counterpoint. Advertisers suddenly began to appeal directly to one's internal diabolism as a force that desired luxury products. Hollywood went through a phase of Satanic horror cinema, including the epoch-defining Roman Polanski film *Rosemary's Baby,* which included Church of Satan recruitment cards in the lobbies of movie theaters where it was playing. Curiously enough, one of LaVey's topless *Witches Review* girls from a few years earlier, Susan Atkins, would join the Manson family and be implicated in the murders that claimed the life of Polanski's wife, Sharon Tate. LaVey began traveling America and appearing on national talk shows as well as in major magazines, his fame spreading. Usually set up for ridicule, LaVey gathered more respect by showing his sense of humor, never rising to provocation, but relaying his message of hierarchical self-empowerment and magical will with calm and intelligence.

As with all celebrity, this did not come without a price. As the 1970s progressed, LaVey found himself increasingly exhausted by the endless harassment, sometimes including violent threats to his well-being and to that of his family. He took to carrying a .45 with him wherever he went. He was forced to give up Togare to the San Francisco zoo after his neighbors filed a petition to the police about the animal. He was distressed that the Church of Satan seemed to be attracting increasing numbers of lower quality people who were just there to poke around. He began restructuring membership and offering direct initiation into the highest orders to those he believed had already lived Satanic lives of achievement and success, something that provoked ire in several of the members of his church who began to splinter off, denouncing LaVey's simony, and proclaiming themselves the "true" Satanic Church. He became more reclusive as the 1970s wore on. According to Barton, he was determined to "start practicing Satanism and stop performing it."[4]

By 1984 the second phase of Satanism had begun. The church had attracted new members, and LaVey had now stripped the church back to its essentials, rather than what he had termed a "pen pal club for Satan."[5] Among the new wave of initiates were the publisher Adam Parfrey and the musician Boyd Rice, both of whom had past romantic relationships with Zeena LaVey, who was being groomed to become the High Priestess of Satanism. Much of what fascinated Rice and Parfrey were the more intimate elements of LaVey's world, particularly his teachings pertaining to the Order of the Trapezoid. On the other hand, Zeena and her new partner, Nickolas Schreck, would take up the mantle of public appearances on behalf of the Church of Satan, profiting from the "Satanic panic" of the 1980s, as mass hysteria set in and people began believing in a media-driven Satan-led conspiracy to kidnap or murder children, among other things. Schreck, missing one ear, and flanked by his beautiful and black-clad Princess of Satan, Zeena, indulged prime time talk show hosts such as Bob Larson with his theories of hierarchy, social Darwinism, and fascination with the Manson murders.

While the division in the church was not as binary as the inner sanctum versus the public face of Satanic royalty, internal tensions were reaching a boiling point. LaVey had become particularly fond of Rice and Parfrey, and these hip young arrivals paved the way for others in a second wave of Satanism, ultimately leading to Crispin Glover and Marilyn Manson joining the church. Rice was eventually made Grand Master for life of the Order of the Trapezoid and was therefore inducted into the deeper mysteries, most especially the nuances of the most fundamental Satanic principle of all, "the strong dominate the weak, and the clever dominate the strong."[6] Rice and Parfrey developed an irritation with Schreck and Zeena, believing them to be guilty of intellectual posturing and not applying Satanic principles to their actual lives, preferring to continue the outward performance of Satanism. LaVey was content to have his daughter and soon-to-be son-in-law take care of public duties, as it allowed him to withdraw from those duties and concentrate on fully incorporating Satanism into his daily life—rituals were no longer necessary to call up the powers from below and charge himself with them, as he embodied it all of the time.

LaVey, meanwhile, was being sued by Hegarty for palimony, and in 1986 she applied for a restraining order against LaVey, with which he complied. After twenty-five years as the Queen of Satan, Hegarty had had enough. LaVey was quick to move and soon brought the young blond Barton into the church, and Barton would, in 1993, give birth to LaVey's third child, Satan Xerxes Carnacki.

In 1988 the Church of Satan participated in the 8-8-88 Rally, a Satanic-themed film and music gathering in San Francisco. The rally featured Rice and Schreck's band, Radio Werewolf, providing the Third Reich carnivalesque musical performances, while Rice and company had managed to source the only surviving copy of the Charles Manson film *The Other Side of Madness*. The film is a fairly ludicrous and sensationalist reenactment of the crimes filmed on location at the Spahn Ranch by director Frank Howard and is a pinnacle of bad taste 1970s B-movie schlock. Nowadays it's freely accessible on YouTube, but in the late 1980s it was an extreme rarity, all the other prints of the film having been collected and destroyed by filmmakers Polanski and Warren Beatty. The rally was a success, and Geraldo Rivera brought a television crew over to record it, even though Rice qualified this success by calling the performances awful. People showed up in droves and even rioted— the eye of America was looking at Satan once more, and that's what counted. Photos from the event show what seems to be a happy family atmosphere. LaVey, of course, was overseeing things, and all seemed to be relatively at ease among the Satanists.

In 1990, however, an almighty rupture in the Church of Satan commenced. Zeena renounced Satanism, leaving the church. A power struggle had been brewing for some time, with Zeena, and especially Schreck, aiming to position themselves in the forefront for the post-LaVey era of the church. She accused her father of promoting a self-centered form of spirituality, of plagiarism, and of endangering her life. The latter claim came from an incident where a man who had been aggressively stalking Zeena called LaVey and asked where she was, and LaVey gave her itinerary. LaVey responded by saying he had no idea that the person in question posed a threat to Zeena, but Zeena's fury was unabated. She divorced herself from the family surname and demanded to be henceforth addressed only as Zeena, although she took Schreck's last name as her legal surname. She returned any correspondence addressed to Zeena LaVey, and "feeling naturally aristocratic," she gave up her titles of High Priestess and Magistra. Furthermore, she joined Michael A. Aquino—a former colonel in the US military who had previously been a member of the Church of Satan—in his Temple of Set, one of the rival Satanic organizations that had sprung up after the changes LaVey made to the Church of Satan in the 1970s. The Temple of Set worshipped the Egyptian deity Set and differed markedly from the Church of Satan in taking a more esoteric stance, opposed to LaVey's rationalism, as well as propounding a literal belief in demonic entities (believing Set to be the archetype for reverence leading to personal spiritual discovery) rather than LaVey's atheistic, symbolic system. LaVey's supporters, including Rice, Barton, future leaders of the church Peggy Nadramia and Peter H. Gilmore, and several members of LaVey's family (including Zeena's own children), gathered around to defend him against the accusations made by the Schrecks. The rift would never be healed, and relations remain rancorous to this day.

Zeena would be made the High Priestess of the Temple of Set in 2002, before then renouncing the temple and converting to Buddhism, not before publishing the seminal and truly excellent text on Eastern sex magic *Demons of the Flesh* along with Schreck, and, absurdly, being subject to speculation that she had been cloned and the second Zeena had grown up to become the singer Taylor Swift.

For all his vigor and self-assuredness, LaVey's life had not always been a happy one. The end of his relationship with Hegarty had been a severe emotional blow, and for many years he resigned himself to a life of isolation and feelings of betrayal. He had to sell off some of his prized possessions to pay the alimony and other legal fees, and this strain took its toll on his mind and body. His heart had been damaged during a bout of fever he had contracted during his teens, and by the 1980s his doctors recommended heart valve replacement. LaVey declined the operation, fearing the complications of his body potentially rejecting the artificial valves more than the condition itself. In the 1990s he granted more interviews and devoted more time to writing, but he was unable to fully liberate himself from the feelings of betrayal and rejection that came from the actions of both Hegarty and Zeena. His relationship with Barton and his son brought him comfort, and it seems that LaVey hid his physical deterioration from all but Barton. Even Rice, to whom he gave one of his final and most revealing interviews, was shocked to learn of his death by pulmonary edema on October 29, 1997, shortly after they had spoken. In truth, the final six months of LaVey's life had been a painful decline, with heart issues compounded by a twisted colon, and a general physical downturn. With his eternal eye for ceremony, he indicated that he'd like his death date to be October 31, even if he fell a couple of days short, so his death was kept quiet among the family until after that date. Anton Szandor LaVey, founder of the Church of Satan and pioneer of radical sexual and magical freedom, was cremated at the age of sixty-seven, his ashes kept in an urn at the Black House.

Selected Works by Anton LaVey Concerning Sex Magic

Anton LaVey's writing is available from a variety of publishers.

1971 ✦ *The Compleat Witch: Or, What to Do when Virtue Fails.* Also published as *The Satanic Witch*

1992 ✦ *The Devil's Notebook*

12

Genesis P-Orridge
(1950–2020)

On June 17, 2019, I had the privilege of interviewing Genesis P-Orridge in New York City—less than a year before their death.

In Genesis P-Orridge we see the culmination of the frenzied gathering of the sexual and magical knowledge obtained by the loose family of practitioners presented in this book. P-Orridge's life and work—which crosses an array of music, art, literature, and performance—has coagulated almost the entirety of the ideas and practices of their predecessors. Sigil magic from Spare, cut-ups from Burroughs, ceremony and performance from Crowley, and radical physical manifestations of magic from Parsons and Cameron all show up in their life's work.

Perhaps the most extraordinary manifestation of these influences has been the application of Burroughs's magical cut-up technique to the human body. P-Orridge fused and blended his own physical body with spouse Lady Jaye (born Jacqueline Mary Breyer) in what they termed the Pandrogyny Project. Beginning as husband and wife, they began to morph into one another first in dress, and then through extensive surgical alteration, to form one single plural-pronounced being known as Breyer P-Orridge. The result was the realization of a marriage of artistic and intellectual radicalism, inspired by Burroughs, as well as a desire to fulfill a deeply romantic aspiration to literally become one another. Even after Lady Jaye's death in 2007, P-Orridge maintained the pronoun "they" when being addressed, in acknowledgment of Lady Jaye's continued presence in their physical and spiritual being.

Genesis P-Orridge was born Neil Andrew Megson on February 22, 1950, in Longsight, south Manchester. Longsight is one of Manchester's most notorious areas, with a history of gang violence that reached its peak during the 1990s, before a crackdown on gang culture led to a period of relative calm. During Manchester's Industrial Revolution heyday, Longsight lacked the canals that brought valuable cotton in and out of the city, and so it began to lag economically before it developed into a home for many of Manchester's factories and their workers as industry diversified in a city that was both gloomy and thrilling. In the post-war decades, when a young Megson was growing up there, Longsight was poor and tough but with a near mythical communal togetherness. Much of this social cohesion was literally bulldozed in the 1960s and 1970s in the so-called slum clearances, where the iconic two up, two down houses (referring to the number of rooms on each floor) were replaced with modern high-rise tower blocks. Former residents of the area who had interconnected multigenerational ties of kith and kin were forced out and sent to other parts of Manchester, now separated from their long-established social structures in this aggressive remodeling of the city. The Megsons found themselves away from Longsight, settling in Gatley, Cheshire.

Young Megson had the critical advantage of intelligence and passed the exam known as the "eleven-plus," which was an examination given to all British school pupils at the end of primary education, at eleven years old, to determine whether they would attend technical, secondary modern, or grammar school—the latter reserved for the most intellectually capable. He would attend, first, Stockport Grammar School, before being accepted on a scholarship to the salubrious surroundings of the Solihull School in the West Midlands. At first, the working-class boy arriving on a scholarship among the established ranks of inherited privilege made life a nightmare of bullying. Solihull School, an all-boys fee-paying public school, was one of the institutions that provided Britain with its bankers, politicians, industrialists, and diplomats, and the boys were expected to take on roles of leadership and control later in their lives. Teenaged Megson, wary of this conformity of power, found solace in art and literature, particularly the works of the Beats, thanks to one sympathetic teacher handing him a copy of Jack Kerouac's *On The Road,* strengthening his sense of freedom and individualism. His grandmother had been a medium, and so he was also drawn to works of the occult, most especially those of Crowley. Upon reading Crowley's work *Magick in Theory and Practice,* Megson came to a startling realization: Crowley had visited him in a vision as a child. In 1957, while walking through Gatley's suburban streets, seven-year-old Megson was approached by an old, heavy-set, and bald man who began talking to the young boy. "As he was talking to me all the streets started to change: the houses started to look like they were made of bread. That was how I remembered it at the time. And everything was very unreal and it was as if the street didn't get any shorter or longer as I walked along with him. I was going fast but I wasn't getting anywhere. And then he patted me on the shoulder and left. And I went home. It didn't strike me as very odd until I read that book [*Magick in Theory and Practice*] and I thought, fuck, this is the person I was talking to."[1]

As Megson went through his teenage years, he began to uncover possibilities for rebellion against the constraints of the school world. At that time in London, a youth cultural revolution was taking place, often in the form of "happenings." These were gatherings where things "happened," normally impromptu art or music performances, poetry readings, and radical political speeches. "Happening" had become a media buzzword in England by the mid-1960s, as the more conservative elements of society craned their necks to try to see what was going on in "Swinging London." Inspired by these transgressive events, Megson organized his own "happening" at the school, having told his teachers that he was organizing a school dance. In 1966, Megson put out a school magazine called *Conscience,* set on lampooning and critiquing the school's rules, that he sold outside the school gates. It was quickly banned. Nevertheless, the torments continued, and Megson began to realize that language was as much a means of force as physical violence. He became angry at what he perceived as formalized language used as a "ritual weapon of control,"[2] which led him to begin developing the idiosyncratic and deconstructed form of written English that would characterize later works. Furthermore, stuck in an intellectual environment he classified as being largely obsessed by "dicks and sport,"[3] he noticed that this path to power was paved with quasi-sexual acts, words, and thoughts, which seemed to develop forms of power the more feverishly they were expressed by his schoolmates—in his mind, unquestionably a form of sexual black magic.

It was at this time that Megson's Christian faith began to break. It had been active enough that he found himself as the secretary of the school's Christian Discussion Circle (controversially inviting a member of the British Communist Party to come and speak on one occasion, defending his choice on the basis of "know thine enemy"[4] as well as organizing Sunday School classes throughout his sixth-form years). Around this time, Megson's asthma medication—cortisone and steroids—caused an atrophying of his adrenal glands. Advised to stop the medication, he had an asthma attack that almost killed him but which served as the catalyst for a life that would be devoted to art and magic: "It was at that point I decided I wasn't going to do what was expected of me."[5]

One of the first sacrifices to this personal new order was his name. While throwing names from the Bible at one another, one of his schoolmates suggested that Megson would be Genesis, "because you're creative,"[6] and so was the genesis of Genesis N. A. Megson. His surname, Megson, a popular name in northern England, is a rare matronym, meaning "son of Margaret," a curiosity of gender naming conventions that perhaps forecast the feminine element to come later.

Megson then attended the University of Hull but was soon bored by the continuation of formalized education and examination, finding some interest in organizing sit-ins and student protests that he hoped to film but which in reality turned out to be poorly attended failures. However, a friend of Megson's, John Krivine, had invited the legendary performance art group the Exploding Galaxy to Hull for a performance. The Exploding Galaxy was formed by the Filipino artist David Medalla as a means of combining kinetic art (which combined science and technology with the arts) and happenings to create a multimedia form of living art. Medalla's creation was situated in the commune at 99 Balls Pond Road from early 1967 and was at the heart of London's own summer of love. The group's finest moment was the 14 Hour Technicolour Dream, which was performed at Alexandra Palace in April 1967. Medalla's kinetic art piece *Fuzzdeath* was the main installation, and it involved improvised painting, dancing, light shows, noise, and copious drug taking in cross-disciplinary transmedia. However, by 1969 the authorities had cracked down on the free love and, most especially, drug taking, and Medalla, along with other senior members of the Exploding Galaxy, had been arrested for cannabis possession, with Medalla being refused reentry to the UK after a visit to Holland. Short, then, on performers, the remaining members of the commune offered Megson the chance to perform with them in Hull. It was a successful collaboration, so Megson and Krivine found themselves invited to London to join a new commune born from the remnants of the Exploding Galaxy, called Transmedia Explorations. They hitchhiked down to London, saw Pink Floyd at the Albert Hall and the Rolling Stones in Hyde Park, and began their lives in the new commune at Islington Park Street.

Transmedia Explorations enforced a strict order upon their number with the intent of breaking down attachments to habit and convention. It was forbidden, for example, to sleep in the same place for two consecutive nights, and all clothes were kept in a large tea chest from which members could construct their outfits daily. Strange meals were prepared and served at unusual intervals. Most of all, language was deconstructed, seen as it was as the primary weapon society deployed as a means of social control—constant experimentation was encouraged, and Megson was already interested in word play, having attempted a novel, "Mrs Askwith," which was influenced by Raymond Queneau's Oulipo movement. Though never published, it featured many elements present in Megson's later work, including a character with two personalities who referred to himself by his initial "E" rather than "I" and did not contain the word "the." Megson permanently supplanted "the" with "thee" in all future works.

This regime did soon become tiresome, but Megson was armed with a great many new avenues for experimentation. In late 1969, he launched his first major project, COUM Transmissions, which was conceived following a magical vision during a car journey with his parents in Wales. What he called a "spontaneous alteration of my conscience" involved the words "COUM Transmissions" and the symbol for the group being revealed to him during a moment of disembodiment. "COUM," devoid of any fixed meaning, had nevertheless a distinct sexual and vulgar ring to it, and to Megson it was a spiritual essence to be preached with zeal, and so he set about spreading the word. COUM's artwork was distinctly sexual; their early posters featuring an ejaculating penis formed from the word "COUM" along with the promise "COUM guarantee disappointment"[7] and "Your Local Dirty Banned." Early gigs in local pubs around Hull were not well received—an *NME* magazine review called them "dreadful"—and the fully improvised sonic experience involved Megson making random noises on a violin. Near the end of the year Megson and Krivine moved into new digs in Hull, a flat in an old fruit warehouse by the docks that they named the Ho-Ho Funhouse. At a party, around this time, he saw "the archetypal flower girl with velvets, silks, and heavy eye make-up, obviously very high on acid."[8] He said hello to the flower girl, and at the precise same moment, the elastic in her underwear snapped, which the girl took as something of a sign. She was Christine Carol Newby, but she would soon become known as Cosey (short for Cosmosis) Fanni Tutti, and before long she had moved into Megson's room at the Ho-Ho Funhouse.

Megson and Tutti began to veer away from their full-on drop-out housemates and kept drugs at an experimental level rather than as a complete raison d'être, allowing them to concentrate their energies on COUM performances. Some of these involved impromptu street shows, but in the early days they were largely musical. By 1971 the performances had evolved to incorporate more interactive and visual elements. Audience members were sometimes required to crawl through a tunnel to access the concert, and at others the stage was set up as a living room with tea being served. The shift toward performance and away from music had begun, and Megson legally changed his named to Genesis P-Orridge in early 1971, as another form of himself emerged, this time paying homage to the oatmeal that restored his strength during his teenage illness and that doctors credited with saving his life.

COUM continued to perform and began to attract various media attention, some of it bemused and bemusing, although others, such as being mentioned in an article by John Peel, more welcome. They relocated to London and were given a grant of £250 by the British Arts Council, which funded more performances. P-Orridge took an interest in postal art, mailing black postcards to random addresses, a Blackburn-area phonebook full of holes to John Lennon, and maggots and used sanitary towels to an art exhibition in Canada (these were not accepted for inclusion). Krivine, moved to London at the same time and opened up Acme Attractions in Chelsea. Initially a record store, it began selling clothes and became a hotspot for punks and other musicians—including Debbie Harry, Patti Smith, Bob Marley, and the Clash. Krivine made a lasting impression on subculture fashion by launching the brand BOY London.

In London, P-Orridge began to associate with the local chapter of the Hell's Angels, which required an initiation of giving a menstruating woman oral sex. P-Orridge had already begun incorporating chewing used tampons into his performances, so this was no great task. Performances continued, and the general artistic zeitgeist was becoming much more politicized in art as the mid-1970s arrived. The world was in a financial chokehold, and the previous relative indifference of even the conservative government of Prime Minister Edward Heath toward the increased radicalism and explicit nature of performance art was disintegrating, as the performers became more interested in agit-prop and agendas of Marxism, feminism, and antifascism. National newspapers began to tout outrage over moral concerns, and the government launched its own investigations into pornography as well as applying pressure on the Arts Council to make more orthodox funding decisions.

In 1974, COUM returned to musical performance but now began incorporating ritual magic. A work titled *Marcel Duchamp's Next Work,* presented at the Palais des Beaux-Arts, Brussels, was a reimagining of Duchamp's 1913 *Bicycle Wheel,* only now there were twelve wheels that could be played by audience members, conducted by COUM. The wheels were designated as harps and set in a circle with twelve divisions around a central dot, a formation that came from Tibetan magical ritual and represented the twelve stages of enlightenment. The conductor would be fed the random noises generated by the harps and then have "godlike coumtrol" over the output, which was rooted in magical formulae, key numbers, and the elementals. Later in 1974, *Couming of Age* was performed at the Oval House in Kennington and was dedicated to Burroughs, following the meeting between P-Orridge and Burroughs the previous year, during which Burroughs instructed P-Orridge in the magic of cut-up. *Couming of Age* was also performed largely nude, and the sexual aspect fascinated an audience member who introduced himself after the show, photographer and graphic designer Peter Christophersen. His enthusiasm for all things sexual was enough for P-Orridge to nickname him Sleazy during this first encounter. By 1975, Sleazy had become an integral member of COUM, and his skills with photography and images added another dimension to the group.

COUM were making use of various cooperative art spaces being opened up in London, and one performance at the Art Meeting Place (AMP), on Earlham Street, Covent Garden (first opening its doors in May 1974), would become a major piece of COUM notoriety. The

AMP was run by artists, and artists could book spaces for performances and hold open meetings. P-Orridge proposed a wild party and invited guests to bring cameras and recording devices, while the room would be filled with mirrors. P-Orridge and Tutti had a bed installed and created a kind of medieval-looking club with studs embedded around the shaft and two dildos on either end. For the performance, they shared the dildo in vaginal and anal penetration as a taboo-smashing tribal and ritualistic initiation ceremony, as well as disrupting gender roles— something that was becoming a major theme in their work as both P-Orridge and Tutti dressed in masculine, feminine, and mixed outfits, and embodied the same during performances. At the same time, Tutti gave up her job as a secretary and signed up for a modeling agency, posing for various men's pornography magazines as a new form of income and as a subversive means of expression. COUM were getting more grants and performing with more spontaneity than before, although many of their public performances, featuring live maggots in carriages filled with plastic babies' heads and Tutti's used tampons, were quickly shut down by the police. Tutti's sex work was beginning to inform COUM's performances, which now involved a mixture of the mundane and the erotic, with Christophersen, P-Orridge, and Tutti ending up nude, covered in fake blood, and with various implements such as medical syringes hanging from P-Orridge's anus while erotic stories and the sounds of children playing rang out from tape recordings.

All three principal COUM members had, by now, recognized the limitations of COUM. An entry into popular culture would not be possible under their current guise, and so their attempts to spread their word would be restricted to thoughtful young art students and the occasional confused police officer. So, choosing the thirty-sixth anniversary of Britain's entry into World War II, Throbbing Gristle were formed on September 3, 1975, by P-Orridge, Tutti, and Christophersen, with the artist and musician Chris Carter joining as the final member soon after. Throbbing Gristle were intended to be a more accessible form of COUM, devoid of manifestoes and other art-world appendages, as a kind of merger between the artistic, academic world of theory and radicalism and the popular culture world of rock music.

As Throbbing Gristle began their first tentative gigs, COUM experienced both legal difficulties and then a sudden move into the public eye. P-Orridge was charged with pornography for his postal art, the postcards now featuring increasingly sexual images collaged with pictures of the queen, among other things. They had caught the eye of the authorities, and he was arrested. Burroughs wrote a defense of P-Orridge as an artist, not a pornographer, but to no avail. P-Orridge was fined £100 and so ended the campaign of postal art.

In October 1976, COUM opened their first major art exhibition, titled *Prostitution,* at the Institute of Contemporary Arts (ICA), situated on the Mall in London. The exhibition contained a selection of Tutti's pornography magazine pages; various instruments that had previously been used in live performances by COUM, including the inevitable tampons, as well as chains, anal syringes, meat cleavers, and Vaseline; and photos and press cuttings of the group. The scene was set for British tabloid scandal. The opposition Tory party already had the scent of blood from a feeble and failing Labour government that was guiding the country into its worst economic disaster in decades, and one of the primary means of assault was a combination of what was perceived as wasting public money and a decline of traditional values—two things that COUM were openly encouraging. The Tories sent a Member of Parliament, Nicholas Fairbairn, who then recounted the horrors witnessed at the *Prostitution* exhibition to the conservative media, including the *Daily Mail, The Sun,* and *The Daily Telegraph.* After describing his heroic battle through the hordes of Hell's Angels and men with multicolored hair and lipstick to the *Mail,* he reviewed the exhibition thus: "A sickening outrage. Sadistic. Obscene. Evil . . . Public money is being wasted here to destroy the morality of our society. These people are the wreckers of civilisation,"[9] all accompanied by a picture of attendee rock stars Siouxsie Sioux and Steve Severin. In the *Telegraph* he noted the "photographs which attempted to make prostitutes look like victims instead of the vultures which they are,"[10] while *The Sun,* giving its own thoughts, stated, "Mr P-Orridge is prostituting Britain—and sending us the bill."[11]

Tutti and P-Orridge became household names and, in some quarters, bywords for depravity. They were visited by journalists and caught in a media frenzy, which they found exciting at first, but the excitement quickly turned to tedium. They were invited to defend themselves on television, which they did with calm, reasoned intelligence, and they received support from the left-wing press. However, Tutti was blacklisted by men's magazines once they discovered she had used their images in the exhibition, effectively making her unemployed, and the ICA was subjected to severe budgetary cuts in retaliation for *Prostitution* and the ensuing moral panic. It would signal the beginning of the end for COUM as P-Orridge and Tutti became fatigued with the art world and began investing more energy into Throbbing Gristle. Before that, however, they were invited to perform as COUM at two galleries in New York, L.A. Institute of Contemporary Art and IDEA Gallery. The performance, called *Cease to Exist,* was a further advance into ritualistic sex magic as performance, as well as other forms of bodily transgression. It was a drastic development of the sex magic philosophy dating back to Randolph of the power of bodily fluids. P-Orridge began by holding all the muscles in his body taut while drinking a pint of half milk, half urine, letting it run down his body. Tutti, meanwhile, was naked with wounds on her breasts and a wound running from her vagina to her navel. She sutured the breast wounds herself and then took a hypodermic needle and filled it with blood from her breast before putting it into the wound in her stomach, injecting it into her vaginal cavity so it dripped out of her vagina into a puddle on the floor. She took a second needle, filled with blood and milk, and injected it into her vagina. Next, Genesis put a needle into one of his testicles and filled it with blood before injecting it into a black egg. Tutti cut a flap of skin out of her forearm and placed a passport photograph of P-Orridge under it, licking off any excess blood, while he continued to draw blood from his testicles and inject it into his forearm and into six more black eggs, all while standing on shards of ice and nails. Tutti then masturbated, and P-Orridge used a syringe to fill his anus with blood and milk, before urinating and releasing the blood-milk concoction onto the floor, which Tutti slathered herself in and rubbed into her vagina. P-Orridge made himself vomit by pushing a long steel nail down his throat, and, lying in the pool of vomit, purified and purged by this violation of the bodily boundaries of pain, they had sex.

Present at the first breaths of punk, Throbbing Gristle went along with the new movement, albeit somewhat uncomfortably. Their aggressive, disorienting, experimental sound was firmly rooted in the art scene, and not the nascent punk that was primarily souped-up pub rock in wild outfits. The look of the band became more conservative—they started to look like a punk band, clean shaven, short haired (except Tutti), leather jackets, and jeans, as well as a great deal of Fascist- and Nazi-inspired symbolism, all being an attempt to give an impression of relative normality when the reality would be much different. Conventional punk venues in pubs around England's midsize towns sometimes vowed never to have them back after being subjected to Throbbing Gristle's cacophony, with songs about serial killers Myra Hindley and Ian Brady (a song titled "Very Friendly") among their most accessible works. By 1979, though, the Sex Pistols had imploded and been reborn as John Lydon's Public Image Ltd., and the punk scene opened up enormously to artistic experimentation, and this year would see the release of Throbbing Gristle's third album, *20 Jazz Funk Greats,* the title a deliberate and amusing attempt to mislead the casual record store browser (not least due to it only containing eleven tracks). While not making the band any money, the records had sold well, given their extreme nature, and Throbbing Gristle could count Elton John and Frank Zappa among their fans. However, within the band tensions were beginning to arise, particularly between Tutti and P-Orridge, due in part to the affair that had developed between Tutti and Carter. Arguments became violent, with Tutti claiming that

P-Orridge threw a plant pot at her from a balcony in an attempt to kill her, while accusations of P-Orridge's capacity for manipulation and a dictatorial approach to both COUM and Throbbing Gristle have remained to this day. At the same time, P-Orridge felt that the remaining members of the band were losing interest and had betrayed the founding principles of COUM, and now that they had become an established and famous act, he was expected to put in all of the work (although even P-Orridge himself admitted this was more of a feeling than necessarily the truth of the situation).[12] Believing that COUM and Throbbing Gristle were deserving of a kind of religious purity, P-Orridge decided to push himself to further extremes of bodily torture and sacrifice to the true aims, both magical and artistic. On one occasion, he ritualistically inserted rusty nails into his body and chewed the twigs of a poisonous plant while drunk on whiskey and gave himself blood poisoning that was very near fatal, causing him to collapse on stage in the middle of a performance.

The record label the band had created in 1976, Industrial Records (and which in turn gave the name to the genre of music Throbbing Gristle made), began releasing records by other industrial artists such as Cabaret Voltaire, Clock DVA, the Leather Nun, and some of Burroughs's spoken word records. P-Orridge was living in Hackney by 1980, which was then a terrifying place of crime, violence, and race battles. In response to this, P-Orridge and his new friend, the American artist Monte Cazzaza, a specialist in transgression and shock, began adopting a distinctly authoritarian look, sourcing their outfits from army surplus stores and modifying them for a fascistic flair. They also remodeled their home as a kind of fortress after running into trouble with some Irish travelers who had parked up nearby, going as far as constructing a "sonic weapon" to use against the tinkers.

Following the fourth Throbbing Gristle album, a live record called *Heathen Earth,* the band ended. Only around thirty live performances had taken place as Throbbing Gristle, and the band had referred to these not as gigs or concerts but as "psychic rallies." The power and frenzy of Throbbing Gristle's sound was specifically designed to evoke powerful emotional, physical, and psychic states in the audience, sexual and nauseating at times. The band was a vehicle, and the performances were a means of transmitting the medium activities of the group to all present, the sound, always improvised, being something collected from the beyond and transmitted sonically, a magical process. During one hiatus from performances, the group had sex with each other every weekend for a year as a means of magically and sexually charging themselves in ritual, so that their sensitivity and ability to transmit magical forms at the psychic rally that would come at the end of it all would be extremely powerful. This interaction among the performers and the audience is a cut-up of traditional magical invocation, where the music is, in some sense, the magic and the band is the demonic entity, initially separated from the thousand or so magicians calling for them, and then becoming one with them.

In 1980, P-Orridge met two more new friends who would set him on a path toward the most magical phase of his life. First was the young musician David Bunting, to whom P-Orridge would give the name David Tibet. Then, in Paris, P-Orridge met Gysin and began to understand the true power of cut-up as a magical means of transcendence and transformation. Tutti and Carter, now liberated from the tense and complex relations they had with P-Orridge, formed a working and romantic partnership that has produced some of the finest and most critically acclaimed music to arise from the Industrial Records stock, and Tutti—still estranged from P-Orridge and at odds over the true history of both their relationship and Throbbing Gristle—has had her artwork exposed internationally.

Following the demise of Throbbing Gristle, P-Orridge launched two new projects that were inextricable, the band Psychic TV and a magical fellowship named Thee Temple ov Psychick Youth (TOPY). Psychic TV was formed by P-Orridge and Alex Fergusson, a member of the band Alternative TV, and they were soon joined by Sleazy and P-Orridge's new wife, Paula, a Tesco checkout girl and performer who played drums. P-Orridge described the band as a "video group that does music,"[13] in opposition to most groups who made music first and then shot music videos to go with them—the principle being that television was an esoteric means of counterattacking the establishment, who were at the same time using television as a method of popular mind control. Psychic TV's video art would warp the viewer away from the regular messages they were used to hearing and seeing. The videos and songs themselves were designed to work as forms of sigil magic, in just the same way Spare's sigils worked, albeit now as moving images. Spare's work in chaos magic had, by this time, been considerable and elaborated on by Carroll and Sherwin in their works *Liber Null* and *Psychonaut;* chaos magic was the system that both Psychic TV and TOPY were borne from. Carroll describes his work, in referencing his magical organization the Illuminates of Thanateros, announced in 1978, as a mixture of Thelema, Tantra, and Spare's defunct Zos Kia Cultus. The Illuminates, by the late 1980s, had expanded their number considerably and included Timothy Leary, Robert Anton Wilson, and Burroughs, before a schism.

In autumn 1982, Psychic TV made their live debut at an event dedicated to and featuring Burroughs, alongside other cut-up influenced and industrial acts including Cabaret Voltaire, 23 Skidoo (a reference to the 1920s esoteric fascination with the cursed number twenty-three that had long fascinated Burroughs), Z'EV, John Giorno, and Gysin. Psychic TV's musical approach was to use cut-up recordings of their works mixed with the precise tempo and loud volume of rave music, which tended to produce a loss of inhibition and feelings of euphoria, with P-Orridge's words then better able to reach the unconscious mind of those there dancing and being initiated. The first album, *Force the Hand of Chance,* was released in November, and a single, the melancholic and gentle "Just Drifting," followed it in December. P-Orridge's use of a kangling, a Tibetan instrument made of a human thighbone and introduced to him by David Tibet, caused some controversy. They were joined by contributors Marc Almond and John Balance, the latter of whom would go on to form the equally esoteric group Coil with Sleazy. P-Orridge then became acquainted with LaVey, who performed on the track "Joy," reading The Lord's Prayer in reverse. In 1983, Psychic TV released a second album, *Dreams Less Sweet,* which was critically well received for its Dadaist melodies. Then in 1986, the band launched an ambitious magical working in which they would play twenty-three live shows in twenty-three different countries, each on the twenty-third of the month for twenty-three consecutive months, and each show would be given an official release on Temple Records. Although the project was abandoned after seventeen months, the run gave the band a mention in the *Guinness Book of World Records.* In 1988 the third album written by Fergusson and P-Orridge, albeit without Sleazy, *Allegory and Self,* was released. Fergusson left Psychic TV after the release of *Allegory and Self,* and P-Orridge decided to take the band in a new direction, heavily influenced by new sounds arising in acid house and techno music.

Concurrent with all of this, TOPY grew throughout the 1980s. It was formed by P-Orridge and Tibet, along with Balance and former members of the Process Church of Final Judgement, a magical order that has gone through a bizarre number of transformations since its inception in London in 1966 by husband and wife Mary Ann McLean and Robert de Grimston Moore. Former Scientologists, they were excommunicated from the church by Hubbard in 1962 and so decided to form the Process Church. Beginning in a commune in Mayfair, London, the Process Church opened a coffee shop called Satan's Cavern and began attracting the likes of Marianne Faithfull, and they preached their Satanic doctrines to the young and hip of London. The church made a pilgrimage to Cefalù to visit the Abbey of Thelema, by then partially ruined, and then decamped first to the mystical Mayan lands of Xtul in Mexico, before moving on to New Orleans. Prosecutors in the Charles Manson case attempted to implicate the Process Church in the killings, but no link was ever proved—most of the suspicions came from Manson himself when he claimed that he and de Grimston Moore were "one and the same" person.[14] The Process Church's rituals and systems were incorporated by P-Orridge into the TOPY rituals, which blended them with chaos magic and the then defunct O.T.O.'s magical teachings. Later, the Process Church would remove all religious and spiritual affiliation and become officially registered as an animal rescue center, operating the largest no-kill animal shelter in the United States from its base in Utah. Before that, however, the church went through various offshoots and incarnations, including as the Unit, which was influenced by Pentecostalism and taught communication with aliens, dolphins, and angels; then as a millenarian organization associated with the Mormons; and finally as an explicitly Christian organization called the Foundation Church of the Millennium.

TOPY differed from its spiritual predecessors in that no formal instruction was offered. Instead it operated as a kind of occult forum, in which the exchange of ideas was encouraged. Sigil magic was important, but so were punk ideals and radical artworks, such as that of the Viennese Actionists, like Herman Nitsch, Rudolf Schwarzkogler, and Gunter Brus, who used their own blood and bodily fluids in art. TOPY encouraged the charging of sigils with blood and semen and instructed initiates to perform "Thee Sigil Ov 3 Liquids" working. The working was performed as follows: the initiate must be naked with only a candle flame as light, and they should then write on a piece of paper their most intense sexual fantasy. The sigil is then charged with spit, blood, and sexual fluid following orgasm, while concentrating on the fantasy at the moment of orgasm. A lock of head hair and some pubic hair should be attached to the paper, with instruction to deploy some artistic freedom in how the whole thing is arranged. Once dry, the paper should be sent to the Station (one of the TOPY churches) in a plastic bag where it will be stored in a locked vault—once the initiate has completed this once a month for twenty-three months, full initiation of the temple would be attained. This meant that on the twenty-third day of any given month, the potential number of sex magic workings might be enormous, Genesis noting, "We did coumthing unique and co-ordinated, as far as linear coumcepts ov T.I.M.E. allowed, (once or twice) thousands ov Individuals to do their version ov thee SIGIL OV THEE THREE LIQUIDS so a mass ov FOCUSSED orgasms were released close to simultaneously."[15]

P-Orridge, having learned his lesson during the blood poisoning episode, began to adapt his own rituals to something less immediately life-threatening. Rather than performing public rituals, Genesis began workings in private, with TOPY assistants on hand should anything go wrong. One of the primary rituals was "Thee Stations ov Thee Cross," in which "a hood is placed over the subject's head. This simulates sensations of disorientation which immediately changes the state of the subject's consciousness . . . enables the gaze of the subject to expand inward."[16] This is a form of psychic projector, allowing the subject to transcend their own sense of existence and begin to regard their own inner workings in a dispassionate way. The subject becomes a shaman, nameless and at liberty to wander the vastness of the atavistic subconscious mind. This can be combined with psychedelic drugs, which place yet another hood upon the user, obscuring the ability to recognize the mundane world at all. These techniques were designed primarily as a simplification of ritual: "One key point to TOPY was to demystify that existing Museum Ov Magic and say, look, here are coum actually very simple techniques and/or tools that in OUR experience seem to work, to be positive way beyond any random appearance ov 'success.' We share them. No need to join anything, learn hundreds ov texts, Gods, Egyptian heiroglyphs blah blah."[17]

In 1991, P-Orridge left TOPY and formally ended its existence, stating that he had never wanted to become any kind of leader of the Temple. TOPY has been maintained by its fans ever since, and its most important works, including *Thee Psychick Bible,* remain in print. The following year P-Orridge was in Nepal in a kind of self-imposed exile with Paula meeting with Tibetans on a famine relief program when the British television network Channel 4 aired an episode of its investigative documentary series *Dispatches,* which focused on cases of Satanic abuse. No doubt encouraged by the Satanic panic of the previous decade, the show claimed to have discovered footage of P-Orridge inflicting sexual abuse on children in a ritualistic, Satanic setting. Following the broadcast, police raided P-Orridge's home and confiscated artwork. Threatened, and above all terrified of the possibility of being separated from his two children, Caresse and Genesse, P-Orridge refused to return to the UK, believing himself to be the target of a Christian fundamentalist plot to frame him as a child abuser. It turned out that the videotapes acquired by Channel 4 were of a consensual, adult sex magic rite performed in the early 1980s, featuring the filmmaker Derek Jarman reading from Chaucer as P-Orridge and others performed sex magic. Ironically, this particular performance had, in fact, been partially funded by Channel 4 at the time. A humiliated Channel 4 released a retraction of their accusations, but for P-Orridge it was enough—having divorced Paula in Nepal, Genesis moved himself and his children directly to the United States and would not return to England for many years.[18]

In early 1993, P-Orridge met Jacqueline Breyer, also known as Lady Jaye, who would become his second wife, and they moved to her home neighborhood of Ridgewood, Queens, New York City. Here, P-Orridge's devotion to cut-up would elevate the idea to new heights, far beyond those ever attained by Burroughs or Gysin in terms of radical and literal application, at least. Jaye and P-Orridge conceived the Pandrogeny Project, whereby, little by little, they would surgically alter themselves so that they would resemble one another in a single all-gendered pandrogynous being known as Breyer P-Orridge. They admit that at first Genesis was "still dressing and technically behaving male,"[19] but soon enough both were "running around in mini-skirts"[20] and feeling very free in New York's tolerant atmosphere. Breast, cheek, and chin implants, nose jobs, hormone therapy, tattoos, and other various surgeries ran to a cost of $200,000 as they morphed together, now adopting alternating and neutral gender pronouns (which I will use from hereon when referring to Genesis). Partly this was an artistic expression of how they believed that the true self—one of pure consciousness—was caged by the genetic form of the body and could be liberated by cutting up the body, but it was also an expression of devoted and romantic love, to be one whole, an evolved variation, perhaps, of the better and idealistic intentions of Christian marriage. This was perhaps the purest expression of P-Orridge's artistic vision, and it was put into so many words by Lady Jaye, who would often remind them that "mutation is the law of evolution, nothing is fixed, all is instantly redundant." Flux and mutation were the means of throwing off the shackles of control— "This means ANY dogmatic, embroidered, belief system is actually a restrictive cage, preventing wisdom and revelation."[21]

Over the next few years Breyer P-Orridge would release several records, some in collaboration with other artists, and then as PTV3, a reformation of the original intentions of Psychic TV. They also won a $1.5 million lawsuit after being injured while escaping from a fire at producer Rick Rubin's house, suffering a broken wrist, broken ribs, and a pulmonary embolism. A book of their artwork was released in the mid-1990s, titled *Ooh You Are Awful . . . But I Like You!* named for the catchphrase of the English comedian Dick Emery's character, Mandy, a sex-starved peroxide blonde played by Emery himself in drag, somewhat resembling Jayne Mansfield.

In 2007, Lady Jaye died of a heart condition that arose as a complication of stomach cancer, a devastating emotional blow for Breyer P-Orridge. They canceled all tour dates for Psychic TV that year, but then decided to continue the Pandrogyny Project, with P-Orridge representing Breyer P-Orridge in the material world, while Lady Jaye would now represent them in the immaterial world, with the collaborations and love affair now interdimensional.

In 2009 they retired from touring, although sporadic returns have occurred in the intervening years, as has involvement in a multitude of art, music, and cinema projects. In 2017, Breyer P-Orridge were diagnosed with chronic myelomonocytic leukaemia, and in March of 2020 they "dropped their body" as Genesis would have had it, finally departing the physical realm at the age of seventy.

"Sex Magick in particular, as WE view I.T. alongside its cousins thee cut-ups, permutations, and a total rejection ov Either/Or remains a potent tool in keeping thee possibilities alone endless. Our humanE species MUST lose its attachment to linearity ov any kind. Our humanE species MUST break up its atrophied behaviour patterns and linguistic oppression and be retrained to constant preparedness for CHANGE ITS SELF."[22]

Selected Works by Genesis P-Orridge Concerning Sex Magic

Genesis P-Orridge's writings are available from a variety of publishers.

2010 ✦ *Thee Psychick Bible: Thee Apocryphal Scriptures ov Genesis Breyer P-Orridge and Thee Third Mind ov Thee Temple ov Psychick Youth*

2020 ✦ *Genesis Breyer P-Orridge: Sacred Intent: Conversations with Carl Abrahamsson 1986–2019*

2021 ✦ *Nonbinary: A Memoir,* published posthumously

CONCLUSION

Following the Open Path

There has been, as this book has hopefully illustrated, a long line of sex magic descent that began with Randolph and has continued, more or less unbroken, to figures who were with us right up until 2020, when we sadly lost Genesis P-Orridge. A baton (or perhaps wand or sword) has been dropped at the passing of the foremost practitioner of sex magic at any given moment, often picked up by someone who was already close to the epicenter. The next in line to this shadowy yet illuminated throne will have to be someone with the same desire to push and prove the West's perennially prudish attitude toward sex and magic, just as every figure in this book managed to do.

Our experience in the West is that of a society that is somewhat enlightened in its attitude when we consider our many freedoms, especially freedom of spirituality and of sexual enjoyment. There are, of course, parts of the world where both of these things are stifled and even violently oppressed still. But are we as comfortable with our sexual and spiritual selves as we ought to be? A renewed interest in sex magic has sparked during the past decade as a generation tries to make sense of the swath of soulless online pornography, the cattle-like behavior of Tinder and hook-up culture, and a disastrous aftermath of the sexual revolution of the 1960s that has resulted in soaring levels of sexual abuse, neuroses, and new forms of moralistic puritanism that, once again, threaten one of humanity's most fundamental instincts.

Sigmund Freud is far from the only notable thinker to remark on the sexual and spiritual failures of Western woman and man leading to deep psychological distress. Much of our world may be broadly considered post Judeo-Christian, but we seem not to have lost our love of suffering, and moreover of creating social climates that favor angst and prevent true expression. Underneath it all, there is still a pagan soul somewhere that spills out here and there, and moments of spiritual-sexual ecstasy can be experienced by even Westerners in an authentic and positive way. Anyone who has ever attended a rave can attest to this. It is curious to note that authorities across our lands have also been slowly but surely turning great musical gatherings—whether rock festivals or "illegal" raves—into anodyne corporate experiences, if not proactively banning them altogether. Is it because of a genuine regard for social well-being and a wish to protect the vulnerable from the dangers of drugs and alcohol? Or is there something about these gatherings that smell (and they can be pungent) much too strongly of ritual spiritual and sexual awakening? How curious it was to see that during the global Covid-19 pandemic, the first instinct of many people was to gather in secluded woodlands with intoxicants and loud music and dance to forms of music that replicate the primal, prenatal sonic experience of the womb; the pound of the heartbeat, the endless droning rush of the blood. Sensorial, ritualized experiences make us feel both safe yet also thrilled by the element of danger, a proximity to radical nature in the literal sense of "radical." And nature is abundant due to its explosive reproductive vitality, while remaining deeply mysterious, always presenting the eternal unanswerable question of "Why?" Sex magic practice cannot answer this question but the practitioner can be part of the question rather than burdened with the impossible task of trying to rationalize an answer.

There is something intrinsically erotic about religion, in spite of, or perhaps because of, how much organized religion has tried to resist sexuality. The decadence of Catholicism, not to mention its relentless sexual symbolism, makes it seem that sexual repression must have been an afterthought. Protestantism attempted to bring a wall-to-wall austerity when it came to sexuality but succeeded in creating an even kinkier cult than its predecessor. In the past fifty years or so, Islam has once more become a significant presence in the West, and curiosity about the sexual possibilities of the Muslim faith has suddenly become a major source of fascination in Western countries. The pagans of old Europe, wiser than both their monotheistic and agnostic-atheist successors, understood that sexuality deserved a place in religion. But for the vast majority of modern Western people, there will be no turning back to monotheism, let alone the polytheistic beliefs of long extinct cultures. Sexual magic will likely never be reinstated as a centerpiece of a ritualized national culture. Its future lies in providing transcendent experiences to those who live in atomized and disconnected societies, with the special ability to unite people in ways that little else can. It will always be feared by some and therefore is hardwired into the occult. But perhaps not everything valuable must be democratized. Some things can remain self-selecting to those with the courage and curiosity to indulge dangerous ideas.

I began with a fascination for the great provocateur and outrager of moral decency that was Crowley, developed a fascination for Spare and the interzone of magic and visual arts, before attending the elaborate rituals of the O.T.O., and finally coming to my own personal interpretation of the function and power of magic. But such a state could never have come without the incoherent adventure and exploration of as many avenues as were open to me, resulting in me organizing a Gnostic Mass in Paris before an audience partly fascinated, partly terrified of the invocations of the priest and naked priestess. No passage will be the same, and it's rare to meet fellow travelers through the darkness, since so much of this spiritual self-discovery will be undertaken alone. And that is, paradoxically, what brings enlightenment.

What sex magic can actually do remains entirely up to the practitioner to discover—and truly, there is no amount of reading that can compare with actual practical learning. But even if there are some "armchair magicians" or even skeptics here, one thing can at least be demonstrated by the selection of biographies presented here: practicing sex magic almost guarantees that a person will live an interesting life, and often an enlightened one that encourages free thought and self-awareness—which ought to be the very least responsibility of every one of us.

Notes

INTRODUCTION

1. Crowley, *Magick in Theory and Practice,* VIII.
2. Kumar, S., Boone, K., Tuszyński, J. et al. "Possible existence of optical communication channels in the brain."
3. Livy, *Books XXXVIII-XXXIX with an English Translation.*
4. Flint, "The Demonization of Magic," 196.
5. Murray, *The Witch-Cult in Western Europe,* 149.
6. US Census Bureau, Statistical Abstract of the United States: 2011, Table 75. Self-Described Religious Identification of Adult Population: 1990 to 2008.

I. PASCHAL BEVERLY RANDOLPH

1. Pluquet, Marc, *La Sophiale.*
2. Randolph, *After Death,* 14.
3. Randolph, *After Death,* 14.
4. Sabbatini, "The History of Shock Therapy in Psychiatry."
5. Naglowska & Randolph, *Magia Sexualis.*
6. Randolph, *Dhoula Bel,* 20.
7. Deveney, *Paschal Beverly Randolph,* 94.
8. Randolph, *Eulis!,* 48.
9. Randolph, *Curious Life,* 15–16.
10. Reynolds, *Secret Societies.*
11. Deveney, *Paschal Beverly Randolph,* 311.

12. Randolph, *Eulis!*

13. Deveney, *Paschal Beverly Randolph,* 254.

14. Jones, "Suicide," *Religio-Philosophical Journal,* 18.

15. A. H. Greenfield, *The Roots of Modern Magick: An Anthology,* 95.

2. IDA CRADDOCK

1. Chappell, *Sexual Outlaw,* 235.

2. Chappell, *Sexual Outlaw,* 232.

3. Lincoln Steffens, *The Shame of the Cities,* 136.

4. Chappell, *Sexual Outlaw,* 144.

5. Schmidt, *Heaven's Bride,* 12–13.

6. Schmidt, *Heaven's Bride,* 17.

7. Schmidt, *Heaven's Bride,* 16.

8. Chappell, *Sexual Outlaw,* 144.

9. Chappell, *Sexual Outlaw,* 11.

10. Chappell, *Sexual Outlaw,* 20.

11. Schaechterle, "Speaking of Sex."

12. Chappell, *Sexual Outlaw,* 30.

13. Chappell, "Martyr for Freedom."

14. Chappell, *Sexual Outlaw,* 22.

15. Chappell, *Sexual Outlaw,* 239.

16. Shaw, *New York Times.*

17. Crowley, *Equinox.*

18. Chappell, *Sexual Outlaw,* 244.

3. ALEISTER CROWLEY

1. Kaczynski, *Perdurabo,* 26.

2. Crowley and Mathers, *The Battle of Blythe Road.*

3. Sutin, *Do What Thou Wilt.*

4. Kaczynski, *Perdurabo,* 120.

5. Cummings, "Beyond Belief."

6. Crowley, *Solitude,* chapter 62.

7. Crowley, *The Vision & The Voice,* 46.

8. Crowley, *Confessions,* 708.

9. Spence, *Secret Agent 666.*

10. Crowley, *White Stains,* ix.

11. Kaczynski, *Perdurabo,* 477.

12. Crowley to Montgomery Evans, July 20, 1940, Evans Papers.

13. Pearson, *The Life of Ian Fleming,* 110–96.

14. Crowley to Gerald Yorke, September 13, 1941, Yorke papers.

15. Kaczynski, *Perdurabo,* 520.

4. MARIA DE NAGLOWSKA

1. North, *Occult Mentors.*

2. Rogers, *Sex and Race,* 329.

3. Naglowska, *The Sacred Rite of Magical Love.*

4. Livingstone, *Transhumanism,* 110.

5. Naglowska, *The Light of Sex.*

6. North, *The Grimoire of Maria de Naglowska.*

7. Naglowska, *Advanced Sex Magic.*

8. Naglowska, *The Light of Sex.*

9. Naglowska, *Advanced Sex Magic.*

5. AUSTIN OSMAN SPARE

1. Letchford, *From Inferno to Zos,* 33.

2. Letchford, *From Inferno to Zos,* 163.

3. Grant, *Images & Oracles,* 10.

4. Baker, *Austin Osman Spare,* 26.

5. Baker, *Austin Osman Spare,* 101.

6. Grant, *The Magickal Revival.*

7. Baker, *Austin Osman Spare,* 75.

8. Grant, *Zos Speaks!,* 43.

9. Baker, *Austin Osman Spare,* 71.

10. Baker, *Austin Osman Spare,* 151.

11. Grant, *Zos Speaks!,* 18.

12. Baker, *Austin Osman Spare,* 165.

13. Spare, *Self as Hitler,* pastel and charcoal, 1948.

14. Allen, "The Mansion House Tavern of Crossed Destinies."

15. Baker *Austin Osman Spare,* 202.

16. Grant, *Zos Speaks!,* 13.

17. Baker, *Austin Osman Spare,* 216.

18. Baker, *Austin Osman Spare,* 216.

19. Baker, *Austin Osman Spare,* 246.

20. Grant, *Zos Speaks!,* 97.

21. Baker, *Austin Osman Spare,* 256.

6. JULIUS EVOLA

1. Anna Momigliano, "Alt-Right's Intellectual Darling."

2. Evola, *Men Among the Ruins.*

3. Evola, *Cinnabar,* 8.

4. Evola, *Cinnabar,* 14.

5. Welles, "Julius Evola: Paintings and Artistic Career."

6. Evola, *Mithraic Mysteries.*

7. Lippi, *Julius Evola; Qui suis-je?,* 25.

8. Evola, *Le Chemin du Cinabre,* 181.

9. Evola, *Le Chemin du Cinabre,* 82.

10. Evola, *Le Chemin du Cinabre,* 94.

11. Evola, *Méditations du haut des cimes,* 139.

12. Lippi, *Julius Evola,* 39.

13. Engels, *On Historical Materialism.*

14. Gilbert, "A. Harriman to President Roosevelt, 1942," *Winston S. Churchill Documents Volume 17,* 152–53.

15. Evola, *Le Chemin du Cinabre,* 153.

16. Evola, *Le Chemin du Cinabre,* 161.

17. Lycourinos, *Occult Traditions.*

18. Nietzsche, *Ecce Homo,* 96.

7. FRANZ BARDON

1. Franz Bardon, *Frabato,* 17.

2. Lumir Bardon, *Memories of Franz Bardon.*

3. Luhrssen, *Hammer of the Gods.*

4. Luhrssen, *Hammer of the Gods.*

5. Hemberger, "The FOGC Lodge."

6. Cosimano, "Oh Tepaphone."

7. Hemberger, "The FOGC Lodge."

8. Lumir Bardon, *Memories of Franz Bardon.*

9. Scott, *Who Was Franz Bardon,* 62.

8. JACK PARSONS

1. Pendle, *Strange Angel.*

2. Pendle, *Strange Angel.*

3. Pendle, *Strange Angel,* 238.

4. Pendle, *Strange Angel,* 257.

5. Letter from Parsons to Crowley, 1946.

6. Urban, *The Church of Scientology,* 39.

7. Mitchell, "Scientology: Revealed for the First Time."

8. White, *The Eloquent Blood,* 142.

9. Letter to Crowley, 1946.

10. Letter to Crowley, 1946.

11. Letter Aleister Crowley to Karl Germer, April 19, 1946.

12. Telegram from Crowley to O.T.O. office, May 22, 1946.

13. Rolfe, *Believe What You Like.*

14. Mitchell, "Scientology: Revealed for the First Time."

15. Grant, *Outside the Circles of Time.*

16. Pendle, *Strange Angel,* 218.

9. WILLIAM S. BURROUGHS

1. Morgan, *Literary Outlaw,* 33.

2. Morgan, *Literary Outlaw,* 34.

3. Morgan, *Literary Outlaw,* 51.

4. Morgan, *Literary Outlaw,* 629.

5. Burroughs, *The Adding Machine.*

6. Morgan, *Literary Outlaw,* 213.

7. Morgan, *Literary Outlaw,* 239.

8. Rae, *William S Burroughs and the Cult of Rock and Roll,* 50.

9. Ambrose, *Man from Nowhere: Storming the Citadels of Enlightenment with William Burroughs and Brion Gysin.*

10. Burroughs, "Deposition: Testimony Concerning a Sickness."

11. Rae, *William S Burroughs and the Cult of Rock and Roll,* 30.

12. Burroughs, "The Cut-Up Method of Brion Gysin."

13. Morgan, *Literary Outlaw,* 344.

14. Gysin, *Dreamachine Plans.*

15. MacFayden, "A Trip from Here to There."

16. Burroughs, *The Adding Machine,* 182.

17. Morgan, *Literary Outlaw,* 488.

18. Jones, "Espresso Bar."

19. Miles, *A Descriptive Catalogue of the William S. Burroughs Archive.*

20. Stevens, "Nothing Here Now but the Recordings."

21. Burroughs, "Gregory Corso & Allen Ginsberg Interview William Burroughs."

22. Burroughs, *Last Words.*

10. MARJORIE CAMERON

1. Starr, *Lost and Found in California.*

2. Kansa, *Wormwood Star,* 28.

3. Percy, "Ruthless Adventure."

4. Percy, "Ruthless Adventure."

5. Kansa, *Wormwood Star,* 104.

6. Nelson, "Cameron, Witch of the Art World."

7. Kansa, *Wormwood Star,* 122.

8. Kansa, *Wormwood Star,* 127.

9. Kansa, *Wormwood Star,* 134.

11. ANTON SZANDOR LAVEY

1. Barton, *The Secret Life of a Satanist,* 49.

2. Barton, *The Secret Life of a Satanist,* 101.

3. Barton, *The Secret Life of a Satanist,* 97.

4. Barton, *The Secret Life of a Satanist,* 114.

5. Barton, *The Secret Life of a Satanist,* 115.

6. Boyd Rice, interview by Michael William West.

12. GENESIS P-ORRIDGE

1. P-Orridge, *Painful but Fabulous,* 48.

2. Ford, *Wreckers of Civilisation,* 16.

3. Ford, *Wreckers of Civilisation,* 16.

4. Ford, *Wreckers of Civilisation,* 17.

5. Ford, *Wreckers of Civilisation,* 17.

6. Ford, *Wreckers of Civilisation,* 17.

7. Ford, *Wreckers of Civilisation,* 17.

8. Ford, *Wreckers of Civilisation,* 17.

9. Ford, *Wreckers of Civilisation,* 19.

10. Ford, *Wreckers of Civilisation,* 19.

11. Ford, *Wreckers of Civilisation,* 19.

12. P-Orridge, interview by Michael William West, June 17, 2019, New York City.

13. P-Orridge, "Unpublished Conversation," interview by Carl Abrahamsson.

14. Medway, *The Lure of the Sinister,* 106.

15. P-Orridge, interview by Michael William West, June 17, 2019, New York City.

16. P-Orridge, interview by Michael William West, June 17, 2019, New York City.

17. P-Orridge, interview by Michael William West, June 17, 2019, New York City.

18. Evans, *The History of British Magic,* 101.

19. P-Orridge, interview by Michael William West, June 17, 2019, New York City.

20. P-Orridge, interview by Michael William West, June 17, 2019, New York City.

21. P-Orridge, interview by Michael William West, June 17, 2019, New York City.

22. P-Orridge, interview by Michael William West, June 17, 2019, New York City.

Bibliography

Allen, Jonathan. "The Mansion House Tavern of Crossed Destinies." *The Cabinet,* Issue 59: The North, August 31, 2015.

Ambrose, Joe, Frank Rynne, and Terry Wilson. *Man from Nowhere: Storming the Citadels of Enlightenment with William Burroughs and Brion Gysin.* Ireland: Subliminal Books, 1992.

Baker, Phil. *Austin Osman Spare: The Life & Legend of London's Lost Artist.* London: Strange Attractor, 2010.

Bardon, Franz. *Frabato the Magician.* Salt Lake City: Merkur Publishing, 1979.

Bardon, Lumir. *Memories of Franz Bardon.* Salt Lake City: Merkur Publishing, 2004.

Barton, Blanche. *The Secret Life of a Satanist: The Authorized Biography of Anton Szandor LaVey.* Port Townsend, Wash.: Feral House, 1990.

Burroughs, William S. *The Adding Machine.* New York: Grove Press, 2013.

———. "Deposition: Testimony Concerning a Sickness." Published as a preface to *Naked Lunch.* New York: Grove Press, 1992.

———. "The Cut-Up Method of Brion Gysin." In *A Casebook on the Beat.* New York: Crowell, 1961.

———. *Last Words, The Final Journals of William S. Burroughs.* New York: Grove Press, 2000.

———. "Gregory Corso & Allen Ginsberg Interview William Burroughs (Journal For The Protection of All Beings) 1961." San Francisco: City Lights Books. The Allen Ginsberg Project, January 18, 2014. https://allenginsberg .org/2014/01/gregory-corso-allen-ginsberg-interview-william-burroughs -journal-for-the-protection-of-all-beings-1961.

Chappell, Vere. *Sexual Outlaw, Erotic Mystic: The Essential Ida Craddock.* Boston: Weiser. 2010.

———. "Ida Craddock: Sexual Mystic and Martyr for Freedom." Originally presented at the Second National O.T.O. Conference, August 7, 1999.

Cosimano, Charles W. "Oh Tepaphone, Oh Tepaphone." Uncle Chuckie's General Store and Death Ray Works, http://www.charlescosimano.com /tepaphone.html.

Crowley, Aleister. *The Confessions of Aleister Crowley.* London: Arkana Publishing, 1989.

———. *The Equinox: Volume III, Number I.* Paris: Ordo Templi Orientis, 1919.

———. *Magick in Theory and Practice by the Master Therion.* Paris: Lecram, 1929.

———. *The Spirit of Solitude: an Autohagiography: Subsequently Re-Antichristened The Confessions of Aleister Crowley.* London: Mandrake Press, 1929.

———. *White Stains.* London: Gerald Duckworth & Co. Ltd., 1986.

Crowley, Aleister, and S. L. MacGregor Mathers. *The Battle of Blythe Road: A Golden Dawn Affair.* Sequim, Wash.: Holmes Publishing Group, 1997.

Crowley, Aleister, Victor Neuberg, and Mary Desti, *The Vision & The Voice.* Boston: Weiser Books, 1999.

Cummings, Tim. "Beyond Belief." *The Guardian.* July 9, 2004.

Deveney, John Patrick. *Paschal Beverly Randolph: A Nineteenth-Century Black American Spiritualist, Rosicrucian, and Sex Magician.* New York: SUNY Press, 1997.

Engels, Frederich. *On Historical Materialis.* New York: International Publishers, 1940.

Evans, Dave. *The History of British Magic After Crowley: Kenneth Grant, Amado Crowley, Chaos Magic, Satanism, Lovecraft, The Left Hand Path, Blasphemy and Magical Morality.* UK: Hidden Publishing, 2007.

Evola, Julius. *Le Chemin du Cinabre.* Milan: Arché, 1983.

———. *Men Among the Ruins: Post-War Reflections of a Radical Traditionalist.* Rochester, Vt.: Inner Traditions, 2002.

———. *Méditations du haut des cimes.* Paris: Pardès, Puiseaux et Trédaniel, 1986.

———. *The Path of Cinnabar: An Intellectual Autobiography.* London: Arktos Media, 2010.

———. *The Path of Enlightenment in the Mithraic Mysteries.* Sequim, Wash.: Holmes Publishing Group, 1993.

Flint, Valerie Irene Jane. "The Demonization of Magic and Sorcery in Late

Antiquity: Christian Redefinitions of Pagan Religions." In *Witchcraft and Magic in Europe: Ancient Greece and Rome*. London: A&C Black, 1999.

Ford, Simon. *Wreckers of Civilisation: The Story of COUM Transmissions and Throbbing Gristle*. London, UK: Black Dog, 1999.

Gilbert, Martin (editor). "A. Harriman to President Roosevelt, 1942." Letter in *The Churchill Documents, Volume 17: Testing Times 1942*. Michigan: Hillsdale College Press, 2014.

Grant, Kenneth. *The Images and Oracles of Austin Osman Spare*. London: Frederick Muller Limited, 1975.

———. *The Magickal Revival*. London: Frederick Muller Limited, 1975.

———. *Outside the Circles of Time*. London: Frederick Muller Limited, 1980.

Grant, Kenneth, and Steffi. *Zos Speaks! Encounters with Austin Osman Spare*. Somerset, UK: Fulgur, 1998.

Greenfield, Allen H. *The Roots of Modern Magick: An Anthology*. Lulu.com. 2005.

Gysin, Brion. *Dreamachine Plans*. Brighton, UK: Temple Press, 1992.

Hemberger, Adolph. "The FOGC Lodge, The Freemasonic Order of the Golden Centurium." https://freemasonrywatch.org/fogc.html.

Jones, S. S. (editor). "Suicide." *Religio-Philosophical Journal,* no. 22, August, 14, 1875.

Jones, Josh. "How William S. Burroughs Used the Cut-Up Technique to Shut Down London's First Espresso Bar (1972)." *Open Culture,* http://www.openculture.com/2014/12/how-william-s-burroughs-shut-down-londons-first-espresso-bar-1972.html. December 19, 2014.

Kaczynski, Richard. *Perdurabo, Revised and Expanded Edition: The Life of Aleister Crowley*. Calif.: North Atlantic Books, 2010.

Kansa, Spencer. *Wormwood Star: The Magickal Life of Marjorie Cameron*. Oxford, UK: Mandrake of Oxford, 2010.

Kumar, S., K. Boone, J. Tuszyński et al. Possible existence of optical communication channels in the brain. *Sci Rep* 6, 36508 (2016).

Letchford, Frank. *From the Inferno to Zos, Volume III. Michaelangelo in a Teacup: Austin Osman Spare*. Thame, UK: First Impressions, 1995.

Lippi, Jean-Paul. *Julius Evola: Qui suis-je?* Paris: Pardès, 1999.

Livingstone, David. *Transhumanism: The History of a Dangerous Idea*. Self-published, CreateSpace, 2015.

Livy. *Books XXXVIII–XXXIX* with an English translation. Translated by Evan T. Sage. Cambridge, Mass.: Harvard University Press, 1936.

Luhrssen, David. *Hammer of the Gods: The Thule Society and the Birth of Nazism*. Lincoln: University of Nebraska Press, 2012.

Lycourinos, Damon Zacharias. "Evolian Sex, Magic, and Power." In *Occult Traditions*. Geelong, Victoria, Australia: Numen Books, 2012.

MacFayden, Ian. "A Trip from Here to There." *RealityStudio*. https://realitystudio.org/scholarship/a-trip-from-here-to-there. February 28, 2011.

Medway, Gareth. *Lure of the Sinister: The Unnatural History of Satanism*. New York: New York University Press, 2001.

Miles, Barry (editor). *A Descriptive Catalogue of the William S. Burroughs Archive*. London: Covent Garden Press, 1973.

Mitchell, Alexander. "Scientology: Revealed for the First Time." *London Sunday Times*. October 5, 1969.

Momigliano, Anna. "The Alt-Right's Intellectual Darling Hated Christianity." *The Atlantic*. February 21, 2017.

Morgan, Ted. *Literary Outlaw; The Life and Times of William S Burroughs*. New York: W. W. Norton & Company, 2012.

Murray, Margaret. *The Witch-Cult in Western Europe*. Oxford: Oxford at the Clarendon Press, 1921.

Naglowska, Maria de. *Advanced Sex Magic: The Hanging Mystery Tradition*. Rochester, Vt.: Inner Traditions, 2011.

———. *The Light of Sex: Initiation, Magic, and Sacrament*. Rochester, Vt.: Inner Traditions, 2011.

———. *The Sacred Rite of Magical Love: A Ceremony of Word and Flesh*. Rochester, Vt.: Inner Traditions, 2012.

Nelson, Steffie. "Cameron, Witch of the Art World," review of *Wormwood Star: The Magickal Life of Marjorie Cameron* by Spencer Kansa. *Los Angeles Review of Books*. https://lareviewofbooks.org/article/cameron-witch-art-world. October 8, 2014.

Nietzsche, Friedrich. *Ecce Homo*. Mineola: Dover Publications, 2004.

North, Robert. *The Grimoire of Maria de Naglowska*. Lulu.com, 2009.

———. *The Occult Mentors of Maria de Naglowska*. Lulu.com, 2010.

P-Orridge, Genesis. *Painful But Fabulous: The Lives and Art of Genesis P-Orridge*. New York: Soft Skull Press, 2002.

———. "Read an Unpublished Conversation with the Radical Genesis Breyer P-Orridge." Interview by Carl Abrahamsson. *AnOther Magazine*. https://www.anothermag.com/design-living/12519/unpublished-conversation-genesis-breyer-p-orridge-carl-abrahamsson-book. May 18, 2020.

Pearson, John. *The Life of Ian Fleming.* New York: McGraw-Hill Book Company, 1966.

Pendle, George. *Strange Angel: The Otherworldly Life of Rocket Scientist John Whiteside Parsons.* Boston: Mariner Books, 2006.

Percy, Margaret. "Ruthless Adventure: The Lives of L. Ron Hubbard." BBC Radio 4. August 11, 1987.

Pluquet, Marc. *LaSophiale: Maria de Naglowska, sa vie & son oeuvre.* Paris: Ordo Templi Orientis, 1993.

Rae, Casey. *William S. Burroughs and the Cult of Rock 'n' Roll.* Austin: University of Texas Press, 2019.

Randolph, Paschal Beverly. *After Death; Or, Disembodied Man. The World of Spirits; Its Location, Extent, Appearance; the Route Thither; Inhabitants; Customs, Societies: Also Sex and Its Uses There, Etc., Etc.; with Much Matter Pertinent to the Question of Human Immortality. Being the Sequel to "Dealings with the Dead."* Boston: Colby & Rich, 1873.

————. *Eulis! The History of Love, Its Wondrous Magic, Chemistry, Rules, Laws, Moods and Rationale: Being the Third Revelation of Soul and Sex: Also, Reply to "Why is Man Immortal?", the Solution of the Darwin Problem, an Entirely New Theory.* Boston: Randolph Publishing Company, 1896.

————. *P.B. Randolph, the "Learned Pundit," and "Man with Two Souls." His Curious Life, Works, and Career. The Great Free-Love Trial. Randolph's Grand Defence. His Address to the Jury, and Mankind. The Verdict.* Boston: Randolph Publishing Company, 1872.

————. *Dhoula Bel, or The Wonderful Story of Ravalette.* Boston: Randolph Publishing Company, 1871.

Randolph, Paschal Beverly, and Maria de Naglovska. *Magia Sexualis.* Rochester, Vt.: Inner Traditions, 2012.

Reynolds, John Lawrence. *Secret Societies: Inside the World's Most Notorious Organizations.* New York: Arcade, 2011.

Rogers, J. A. *Sex and Race Volume 2 : Negro-Caucasian Mixing in All Ages and All Lands—the Old World.* New York: Helga M. Rogers, 1942.

Rolfe, C. H. *Believe What You Like: What happened between the Scientologists and the National Association for Mental Health.* London: Andre Deutsch Limited, 1973.

Sabbatini, Renato M. E. "The History of Shock Therapy in Psychiatry." *Brain & Mind, Electronic Magazine on Neuroscience.* https://cerebromente.org.br /n04/historia/shock_i.htm. January 30, 2008.

Schaechterle, Inez. "Speaking of Sex: The Rhetorical Strategies of Frances Willard, Victoria Woodhull, and Ida Craddock." Electronic Thesis or Dissertation. Ohio: Bowling Green State University, 2005.

Schmidt, Leigh Eric. *Heaven's Bride: The Unprintable Life of Ida C. Craddock, American Mystic, Scholar, Sexologist, Martyr, and Madwoman.* New York, NY: Basic Books, 2010.

Scott, Tim. *Who Was Franz Bardon.* Frabato.org Archive, 1991. https://www.moryason.com/Frabato/html/timscott.html.

Shaw, George Bernard, "Bernard Shaw Resents Actions of Librarian," *New York Times.* Sept. 26, 1905.

Spence, Richard B. *Secret Agent 666, Aleister Crowley and British Intelligence in America 1914–1918.* Port Townsend, Wash.: Feral House, 2008.

Starr, Sandra Leonard, interview with Cameron. In *Lost and Found in California: Four Decades of Assemblage Art, July 16 to September 7, 1988: An Exhibition.* Santa Monica, Calif.: James Corcoran Gallery, 1988.

Steffens, Lincoln. *The Shame of Cities.* New York: S. S. McClure, 1904.

Stenslie, Ståle. "Cybersex." *The Oxford Handbook of Virtuality.* Oxford, UK: Oxford University Press, 2014.

Stevens, Matthew Levi. "Nothing Here Now but the Recordings." *RealityStudio.* https://realitystudio.org/biography/nothing-here-now-but-the-recordings. July 29, 2013.

Sutin, Lawrence. *Do What Thou Wilt: A Life of Aleister Crowley.* New York: St. Martin, 2000.

Urban, Hugh B. *The Church of Scientology: A History of a New Religion.* N.J.: Princeton University Press, 2011.

Welles, Manon. "Julius Evola: Paintings and Artistic Career." *Aristocrats of the Soul.* http://aristocratsofthesoul.com/the-paintings-of-julius-evola. August 24, 2013.

White, Manon Hedenborg. *The Eloquent Blood: The Goddess Babalon and the Construction of Femininities in Western Esotericism.* Oxford: Oxford University Press, 2019.

Index